Applied Communication
in the 21st Century

Applied Communication in the 21st Century

Edited by

Kenneth N. Cissna
University of South Florida

Routledge
Taylor & Francis Group

NEW YORK AND LONDON

First Published by

Lawrence Erlbaum Associates, Inc., Publishers
10 Industrial Avenue
Mahwah, New Jersey 07430

Transferred to Digital Printing 2009 by Routledge
270 Madison Ave, New York NY 10016
2 Park Square, Milton Park, Abingdon, Oxon, OX14 4RN

Library of Congress Cataloging-in-Publication Data

Applied communication in the 21st century / edited by Kenneth N. Cissna.
    p.   cm.
    Includes bibliographical references and index.
    ISBN 0–8058–1475–2. — ISBN 0–8058–1852–9 (pbk.)
    1. Communication—Research.   I. Cissna, Kenneth N.   II. Title: Applied communication
in the twenty first century.
    P91.3.A68   1995   95–2003
    302.2—dc20   CIP

Publisher's Note
The publisher has gone to great lengths to ensure the quality of this reprint
but points out that some imperfections in the original may be apparent.

To Gerald R. Miller
whose passion for inquiry inspired so many

Contents

I   THE STATE OF APPLIED COMMUNICATION RESEARCH

Introduction

Kenneth N. Cissna
University of South Florida

Communication as a field had its genesis in concerns for practice, and our public speaking pedagogy remains our greatest practical contribution. The future of our field, however, lies in our ability to produce a socially relevant scholarship, without which communication is unlikely to attract the best students, command significant societal resources, or make its greatest contributions to the world's store of knowledge.

In 1968, the field of communication held its first discipline-wide national research conference, the New Orleans Conference on Research and Instructional Development (Kibler & Barker, 1969). This conference had enormous impact in moving the field to accept behavioral science and in setting an agenda for behavioral scholarship. Less noticed was that the conference also addressed issues related to social relevance and engagement, and eight of the recommendations of the conference dealt with this theme. Among other things, the conference participants encouraged us to conduct research concerning the communication dimensions of social problems, apply our research findings to the solution of individual and social problems, and communicate our knowledge and research findings to the general public. Although those recommendations were among the least realized of that important conference, in the years that followed the field did take important steps toward applied and socially relevant scholarship.

Following the New Orleans conference and another nearly simultaneous Speech Communication Association (SCA) conference on social engagement, Mark Hickson III founded the *Journal of Applied Communications*

Research, publishing the first of his semi-annual issues in 1973 (see Hickson, 1973). Subsequently, applied units of SCA and of several of the regional organizations were formed. In 1980 Hickson sold *JACR* to the University of South Florida (USF), which dropped the "s" from *communications* in the journal's name and published its first issue in 1981.

As early as 1985, SCA's Administrative Committee began exploring the possibilities of publishing an applied journal, either by revising *Communication Education* or by initiating a new journal. After 2 years, involving careful study by SCA and discussions with USF, SCA had determined that it wished to acquire *JACR* from USF, and the Legislative Council of SCA approved the acquisition in November 1987. William F. Eadie, SCA's first editor of *JACR,* published his first issue in 1991. About that time, SCA inaugurated an applied communication book series under the editorship of Gary L. Kreps.

In less than 20 years, what began as Hickson's own small, fringe journal to represent an overlooked area had become a quarterly publication of our major professional organization, corresponding to the interests of a significant number in the field. Still, the area needed focus and direction, which gave rise to an SCA-sponsored research conference on applied communication and to this volume.

Meetings and discussions regarding the conference began late in 1987 between Robert K. Avery, chair of the SCA Research Board, and Arthur P. Bochner, chair of the Department of Communication, at USF. By the summer of 1988, the SCA Research Board had committed funds to the conference, and Kenneth N. Cissna, editor of *JACR* during most of its USF years, was selected as conference director.

A steering committee for the conference was formed, consisting of James Gaudino, Mark L. Knapp, Gerald R. Miller, Teresa L. Thompson, and Loyd S. Pettegrew, along with Avery, Bochner, and Cissna. The committee held planning meetings at SCA and ICA conventions in November 1998, May 1989, and November 1989. Its first decision was to charge Cissna with conducting a survey to determine how subscribers to *JACR*, members of the applied section of SCA, and selected opinion leaders across the areas of communication study conceptualize applied communication and applied communication research. The analysis revealed four themes and an underlying dichtomy between (a) views of applied communication as theoretically informed and therefore as closely connected with all communication scholarship, and (b) those who see it as atheoretical, distinctively practical, and largely separate from other concerns of the field. These issues are also reflected in various recent commentaries on applied communication (Cissna, 1982, 1987; Eadie, 1982, 1990, 1994; Ellis, 1991; Gordon, 1982; Hickson, 1983; Johnson, 1991; Kreps, Frey, & O'Hair, 1991; Miller & Sunnafrank, 1984; O'Hair, 1988; O'Hair, Kreps, & Frey, 1990; Pettegrew, 1988; Phillips, 1981; Plax, 1991; Weick & Browning, 1991), although the second position is rejected as a viable conception of applied communication research by most of these commentators and by the authors featured in this volume.

The steering committee identified conference goals and objectives, determined the focus of the conference, discussed the conference name, developed criteria for selection of participants, determined criteria for selecting the conference hotel, and made recommendations for securing outside funding. The goals and objectives for the conference as developed by the committee at that meeting included the following:

1. Legitimizing applied communication research by encouraging applied scholarship and by helping to improve the quality of applied scholarship

2. Fostering dialogue between communication practitioners and communication theorists and researchers;

3. Identifing and promoting theoretical and research-based models for training, instruction, and application;

4. Setting an agenda for the future in applied communication research by assessing research priorities;

5. Enhancing the dissemination of applied communication research;

6. Assessing the current usefulness of applied communication knowledge;

7. Recommending improvements in how we conduct applied communication research; and

8. Recommending changes in graduate education in communication that would result in more and better applied communication scholarship.

To achieve these goals, the committee preferred a format that emphasized discussion rather than paper presentations. In addition, the committee proposed that a well-known person from outside the field be invited to deliver the keynote address. The committee also suggested that senior scholars serve as authors of major position papers and responses, and thought it important to allow an opportunity for invited and self-nominated participants to be included.

Corporate and grant support was sought in order to fund a keynote speaker, provide stipends for presenters, and secure one of Tampa's nicest hotels, while offsetting some expenses for all participants. The conference was set for 3½ days, and 40 was identified as the maximum number of participants that our discussion-oriented format could involve.

Invited participants included members of the steering committee, the keynote speaker, the presenters of the position papers and many of the respondents, a few others with significant applied research programs, and the newly selected SCA editor of *JACR*. Half of the participants nominated themselves in response to an announcement appearing in *Spectra* and mailed to various people around the country. Selections of nominees were made using the following criteria: (a) an active research program, evidenced by publication, in areas related to applied communication; (b) the ability to influence the field regarding its commitment to applied communication scholarship; and (c) appropriate representation of various areas of the field, graduate programs within the field, and regions of the country. A list of participants appears in Appendix B.

As with the New Orleans conference, the steering committee wished the conference to develop a set of recommendations reflecting the conferees' judgments about how the field might foster applied studies. In order to maximize discussion and to encourage the conference to develop a set of recommendations that the conference might adopt, a format for the conference emerged (see Appendix C).

Because insufficient time was available to complete deliberating on the recommendations, a postconference Delphi problem-solving format was utilized during which the recommendations underwent further scrutiny and revision. After three rounds of the Delphi, the recommendations were in final form; they can be found in Appendix A.

This volume is intended both as a report of the Tampa Conference on Applied Communication and as a stimulus to further applied scholarship in communication. The volume opens with the keynote address by Chris Argyris. Part I then describes the state of applied communication research and presents the major position papers and responses. Authors had the opportunity to revise their work prior to inclusion in this volume. Responses were given to each position paper, most of which are included in this volume.

Part II features a set of postconference reflections, two written by conference participants and two written by significant scholars who did not attend the conference. Part III completes the volume: Appendix A presents the recommendations of the conferees to the communication field, and Appendixes B and C serve to document the conference.

The authors included in this volume, among the most distinguished in the field of communication, do not agree on much. The debate among them is lively, and the issues they raise are provocative. The questions they leave with you can last a scholarly lifetime. The goal of the conference and of this volume is to provoke rather than to end conversation. For the most part, these authors do agree that the future of the communication field lies in scholarship that makes a difference to someone besides ourselves. Our scholarship must do more than enhance our vitae and contribute to the literature of our field. In the 21st century, communication scholarship must become, in Bateson's (1972) apt phrase, a "difference which makes a difference" (p. 453).

ACKNOWLEDGMENTS

The conference from which this volume resulted was initially the inspiration of Bob Avery, chair of SCA's Research Board, and Art Bochner, chair of the Department of Communication at the USF. SCA was about to assume ownership of the *Journal of Applied Communication Research*, which we published at USF for 10 years, and we were about to initiate our doctoral program. The conference seemed a timely project for USF, for SCA, and for the field, and we are all grateful to them for recognizing the opportunity.

The Research Board of SCA also provided our initial financial support, and I want to note the efforts of both Bob Avery and later Thom McCain, who succeeded Avery as chair.

My colleague Loyd Pettegrew was instrumental in securing major funding from the Southwestern Bell Corporation and from Johnson & Johnson, without which we would have had a much different conference. Their support of the conference is gratefully acknowledged.

As we were planning the conference, the Research Council at USF began a new program to provide significant support to university-sponsored research conferences, and ours was the first to receive financing from this program. My thanks to Ken Wieand and Bill Shea, chairs of the Research Council, and to Frank Lucarelli and Richard Streeter, directors of the Division of Sponsored Research.

The Department of Communication also committed funds to the conference, and I appreciate the confidence and support my colleagues in this effort.

The willingness of Jim Gaudino, Mark Knapp, Gerry Miller, and Teri Thompson, along with Bob Avery, Art Bochner, and Loyd Pettegrew, to give of their time to the conference steering committee enabled the conference to become a reality.

Many others members of the communication profession—far too many to list—contributed their time and ideas in shaping the conference, and I thank them for their commitment to the future of applied communication studies. Larry Frey helped me locate the source of Kurt Lewin's famous quotation, "There is nothing so practical as a good theory," which is cited in several chapters and for which no one seemed to know a citation.

I also want to acknowledge Laura Ellenberg, of USF's Division of Conferences and Institutes, who did an outstanding job of managing the details of the conference.

Finally, I want to thank Jennings Bryant and Teri Thompson, series and advisory editors in communication for Lawrence Erlbaum Associates, who believed in this volume, and Hollis Heimbouch, my editor at LEA, who is not only an excellent editor but a terrific person as well.

REFERENCES

Bateson, G. (1972). *Steps to an ecology of mind.* New York: Ballantine Books.
Cissna, K. N. (1982). Editor's note: What is applied communication research. *Journal of Applied Communication Research, 10,* i–iii.

Cissna, K. N. (1987). *Applied communication: A research perspective.* Paper presented at the Eastern Communication Association convention, Syracuse, NY.

Eadie, W. F. (1982). The case for applied communication research. *Spectra, 18*(10), 1–2.

Eadie, W. F. (1990). Being applied: Communication research comes of age. [Special issue]. *Journal of Applied Communication Research,* 1–6.

Eadie, W. F. (1994). On having an agenda. *Journal of Applied Communication Research, 22,* 81–85.

Ellis, D. G. (1991). Applied intelligence. *Journal of Applied Communication Research, 19,* 116–122.

Gordon, R. (1982). Practical theory. *Spectra, 18*(9), 1–2.

Hickson, M., III. (1973). Applied communications research: A beginning point for social relevance. *Journal of Applied Communications Research, 1,* 1–5.

Hickson, M., III. (1983). Ethnomethodology: The promise of applied communication research? *Southern Speech Communication Journal, 48,* 182–195.

Johnson, J. (1991). Some critical attributes of applied communication research. *Journal of Applied Communication Research, 19,* 340–346.

Kibler, R. J., & Barker, L. L. (Eds.). (1969). *Conceptual frontiers in speechcommunication: Report of the New Orleans Conference on Research and Instructional Development.* New York: Speech Association of America.

Kreps, G. L., Frey, L. R., & O'Hair, D. (1991). Applied communication research: Scholarship that can make a difference. *Journal of Applied Communication Research, 19,* 71–87.

Miller, G. R., & Sunnafrank, M. J. (1984). Theoretical dimensions of applied communication research. *Quarterly Journal of Speech, 70,* 255–263.

O'Hair, D. (1988). Relational communication in applied contexts: Current status and future directions. *Southern Speech Communication Journal, 52,* 315–330.

O'Hair, D., Kreps, G. L., & Frey, L. R. (1990). Conceptual issues. In D. O'Hair & G. L. Kreps (Eds.), *Applied communication theory and research* (pp. 3–22). Hillsdale, NJ: Lawrence Erlbaum Associates.

Pettegrew, L. S. (1988). The importance of context in applied communication research. *Southern Speech Communication Journal, 52,* 331–338.

Phillips, G. M. (1981). Researchers as brethren. *Spectra, 17*(7), 2.

Plax, T. G. (1991). Understanding applied communication inquiry: Researcher as organizational consultant. *Journal of Applied Communication Research, 19,* 55–70.

Weick, K. W., & Browning, L. D. (1991). Fixing with the voice: A research agenda for applied communication. *Journal of Applied Communication Research, 19,* 1–19.

About the Authors

THE EDITOR

KENNETH N. CISSNA (PhD, University of Denver, 1975) is Professor of Communication, University of South Florida. He was Editor of the *Journal of Applied Communication Research*, and is a former Chairperson of the Applied Communication Section of the Speech Communication Association. He is presently on the editorial boards of *JACR* and of the SCA Applied Communication Book Series. His articles have appeared in a variety of journals and edited volumes, and he recently co-edited *The Reach of Dialogue*.

THE CONTRIBUTORS

CHRIS ARGYRIS (PhD, Cornell University, 1951) is James Bryant Conant Professor Emeritus, Harvard University. His current interests are in actionable knowledge and organizational learning. Recent books include *Knowledge for Action* and *Overcoming Organizational Defenses*.

SAMUEL L. BECKER (PhD, University of Iowa, 1953) is University of Iowa Foundation Distinguished Professor Emeritus of Communication Studies, University of Iowa. His books and articles have focused largely on mass communication processes and rhetorical and communication theory. His most recent applied research has concerned means for reducing children's tobacco use.

DWIGHT CONQUERGOOD (PhD, Northwestern University, 1977) is Chair of Performance Studies, and Faculty Fellow, Center for Urban Affairs and Policy Research, Northwestern University. In addition to scholarly publication and videomaking, he has served as ethnographic consultant for the International Rescue Committee (Thailand) and the Palestine Human Rights Information Campaign (Gaza Strip), and he has testified in courtrooms and parole boards on behalf of refugees, illegal aliens, and prisoners.

ROBERT T. CRAIG (PhD, Michigan State University, 1976) is Associate Professor of Communication, University of Colorado at Boulder. His articles have addressed a variety of topics in communication theory and discourse analysis. In addition to serving as Editor of *Communication Theory*, his current projects include a book about communication as a practical discipline.

LOUIS P. CUSELLA (PhD, Purdue University, 1978) is Professor of Commmunication, University of Dayton. He has published articles in such journals as *Human Communication Research*, *Quarterly Journal of Speech*, *Health Communication*, and *Journal of Applied Communication Research*. His principle research interests concern communication processes in organizations.

WILLIAM F. EADIE (PhD, Purdue University, 1974) is Associate Director of the Speech Communication Association. His duties for SCA include promotion of the communication discipline's scholarship to a variety of audiences. He was the first SCA editor of the *Journal of Applied Communication Research*, and he chaired SCA's Applied Communication Section.

VICKI S. FREIMUTH (PhD, Florida State University, 1974) is Professor of Communication at the University of Maryland. She has worked in the area of public health and communication for many years. Her research on public communication health campaigns has been published in numerous articles, chapters, and books.

H. L. GOODALL, JR. (PhD, Pennsylvania State University, 1980) is Professor of Speech and Communication Studies, Clemson University. His organizational ethnographies include *Casing the Promised Land* and *Living in the Rock n Rock Mystery*, and he recently co-authored *Organizational Communication*.

KATHLEEN HALL JAMIESON (PhD, University of Wisconsin, 1972) is Professor and Dean of the Annenberg School for Communication of The University of Pennsylvania. She is the author of *Packaging the Presidency*, *Eloquence in an Electronic Age*, *Dirty Politics*, and most recently *Beyond the Double Bind*.

THOMAS A. McCAIN (PhD, University of Wisconsin, 1972) is Professor of Communication and Director of the Center for Advanced Study in Telecommunications at the Ohio State University. His research interests focus on the relationships between communication technologies and society. He is the author of numerous articles and book chapters, and he recently co-edited *The 1,000 Hour War: Communication in the Gulf*.

GERALD R. MILLER (PhD, University of Iowa, 1961) was Chair of the Department of Communication and University Distinguished Professor of Communication at Michigan State University. He served as President of the International Communication Association and was founding Editor of *Human Communication Research*. He was a Fellow of the International Communication Association and the American Psychological Association, and a Distinguished Scholar of the Speech Communication Association. He succumbed to cancer in 1993.

DAVID R. SEIBOLD (PhD, Michigan State University, 1975) is Professor of Communication, University of California–Santa Barbara. Author of nearly 100 articles on group decision making, interpersonal influence, health communication, and organizational change, he currently serves on the editorial board of *Communication Monographs*. He also works closely with many business, government, and health organizations.

TERESA L. THOMPSON (PhD, Temple University, 1980) edits the journal *Health Communication*. Her research focuses on communication between disabled and able-bodied individuals and on the interaction between health care providers and patients. She has written two books and is currently Professor of Communication at the University of Dayton.

PHILLIP K. TOMPKINS (PhD, Purdue University, 1962) is Professor of Communication and Comparative Literature, University of Colorado at Boulder. His articles in *Esquire, James Joyce Quarterly, Human Communication Research, Quarterly Journal of Speech*, and *Communication Monographs* instantiate his interests in communication as a social scientific and literary-rhetorical phenomenon.

JULIA T. WOOD (PhD, Pennsylvania State University, 1975) is Nelson R. Hairston Distinguished Professor of Communication Studies at the University of North Carolina at Chapel Hill. She has written 10 books, edited 6 others, and published over 50 articles and chapters. She is currently Editor of the *Journal of Applied Communication Research*, and is co-founder of the National Conference on Gender and Communication Research.

1

Knowledge When Used in Practice Tests Theory: The Case of Applied Communication Research

Chris Argyris
Harvard University

How can scholars create theory that practitioners can use to produce action and when they do, create also a genuine test of features of the theory? I am interested in this question for two reasons. First, I believe that practitioners will gain by using research-based knowledge. Second, I believe that scholars will gain because knowledge that is usable in practice and testable by practice will have to be conceptually more rigorous, and methodologically more demanding. I illustrate these claims by using research reports primarily from the field of applied communication.

APPLICABLE AND USABLE KNOWLEDGE

Social scientists have been, and continue to be, concerned about producing applicable knowledge. Applicable knowledge is relevant to the world of practice. Social scientists enhance applicability by striving to increase its external validity (Campbell & Stanley, 1963).

Whereas *applicability* refers to relevance, I define *usability* as implementing applicable knowledge; to carry into effect, to fully fulfill, to bring to full success whatever the propositions of applicable knowledge assert. Textbooks on research methodology contain applicable knowledge. Those who conduct research know that implementing such knowledge requires more knowledge than is typically found in textbooks.

Usable knowledge, as I use the term here, specifies the actual sequence of actions that leads to specified consequences. It is knowledge that can be used to bring about intended consequences.

Typically, social scientists produce knowledge that can be used to predict someone's (or some social unit's) actions. The prediction is used as evidence that the researchers understand and are able to explain the phenomena. Another type of knowledge is used to influence and to control others' thoughts and actions. This type of knowledge appears to be at the heart of applied communication. For example, Haslett (1987) noted that a major focus of much research on communication is on how to produce compliance.

A third type of knowledge that can be produced is knowledge that actors can use to control or influence their own actions. This action may include influencing others, but the actors are causally responsible for the attempt to get others to comply. Such knowledge contains directions and specifies sequences of actions that the actors can use. It helps actors to act effectively under real-time conditions in the world of practice. It empowers human beings in the everyday world. I found very little such knowledge in communication literature and, by the way, I found the same to be true in organizational behavior and public administration and public management.

MY BIASES ABOUT THEORY, EMPIRICAL RESEARCH, AND USABLE KNOWLEDGE

I begin by making explicit eight of my biases. They influenced the way I read, interpreted, and evaluated the research that I reviewed. These biases are not presented as claims about truth but as insights into how I interpreted this research.

Bias 1.   I believe that usable knowledge for effective action is one of the most important resources that scholars can produce for society. I call such resources theories of action, or more accurately, theories about designing and producing action. *Action* is defined as a sequence of activities given meaning by the actor, which is intended to produce specified consequences.

In order for theories of action to be usable, their proposition will have to be crafted in the service of taking action. Such propositions will specify action strategies that lead to specifiable intended consequences. They will also specify how the action strategies and intended consequences are connected to and driven by governing values.

Bias 2.   Governing values and their action strategies represent personal choices. They are not objectively true. Therefore, theories of action are normative theories. Although theories of action are not theories of objective truth, they do contain predictions as to what will occur given specified conditions. The truth of those predictions can be tested (disconfirmed) in real life. I am concerned that knowledge be developed that questions the status quo and suggests new alternatives (Srivasta, Cooperrider, & Associates, 1990; Unger, 1987).

Bias 3.   Action can be viewed as the result of a generic process that human beings implement. The process begins with discovering a problem, inventing a solution to the problem, implementing the solution, and evaluating the effectiveness of the implementation. This is a process of learning. Usable knowledge is, as is seen here, implementing the discoveries and the inventions under real-time constraints of everyday practice. Usable knowledge is used to implement applicable knowledge.

I question the assumption that theory and research in the service of discovery and invention will necessarily add up to applicable and usable knowledge. Theories and methods to produce usable knowledge may be different from what is required to produce applicable knowledge. For example, typical normal science theories and methods focus on precision and clarity. Theories that are usable in everyday practice may have to focus on how actors can act by being precisely imprecise, and by being clearly vague and still be able to subject their actions to public tests in the world of practice.

Bias 4.   Another feature of theories for producing usable knowledge is that the correct implementation of the theory should not inhibit the learning process described here. Theory for action should not be a self-limiting learning theory. We should not produce theories, for example, that require manipulation or the cover-up of manipulation, and that make manipulation impossible to discuss, because such theories make it difficult to detect and correct errors. Elsewhere, I have suggested that such theories are frequently produced by normal science researchers because of their requirements for cover-up (Argyris, 1980). This is also true for some of the research that I review later.

It is no accident that much normal science research produces knowledge that if used creates top–down hierarchical conditions. This happens because the theory of action embedded in some normal science research procedures results in conditions under which the researcher is primarily in control of the design, the experimental manipulation is understandably kept secret, the purpose of the research is often kept secret until after the data are collected, and the subject's time perspective is controlled by the researcher. These conditions should be included in every proposition produced using such normal science methodology. Thus, when scholars predict the consequences of a specified set of reinforcements, they do so under conditions in which they are in control. These conditions should be added to the generalizations that are produced. If we state that A leads to B, we should also state that this prediction is likely to hold when the conditions in real life are similar to the conditions required by top–down theory of action of rigorous research (Argyris, 1980).

Bias 5.   Theories of action that people actually use can be divided into two kinds: the theory that actors say they use, their espoused theory, and the theory that they actually use, their theory-in-use (Argyris & Schön, 1974).

What is peculiar about theories of action is that under conditions of dealing with complex, embarrassing, and even threatening problems, individual's espoused theories and theories-in-use tend to be inconsistent. Moreover, the actors are unaware of the inconsistency. This means that they have theories-in-use to keep them unaware and that they are unaware of these theories in use. Human beings are limited learning systems precisely when these limits are likely to be crucial (Argyris, 1982). I might add that we have found that human beings within any organization create contexts that encourage and reward limited learning systems even though the espoused theory is for vision, risk taking, responsibility, and courage (Argyris & Schön, 1978).

Bias 6.   Human beings are causality producing organisms. Human beings reflecting on their actions can be heard saying, "I did this because . . ." or "In order to . . . I acted as I did," or "I expected so and so to say such and such when I acted as I did." As Shoham (1990) stated:

> If causal reasoning is common in scientific thinking, it is downright dominant in everyday common sense thinking. All one needs to do is scan a popular publication and verify that causal terms—causing, preventing, enabling, bringing about, invoking, resulting in, instigating, affecting, putting an end to, and so on—appear throughout it. (p. 214)

Fritz Heider (1958) developed a perspective to understand human behavior in which the actor was seen as a naive scientific trying to understand the causality in his everyday world. It is the task of researchers to discover the causal reasoning that human beings use in everyday life and in the world of practice.

Bias 7.   Knowledge that is intended to be usable should be subjected to as tough a test as we can produce. Testability, falsifiability, disconfirmability are required if we are to assure the users that we have done our best to make sure that our claims of usability are justified. Also, we should seek to identify any second or third order consequences, especially those that may lead to inconsistencies.

Bias 8.   Human beings make life manageable by imposing on it behavioral routines, norms, and cultural values that guide their actions as well their understanding of others' actions. These features are so much an integral part of every day life that they are taken for granted.

Those of us who strive to produce usable knowledge have, I believe, a responsibility, on the one hand, to respect the taken for granted, while on the other hand, to use research methods that do not take it for granted that usable knowledge will be produced (Argyris, 1980; Hickson, 1983).

I now turn to an examination of selected applied communication literature. I do not focus on questioning the research methods, nor do I question the substantive findings. I base my discussion on the usability of the research.

A REVIEW OF RESEARCH WITH SPECIFIC APPLICABILITY

I begin with a study describing the development of an adolescent smoking prevention program (Burke, Becker, Arbogast, & Naughton, 1987). The objective of the interesting intervention was to prevent adolescents from smoking. The authors culled the scientific literature and identified several theories (e.g., theory of reasoned action, social learning theory, inoculation theory) that were relevant to their problem. The reasoning that the researchers used was enhanced by existing theories. For example, from inoculation theory they reasoned that arguments against smoking should be given in small doses. The arguments should work against attempts to pressure adolescents to smoke if the attempts are crafted in the language and use the reasoning that is answered by the refutations. Building adolescents' resistance to different arguments requires exposing individuals to arguments and allowing them to practice actively defending against them.

On the basis of such reasoning, the authors developed interventions consisting of an educational curriculum, competition and rewards, community activation, and student activation. The underlying strategy of the first three interventions was to create forces that would enable the adolescents to stop or reduce smoking. The educational curriculum gave relevant knowledge about the consequences of smoking. The competition and rewards provided positive reinforcement designed to elicit the desired behavior. The community activation program developed people in the community to create programs that would support all three activities just described.

How implementable are these interventions? Although the researchers did not provide an answer to this question because the programs had yet to be fully implemented, I assume that they are implementable. This assumption is fair because the gap between the knowledge and skills required to invent the programs and the knowledge and skills required to implement them is not large. The implementors do not require a new set of subtle skills. With a thoughtful selection process the creators could find citizens and teachers who could implement the four programs. The knowledge therefore is usable because the gap between ideas and action is small.

I suggest that the same is true in a study of the effectiveness of the newsletter (Seibold, Meyers, & Willihnganz, 1984) as well as a study on encouraging refugees to inoculate their dogs against rabies and to keep their camp clean (Conquergood, 1988). In both cases, if the recipients chose to read the newsletter or chose to clean up their camp, they had the skills to read or to clean up.

The same can also be said, I believe, for the study by Miller and Fontes (1975). Consistent with Miller's (1975) plea to integrate scientific and applied research, the authors conducted a series of interesting experiments that used simulation in ways that approximated "real" conditions in court. The results are usable, in that the findings could be applied in the courtroom by judges and lawyers.

If the gap between knowledge and action were large, in that the creators would have to learn skills that they did not have, then in order for the knowledge to be implementable the researchers would have to specify how to close the gap. For example, in the essay by Stewart (1983) the recommendations that he suggests are applicable, but the gap to produce them is large. It is not easy for consultants to carefully assess their interpersonal style, to be proactively opportunistic, and to function effectively under uncertainty. In my experience the gap between knowing and believing the ideas on the one hand, and producing them on the other, is quite large. Most human beings who espouse or value such concepts are unable to produce them, especially under conditions of embarrassment or threat, and are unaware of their inability to do so (Argyris, 1982, 1985, 1990).

The same is true for the research by Tompkins (1977). He discovered several profound communication problems in the Marshall Center. A key issue was lack of lateral openness. There was insufficient lateral or horizontal communication between two key units. Tompkins then invented a solution which was to generate a candid discussion among the key managers of the two units and the top management.

In my experience, such workshops are likely to be useful if the players are able to be candid, if they feel that they will not be harmed, and if they feel that others are able and willing to be candid. Under these conditions the outside consultant can be of help because her or his presence permits the players to project the responsibility for their becoming candid onto the consultant and the top management who agreed to have the meeting.

These types of workshops often do not deal with the underlying problem. For example, if there was poor communication, the theory-in-use of the players must have been to produce poor communication. The players must have been highly skillful at bypassing the embarrassing and threatening issues identified by Tompkins. In order for any bypass to be effective, it must be covered up. The players must therefore be skillful at cover-up. In order for the players to bypass and cover-up, they must have organizational norms that encourage them to do so. The organizational theory-in-use is to encourage bypass and cover-up.

We have now gone from a "let's be candid session" to a session that examines the skillful actions that produce ineffectiveness and the organizational conditions (formal and informal) that sanction such actions. It is the latter factors that are the causal ones. Identifying these factors in a way that is constructive requires skills that the participants do not have and an organizational culture that does not exist to support such skills. These are large gaps, which is why I suggest that Tompkins' solutions, as presented in the paper, were applicable but not usable.

Let us now turn our attention to the recipients. How usable is the knowledge that researchers produce? Recalling the adolescent study, the intent was to inoculate them against smoking and keep them from succumbing to peer pressures to smoke. Let us assume for the moment that the four intervention activities would work when their message to not smoke was consistent with the intentions of the adolescents. The gap then would be small.

The gap was large with the adolescents who would like to smoke or those who were ambivalent. The theories-in-use of these two groups was different from the theory-in-use of the one described earlier. This is the case because the adolescents in the two latter groups held theories-in-use that would lead to smoking or ambivalence about smoking. If I read the article correctly the educational reward and other interventions did not differentiate among the first, second, and third groups. Hence it is difficult to specify how usable the knowledge was by the adolescents who favored smoking or were ambivalent.

This does not mean that the compliance dimensions of the knowledge may not have positive effects. The point is that the communication research did not lead to knowledge that could empower the adolescents because it did not deal with their theories-in-use. Nor did it deal with the task of unfreezing the present theories-in-use and introducing new ones.

The same may be said for Seibold, Meyers, and Willihnganz's (1984) research on health information and for Meyers and Seibold's (1985) segmentation approach to a health services organization. Both provide applicable knowledge about who is likely to do what the creators wish them to do. The study on segmentation suggests that high involvement may be a better predictor of success. The study does not say how to increase the involvement.

But, could not research be conducted to identify these factors? I believe the answer is yes. I also believe that research designs would be required that incorporate different features from those illustrated by the research cited. For example, in the smoking study the adolescents should be helped to discover their existing theories-in-use and their skilled incompetence to deal with peer pressure. Next, the design should help them learn a new theory-in-use to deal effectively with the pressure. This research goal is achievable but it would require educational experiences different from those reported in the study (Argyris, 1982).

In this connection, it is interesting to note that during the student activation component the adolescents were asked to generate antismoking slogans to be used on their fellow adolescents. The idea was that creating these slogans would inoculate the creators and might influence the receivers. There were two models of communication implicit in this strategy. The one used by one adolescent to influence another was consistent with the external commitment model described previously. The one used by the creator required that the intention be kept secret from the adolescent. Was it likely that adolescents could be helped to inoculate themselves if they were told that the reason they should create slogans for others was to strengthen themselves?

To use the language of research, slogan creation, in this case, was the experimental manipulation. Normal science experimental procedures require that the reasoning behind as well as the actual experimental manipulation used be kept secret from the subjects in order not to confound the explanation or the cause of the effect. An analysis of a large number of such studies shows that if the results were used by practitioners, in order for them to work as predicted, the built-in secrecy would necessarily have to be continued in the world of practice (Argyris, 1980). For example, in the research on trust and credibility, one study indicated that the same message would have to be communicated differently depending on the brightness of the audience. The author held that if the audience is bright, several alternatives should be communicated. If the audience is not so bright, only one alternative should be communicated (Aronson, 1972). Let us assume that this finding is true. Should the users then tell the not so bright audience why they are being given one alternative or would this cause the users to lose their credibility? What are the ethics of producing knowledge that "works" when the reasoning behind its use must be kept secret?

Similar questions may be asked regarding the Conquergood (1988) study. He and his colleagues decided that the best strategy to influence the refugees was a grand, clamorous, eye-catching Rabies Parade led by an individual in a tiger costume followed by someone in a chicken costume. What would have happened if the researchers had told the audience that they were using the chicken because in Hmong lore chickens are believed to have divine powers?

The program was a success. Scores of dogs were inoculated and camps were cleaned up. If one were interested in empowering the refugees so that they did not need the parade in the first place, what sort of communication efforts would be required? The authors in the smoking study would suggest that the intervention would require more involvement of the refugees in dealing with the reasons that the refugees had that led them not to worry about rabies and about camp cleanliness (Burke et al., 1987). Please recall that the actions these authors report that they designed to get students more involved was to encourage them to produce antismoking messages that could be disseminated to their peers (p. 12). They were teaching adolescents to be users and their fellow adolescents to be recipients.

A REVIEW OF RELATIONSHIPS AMONG VARIABLES RESEARCH

In a careful set of three field studies, Eadie, Komsky, and Krivonos (1984) investigated the relationship between credibility and distortion in the context of a faculty unionization campaign. In my opinion, the authors showed ingenuity in studying a very difficult and timely issue in such a way that they could produce applicable knowledge. The problem with the knowledge produced is, in my opinion, not with its external validity but with the possible unintended consequences if used by others in order to create similar interventions in other contexts.

For example, the authors reported that initially the credibility of the source of the message could act to overcome initial concerns about distortion. Once expectations were formed, credibility and distortion were related in more complex ways. The distortion in early messages was forgiven by auditors as being necessary to persuade. This was especially true for highly involved recipients when the message came from the preferred source. Recipients were also willing to recognize that the competing source had to distort the message in order to make its case. But the recipients used the distortion by the competing organization as a means for distinguishing the "good guys" from the "bad guys." Finally, the authors concluded that neither strategy made a significant difference in influencing the final outcome because the long years of campaigning had firmly set opinions.

It is true that the study clarified the complex relationship between credibility and distortion. The clarification was largely at the level of discovery. The authors provided no solutions or ways to produce the solutions to the problems of how to communicate when attitudes are set. A study could be conducted to involve human beings in exploring the conditions under which they would alter their vote. A study could be conducted in which the senders admit at the outset that they realize that they are facing an audience with attitudes that are largely set. They could then invite the audience to design a communication program in which the recipients educate the senders as to how they could communicate more effectively with the recipients.

The second thoughtful study that focused primarily on discovery was one by Cissna, Cox, and Bochner (1990), designed to make intelligible the experiences of adults who have reorganized into a stepfamily structure. The study used largely clinical interpretive methods of inquiry. Like the previous one, it did not attempt an intervention.

The primary research methodology was in-depth interviews that were administered to each adult separately and then a second set of in-depth interviews with the partners together. There were no data reported on the children's views and experiences.

There was, in the parents' views, a top–down relationship with the children. The authors appeared to go along with this view in their research. For example, the authors concluded that managing the interface of marital versus parental relationship involved two tasks. The first task was to establish the solidarity of the marriage in the minds of the stepchildren. The second task was to establish parental authority, particularly the credibility of the stepparent. In my language these two tasks were solutions to the discovery of the tension between marital and parental relationships.

How did the parents accomplish these tasks? The authors either did not tell us what the parents said or if they did, one had to infer that the parents acted in ways that were counterproductive to the very bonding that the parents were trying to create. An example of the former is when Paul said that he used to tell Cynthia (his daughter) that she was holding out to get her original parents together. In order for us to know how he produced this solution, there should be either excerpts from the actual conversation or at least recollections of it. Do the authors mean to imply that the validity of intelligible descriptions does not require knowing how Paul crafted his conversation?

An example of the latter is John quoted as saying, "Look, kids, you're not splitting us up. If you want to leave, leave. We're here to stay and it's your option." Or when Jim reports that he said to his daughter, "We are not going to get into a courtroom session. When Mommy comes home and tells me how everything happened, it is as good as if I have been there." These comments suggest a top–down, one-way communication. (It is consistent with the theory-in-use that we have observed most human beings use). Such conversation tends to limit learning as well as discourse. It is not consistent with authentic communication of the kind recommended by Bateson and Watzlawick, two scholars who are quoted approvingly by the authors.

It appears to me that the authors took John's and Jim's mode of communication for granted. They speak of going meta on studying communication but, if I read the article correctly, they did not go meta on why John nor Jim did not examine their modes of communicating. Would not such inquiry produce knowledge that could help John and Jim surface their respective reasons for the way they crafted their conversation? Would that not, in turn, help the authors develop analyses of second order consequences of the conversations as crafted? Would not both types of analysis help enrich our understanding of the cues and propositions that John and Jim used to codify and to create their relationships, which the authors say are central to understanding metacommunication?

This study also raises the question of how those of us studying human beings' dialogue strive to make sure that we are not unrealizingly kidding ourselves or others. For example, the authors point out that interpretive studies seek intelligibility rather than predictability and change. Their goal is to make sense of behavior rather than to explain it. But, how do we know that the sense we make of the dialogue is valid? One answer is to build on a basic assumption of the interpretive approach which is to embrace the burden of choice made by the actors to keep the conversation going. What does "going" mean? Could one have more or less effective ways of going? If so, how would the reader know what they might be?

Would not such information be of help to John and Jim? If so, then does this not mean that the researchers chose not to produce knowledge that would help John and Jim become more effective? The authors could have produced knowledge that would help John and Jim learn how to go meta when they are dealing with their children. The authors appear to take for granted the burden of choice (to use their concept) made by Jim and John in how they engaged in dialogue with their children.

From the point of view of producing usable knowledge, does it not matter how the choices are made to keep the conversation going? Are Jim's, John's, and Mary's choices all equally desirable? Can we understand how to keep conversation going in these families without including the children?

Finally, although the authors appear to shun explanations and causality, they do crop into their analysis. For example, the authors report that the parents establish their identity and unity of the new marriage in the eyes of the children by appearing to agree even when they may not *because* [italics added] marital dissension makes the couple, and especially the stepparent, vulnerable to harassment or "courtroom accusation" from the stepchildren (p. 53).

Moreover, the authors appear to predict that the parents may have to play games of deception (appear to agree even when they do not) in order to solidify the family. Again, if one were to want to use these data, would the authors recommend the use of these games? What might be the second order effects of designed lying and coverup within the family?

Summary, So Far

To summarize, the research studies reviewed so far appear to contain biases that inhibit usability by the people from whom the data were obtained:

1. If, as I did at the outset, we assume that individuals have the values and skills to produce the influence conditions required, then some of the research results are usable. To put it another way, the more routine the implemen-

tation, the more likely that the knowledge can be usable. The greater the gap between the inventions or solutions produced by the researchers and the skills and competencies of the willing implementors, the less likely that the results will be usable. Most of the research reviewed did not make this distinction.

2. Much of the research reviewed was aimed at producing conditions of unilateral influence over others. Little knowledge was produced on how the recipients of the influence could deal with the influencers other than to comply. The research empowers the influencers but not those being influenced.

If those being influenced tried to remedy the inequality by using the same knowledge, they would create the same inequality for others that the original influencers created for them.

3. If it is true that espoused theories may differ significantly from theories-in-use and if individuals tend to be unaware when they are acting inconsistently, the research cited appears to assume that this problem does not exist. Or, if it does exist, it can be ignored without harming the potential users.

4. When researchers study actors who use games of bypass and cover-up, the researchers tend to be unaware that their empirical generalizations contain these bypass and cover-up processes; the researchers take them for granted (as do their subjects).

SOME DILEMMAS OF IMPLEMENTING NATURALISTIC, HUMANISTIC, INTERPRETIVE (NHI) APPROACHES

In the papers that I reviewed about theory and method the authors take positions that range from the belief that applied research and basic research can profit from each other to the position that they overlap greatly (Cissna, 1982; Eadie, 1982; Miller & Sunnafrank, 1984; Pettegrew, 1988). Some authors (Bochner, 1985; Eadie, 1982; Ryan, 1986) suggested ways to integrate what they refer to as scientific or basic versus applied research.

Bochner (1985) proposed an applied science that strives to make the universe intelligible. The goal is edification of which one mode is the pursuit of prediction and control. The goal is less to collect facts that will produce objective truth and more to generate descriptions that will enable us to keep the conversation going. I turn to exploring some features of the current debate between normal science and NHI approaches (Hirschman, 1989; Hunt, 1989). The purpose is to ask the NHI proponents to examine several consequences that flow from the implementation of their approach that are, I believe, contradictory the values of world view that they hold.

Again, I begin with making my biases explicit. I am a critic of normal science methodology because the correct use of it will necessarily lead to limited learning and an unawareness of the limitation (Argyris, 1980). Briefly, the argument is as follows. Human behavior may vary widely but the theories-in-use to produce it do not. Young and old, wealthy or poor, well educated or poorly educated, male or female, minority or not, they all have the same theory-in-use (Argyris, 1982).

The theory-in-use most often found has been modeled and we call it Model I. This model is helpful as a theory of learning in which the learning is routine and does not require questioning the underlying values of the players nor the underlying organizational or societal values. Model I not only leads to limited learning individuals, it leads to limited learning systems (Argyris & Schön, 1978).

Research methodology is also a theory of action. It too has a theory-in-use. The theory-in-use of much of normal science is almost identical to Model I. When Model I human beings use Model I research methods, the result is research that conforms to the status quo. Even when the research is intended to produce possible new alternatives, it does not (Argyris, 1980).

Given these views when I read that NHI proponents seek to understand meaning, to be flexible, and to create open dialogue, I became interested to say the least. However, by the time I finished the reading I had developed some concerns that I should like to share.

I begin by describing how the proponents of NHI characterize their approach and the resistance and barriers that they report they experience. As to the former, NHI is described as an epistemic, self-consciousness framework, in which interpretations can be disciplined and rule bounded; and as an imaginative way of seeing experience (Holbrook, Bell, & Grayson, 1989). NHI is less concerned with causality and more with interpreting text to surface the meanings, especially those that are taken for granted. It involves hermeneutics rather than statistics or experimentation. There is a dependence on the researchers' personal introspection and subjective judgment. It finds its major supporting evidence in the body of the text (Hunt, 1989).

NHI proponents report that normal social scientists see its perspective as inappropriate and inherently nonscientific. At best it can be used for hypothesis generation for the logic of discovery but not for the logic of refutation or demonstration (Anderson, 1989; Hirschman, 1989).

Some NHI proponents agree that the approach is not best suited for refutation. Others (Anderson, 1989) suggest there are no fundamental differences separating the sciences and the nonsciences. Still others (Peter & Olson, 1989) suggest that no one has solved the problem of demarcation and that any claim of refutation is often easily refuted. Finally, there is the appeal to cooperate (Holbrook, Bell, & Grayson, 1989) because there are many legitimate approaches to science and inquiry (Peter & Olson, 1989).

I agree with the call for cooperation. I agree that there are many reputable modes of inquiry to achieve understanding. But, when we intend to produce knowledge that human beings can use, then I believe that even if the arguments discussed earlier are valid they bypass central ethical problems involved in producing usable knowledge. If it is true that usable knowledge is based on normative theories, and if it is true that normative theories are not theories of objective truth, then those who produce usable knowledge have the responsibility to make it clear how usable is the knowledge and under what conditions. They also have the responsibility of making disconfirmable any explicit dysfunctional consequences that arise if the knowledge is used correctly (not simply if it is used incorrectly).

In our work, much of which is biased toward the NHI perspective, we do not have difficulty in designing and implementing predictions that, I believe, are genuinely disconfirmable. First, we begin with tests with the use of consensus. Next we strive to generate predictions about what will and will not happen in a given situation, in the same situation over time, and in different situations. Next are the predictions that are not disconfirmed even after (a) we tell the subjects the prediction ahead of time, (b) even after they disagree with the predictions, and (c) even after the test is created jointly by the researchers and the subjects and the tutors are the subjects themselves. Moreover, we have found it possible to craft the generalizations in ways that practitioners can use and when they do, test the predictions (Argyris, 1982, 1985; Argyris, Putnam, & Smith, 1985; Schön, 1983).

A NATURALISTIC HUMANISTIC PERSPECTIVE IN THE SERVICE OF COMPLIANCE

Many applied researchers appear to seek research results that produce compliance without making the strategy for compliance explicit. For example, McQuarrie (1989) states that the beauty of resonance in advertising is that it reduces the explicit verbal statements to influence that can be counterargued by the consumer and therefore lead to resistance. With the use of resonance, equivalence is tacit and refutation by the consumer is more difficult.

In my research domain, I would question the advisability of using communication to lower resistance in order to generate compliance. Organizations that produce such compliance also produce defensive routines. The defensive routines create conditions that over protect and inhibit learning (Argyris, 1985). There is a set of third order consequences. Many individuals who comply know that they are complying and come to dislike the system for requiring them to do so, and later themselves for so doing. Others distance themselves from the choice they made to comply. They legitimize the distancing by becoming cynical about organizational change and justice, by mistrusting those in power, and by learning to play subtle games of manipulation. They comply on the surface and resist below the surface. Often these individuals create organizational malaise in which they feel good about their system failing yet deny that this is the case. They get joy out of organizational distress but, of course, deny it (Argyris, 1990).

Could this happen in the world of applied communication in those cases in which the research is in the service of unilateral compliance? Could individuals learn to inoculate themselves against any shame or guilt that they may feel because of choosing to comply? Could they learn to mistrust the compliance methods? Or, could they distance themselves enough from them so that they become tolerant of distortions made in the communication schemes because the creators of the schemes have to do that (Eadie, Komsky, & Krivonos, 1984). Moreover, could they reach the point where they accept distortion because their minds are no longer influenced by the communication enough to produce compliance? It doesn't make any difference because they had already made up their minds.

There exists a dilemma. The proponents of NHI speak of wholeness, choice, understanding, meaning, flexibility, open texts, and dialogue. Yet, if I read the research correctly, most of it is in the service of compliance and ultimately closed dialogue and closed texts (Cohen, 1989). NHI proponents may have a different methodology from normal science but it appears to me that they use it in a way that results in some of the dysfunctional consequences that they decry. May not this dilemma exist for consumers? If so, might they deal with it by developing personal and social defensive routines that will make compliance more difficult while the intentions and strategies for resistance will be covered up and the cover-up also covered up?

As I read the systematic review of consumer research by Cohen and Chakravarti (1990), I noted that whether the propositions are about the ways consumers make judgments and choices or about getting the desired responses to marketer-initiated stimuli, the reasoning embedded in the propositions about how to do each effectively cannot be made explicit to the consumer.

For example, when the research specifies that complex stimuli have such and such influence or emotional content has the following impact, and when marketers use that knowledge to reach the consumer rather than telling the consumers ahead of time, the reasoning behind the marketers' strategies could reduce their effectiveness.

I wrote to Professor Cohen and he kindly responded to my speculations:

> For the sake of discussion let us assume that marketers have acquired some important insights regarding consumers' psychological processes that they feel able to "exploit." Let's assume further that key ethical issues and legal questions have been resolved [specifies them]. . . . Still, it is conceivable that the marketer may wish to consider some type of disclosure (e.g., imagine some "powerful" sales tactics) to overcome objections that the practice is unfair or deceptive. How such a disclosure might weaken the persuasive impact of any specific tactic is probably an empirical question. (personal communication, 1990)

I agree with Professor Cohen's suggestion for empirical research on the impact of specific tactics on persuasion. I also recommend empirical research on the long range impact of the cumulative impact of the present tactics.

NHI Perspective and the Dialogue with Clients

In this section, I shift the attention from the consumer to the client. By client I mean the line manager who is trying to produce and sell a product or service. I asked myself how would I feel if I were a line manager trying to sell the various products described in several chapters in the Hirschman (1989) book? What would be the natural, human dialogue that might occur if my staff (read advertising or marketing professionals) used the reasoning I found in the various chapters?

McQuarrie (1989) quotes approvingly an analysis by Barthes. Barthes is quoted as saying the name Panzoni suggested Italian. Pepper and tomato and tri-color printing suggested "Italianicity." The open string bag from which the vegetables spill suggested both a recent return from shopping and a healthy image of a person who shopped for fresh food. Drawing these together, his advertising staff would then say that the "advertisement connotes a product which is ethnic, perhaps exotic; fresh and wholesome; delectable in the timeless fashions of art" (p. 99). The staff would also communicate (tacitly or explicitly) their belief that this analysis was "more subtle and far-reaching" than the usual social science.

My first thought on this analysis is to recall that NHI proponents caution me against placing too much faith in causality. Interpretation of text is the way to go. So, I listen to their interpretations and I find all sorts of causal statements in them. For example, Panzoni *suggests* Italian; . . . *suggests* Italianicity, . . . *suggests* a healthy image.

They may use the term *suggests* in order to indicate weak causality. But how weak is weak? I note that they combine several "suggests" to conclude that the analysis is more subtle and far reaching. How do weak causal statements add up to robust ones?

When I asked that question I would likely experience my staff as not only playing down causality, but practically denying it. For example, I might be told that the copywriter and art director cannot tell what it does or does not mean, and that the analysis that I just heard should be placed alongside poetry, myth, and dreams.

This reminds me of a scholar who maintained that NHI professionals should be cautious about making policy recommendations because of the tenuous causality in their approach (Hunt, 1989). I remember wondering, "Do I not pay the professionals to make policy recommendations?"

Also, I could not help but reflect that NHI professionals hold that they must get at the meaning of the phenomena from the perspective of the consumers involved (Ozanne & Hudson, 1989). I like that approach; but so far all I get are interpretations of what is likely to be the impact of the advertisement. I get relatively little insight into the meanings the consumer holds as described by the consumers in their own words or their own actions.

Now I can begin to understand Park and Zaltman's (1987) report of the mistrustful attitudes of professionals and line managers that lead to self-sealing defensive patterns. The NHI proponents seek to conduct research to create open texts yet they (as well as those using normal science methods) create, in my opinion, conditions that are similar to closed texts.

For example, managers complain that research is not problem oriented. It tends to provide a plethora of facts, but not actionable data. Researchers are overly involved with techniques. They do not appear to focus on management problems. Researchers defend their actions by citing the rules of science or NHI which means they respond in ways that reinforce the teckie attribution. Teckie responses are compulsively repeated even though they prove ineffective.

The result is a set of circular processes in which both sides are likely to dig in their heels and learning is not going to occur. These self-sealing processes must be interrupted. The skills necessary to do so can be taught to researchers as well as to managers. In our advanced seminars for researchers, we help them to see that their actions that they have available to react to these self-sealing processes are highly skillful and incompetent (Argyris, Putnam, & Smith, 1985). Again, the same is true for managers (Argyris, 1990).

SUMMARY

All of the research that was reviewed is applicable. A smaller portion is usable by practitioners where the use is a test of a feature of a theory. Where the implementation is a test of a theory, it is primarily a test of a theory of unilateral compliance. Research in the domain of organizational behavior suggests that human beings who choose to comply are likely to place the responsibility for compliance on those creating it. This leads to external commitment, a lower sense of learning, and a greater sense of disempowerment.

Research with an NHI emphasis intends to be more humanistic than positivistic research. Its focus is on meaning, choice, and individuality or uniqueness. The NHI researchers question normal science concepts of causality and focus on interpretation. My analysis suggests that most of the NHI research reports rely upon a tacit concept of causality. The NHI studies were difficult to disconfirm yet the researchers intend that the knowledge they produce should be usable. Finally, NHI researchers who question the built-in distancing of positivistic research may also produce their own brand of distancing, which they simply keep tacit.

REFERENCES

Anderson, P. F. (1989). On relativism and interpretivism—With a prolegomenon to the 'Why' question. In E. C. Hirschman (Ed.), *Interpretive consumer research* (pp. 10–22). Provo, UT: Association for Consumer Research.

Argyris, C. (1980). *Inner contradictions of rigorous research.* New York: Academic Press.

Argyris, C. (1982). *Reasoning, learning and action: Individual and organizational.* San Francisco: Jossey-Bass.

Argyris, C. (1985). *Strategy, change and defensive routines.* New York: Harper Ballinger.

Argyris, C. (1987). A leadership dilemma. *Business and Economic Review, 1,* 1–7.

Argyris, C. (1990). *Overcoming organizational defenses: Facilitating organizational learning.* Needham, MA: Allyn-Bacon.

Argyris, C., Putnam, R., & Smith, D. (1985). *Action science.* San Francisco: Jossey-Bass.

Argyris, C., & Schön, D. (1974). *Theory in practice.* San Francisco: Jossey-Bass.

Argyris, C., & Schön, D. (1978). *Organizational learning: A theory of action perspective.* Reading, MA: Addison-Wesley.

Argyris, C., & Schön, D. (1988). Reciprocal integrity: Creating conditions that encourage personal and organizational integrity. In S. Srioasta & Associates (Eds.), *Executive integrity* (pp. 197–222). San Francisco: Jossey-Bass.

Argyris, C., & Schön, D. (in prep.). *Conceptions of causality in social theory and research: Normal science and action science compared.*

Aronson, E. (1972). *The social animal.* San Francisco: Freeman.

Bochner, A. P. (1985). Perspectives on inquiry: Representation, conversation and reflection. In M. L. Knapp & G. R. Miller (Eds.), *Handbook of interpersonal communication.* Beverly Hills: Sage Publications.

Burke, J. A., Becker, S. L., Arbogast, R. A., & Naughton, J. M. (1987). Problems and prospects of applied research: The development of an adolescent smoking prevention program. *Journal of Applied Communication Research, 15,* 1–18.

Campbell, D. T., & Stanley, J. C. (1963). *Experimental and quasi-experimental design for research.* Skokie, IL: Rand McNally.

Cissna, K. N. (1982). What is applied communication research? *Journal of Applied Communication Research, 10,* 1–3.

Cissna, K. N., Cox, D. E., & Bochner, A. P. (1990). The dialectic of marital and parental relationships within the stepfamily. *Communication Monographs, 57,* 44–61.

Cohen, J. B. (1989). An over-extended self? *Journal of Consumer Research, 16,* 125–128.

Cohen, J. B., & Chakravarti, D. (1990). Consumer psychology. *Annual Review of Psychology, 41,* 243–288.

Conquergood, D. (1988). Health theater in a Hmong refugee camp. *Journal of Performance Studies, 32,* 171–208.

Eadie, W. F. (1982). The case for applied communication research. *Spectra, 18*(10), 1–3.

Eadie, W. F., Komsky, S. H., & Krivonos, P. D. (1984). Credibility and distortion in a university collective bargaining campaign. *Journal of Applied Communication Research, 12,* 103–127.

Haslett, B. J. (1987). *Communication: Strategic action in context.* Hillsdale, N.J.: Lawrence Erlbaum Associates.

Heider, F. (1958). *The psychology of interpersonal relations.* New York: Wiley.

Hickson, M., III. (1983). Ethnomethodology: The promise of applied communication research? *The Southern Speech Communication Journal, 48*, 182–195.

Hirschman, E. C. (Ed.). (1989). *Interpretive consumer research*. Provo, UT: Association for Consumer Research.

Holbrook, M. B., Bell, S., & Grayson, M. W. (1989). The role of humanities in consumer research: Close encounters and coastal disturbances. In E. C. Hirschman (Ed.), *Interpretive consumer research* (pp. 19–47). Provo, UT: Association for Consumer Research.

Hunt, S. D. (1989). Naturalistic, humanistic, and interpretive inquiry: Challenge and ultimate potential. In E. C. Hirschman (Ed.), *Interpretive consumer research* (pp. 185–198). Provo, UT: Association for Consumer Research.

McQuarrie, E. F. (1989). Advertising resonance: A semiological perspective. In E. C. Hirschman (Ed.), *Interpretive consumer research* (pp. 97–114). Provo, UT: Association for Consumer Research.

Meyers, R. A., & Seibold, D. R. (1985). Consumer involvement as a segmentation approach for studying utilization of health organization services. *The Southern Speech Communication Journal, 50*, 327–347.

Miller, G. R. (1975). Humanistic and scientific approaches to speech communication inquiry. *Western Speech Communication, 39*, 231–239.

Miller, G. R., & Fontes, N. E. (1975). *Real versus reel: What's the verdict?* East Lansing, Michigan: Department of Communication, Michigan State University, Final Report to National Science Foundation (NSF-RANN grant Apr 75–15815).

Miller, G. R., & Sunnafrank, M. J. (1984). Theoretical dimensions of applied communication research. *Quarterly Journal of Speech, 70*, 255–263.

Ozanne, J. L., & Hudson, L. A. (1989). Exploring diversity in consumer research. In E. C. Hirschman (Ed.), *Interpretive consumer research* (pp. 1–8). Provo, UT: Association for Consumer Research.

Park, C. W., & Zaltman, G. (1987). *Marketing management*. Chicago: Dryden Press.

Peter, P. J., & Olson, J. C. (1989). The relativistic/constructionist perspective on scientific knowledge and consumer. In E. C. Hirschman (Ed.), *Interpretive consumer research* (pp. 24–28). Provo, UT: Association for Consumer Research.

Pettegrew, L. S. (1988). The importance of context in applied communication research. *The Southern Speech Communication Journal, 53*, 331–338.

Rosen, M. (1991). Coming to terms with the field: Understanding and doing organizational ethnography. *Journal of Management Studies, 28*, 1–24.

Ryan, M. J. (1986). Implications from the 'old' and the 'new' physics for studying buyer behavior. In D. Brineberg & R. J. Lutz (Eds.), *Perspectives on methodology in consumer research*. New York: Springer-Verlag.

Schön, D. A. (1983). *The reflective practitioner*. New York: Basic Books.

Seibold, D. R., Meyers, R. A., & Willihnganz, S. C. (1984). Communicating health information to the public: Effectiveness of a newsletter. *Health Education Quarterly, 10*, 263–286.

Shoham, Y. (1990). Nonmonotonic reasoning and causation. *Cognitive Science, 14*, 213–302.

Srivasta, S., Cooperrider, D. L., and Associates (1990). *Appreciative management and leadership*. San Francisco: Jossey-Bass.

Stewart, J. (1983). Reconsidering communication consulting. *Journal of Applied Communication Research, 11*, 153–167.

Tompkins, P. K. (1977). Management qua communication in rocket research and development. *Communication Monographs, 44*, 1–26.

Unger, R. (1987). *Social theory: Its situation and its task*. New York: Cambridge University Press.

Wallendorf, M., & Belk, R. W. (1989). Assessing trustworthiness in natural consumer research. In E. C. Hirschman (Ed.), *Interpretive consumer research* (pp. 69–83). Provo, UT: Association for Consumer Research.

I

THE STATE OF
APPLIED COMMUNICATION RESEARCH

2

Theoria and *Praxis:*
Means and Ends in
Applied Communication Research

David R. Seibold
University of California–Santa Barbara

Article II of the Constitution of the Speech Communication Association (SCA), sponsor of this volume to chart applied communication in the 21st century, states, "The purpose of this Association shall be to promote study, criticism, *research*, teaching, and *application* of the artistic, humanistic, and scientific principles of communication" (italics added). *Research* and *application* are not only inherent in SCA's multifaceted mission, but are endemic to its varied endeavors. They have been wedded explicitly as *applied research* in two principal SCA enterprises: the Applied Communication Section of the Association and the *Journal of Applied Communication Research (JACR)*. Indeed, in an article in SCA's 75th anniversary publication, Work and Jeffrey (1989) concluded their "Historical Notes" on trends and changes in the Association between 1965 and 1989 by observing that "heightened interest in 'applied communication' suggests (a) growing maturity in communication theory-building, and (b) growing interest in practical application of communication principles in a variety of social situations and settings" (p. 56). Even former SCA President Osborne's (1990) defense of the discipline highlighted the prominent role of applied studies by communication researchers: "*[R]esearch* in communication is exploring significant questions in the humanities and the social sciences, on both theoretical and *applied* levels" (p. 2; italics added).

If research and application are inherent in our mission, our structure, our activities, and our self-presentation, why should this be so? What is the relationship between research and practice, and what should be the role of applied research in communication? One answer rests in the fact that, for better or worse, ours is a practical field. As Craig (1988) has cogently argued, our raison d'être resides in the cultivation of "practice." Historically we have existed to help others speak more clearly, argue more persuasively, disseminate information more effectively, relate to others through talk more satisfactorily, and the like. Of course, we cannot do so without explicit communication theory; therefore theory building arguably is our most important goal. But as a discipline we cannot proceed far on this tack without addressing questions of practice: Who can use this theory? For what purposes? In what manner and in which contexts? With what effects? And although we must be mindful of Brief and Dukerich's (1991) cautions about the limits of theory-usefulness interrelationships, the point emphasized thus far is that there is a mutuality to theory and practice. They guide and temper each other.

Communication researchers probably would not object too strenuously to the preceding characterization of our field as both an intellectual and practical endeavor, nor to the depiction of the interdependence of *theoria* and *praxis*. For a variety of reasons that are beyond the purview of this essay (see Kytle & Millman, 1986, on the goals and reward system of social research), there is a tendency among researchers to represent themselves as either "basic" or "applied" in orientation (see Miller & Sunnafrank, 1984, on this distinction in communication). Regrettably, this has led to some ambivalence among discipline members about the importance of having both basic and applied research within communication. Rossi (1980) noted a similar sentiment in his Presidential Address to members of the American Sociological Association: "Our ambivalence consists in believing—at one and the same time—that applied work is not worth our best efforts and our best minds . . . [yet] an important reason for our existence is that sociology will lead to important practical applications" (p. 889).

Researchers' tendencies to label themselves and others as either applied or basic also has encouraged the misconception that these should be separate endeavors conducted by different researchers. This depiction tends to be polarizing and often self-serving, while doing little to advance the discipline's twofold goals of theory and practice. Furthermore, not only have these distinctions falsely fostered the belief that pure and applied research are at 180° to each other, but they may have contributed to the misconception that communication research can be either 100% theoretical or 100% applied. Perhaps most importantly, largely ignored is the fact that both basic and applied research have advantages and disadvantages. Thomas (1983), a former President of the Ford Foundation, expressed this matter eloquently in the *American Council of Learned Societies Newsletter:*

> Good scholarship is not demeaned by taking as its starting point a specific policy issue. And basic research is not necessarily ennobled because it seeks to

satisfy only the scholar's intellectual curiosity. Both modes of inquiry have their advantages and disadvantages. If there is a risk that the quality of problem-oriented research may be impaired by the overly narrow nature of the questions or by constrictive deadlines, unfettered research runs the risk of self-indulgence and irrelevancy. (p. 23)

TOWARD A DEFINITION OF
APPLIED COMMUNICATION RESEARCH

Having set forth these premises concerning the mutuality of theory and practice, and the interrelationships between applied and basic research for achieving the theoretical and practical aims of the communication discipline, let us address another matter. What shall we take applied research in communication to mean, and by extension what should not be construed as applied communication research? For present purposes *applied communication research* will be defined as quantitative and qualitative empirical work that employs communication theory and research methods (a) as a means to applied ends, and/or (b) as a means to test theory in applied settings. In the first sense, "applied ends" may include problem solving, policy analysis and formulation, developing insights that are situation specific, and so forth. No deliberate effort is made to address theoretical issues in the discipline per se, although there may be theoretical implications that are simultaneously recognized by applied researchers or that are pursued later by more basic researchers. For example, in an article published in the *American Journal of Hospice Care*, Seibold, Rossi, Berteotti, Soprych, and McQuillan (1987) reported an evaluation of a hospice volunteer program. Although we necessarily drew upon major research concepts from interpersonal communication theory as well as small group, organizational, administrative, and sociological theories, we did not begin the project with the goal of addressing these traditions. Rather they served as means for understanding why the volunteer program succeeded in retaining some volunteers while losing what program administrators regarded as too many others. We did not set out to test postulates about the effects of role conflict on organizational turnover, for instance, but simply drew upon what insights organizational theory afforded us (cf. Berteotti & Seibold, 1994) as a means to answer a specific question about a specific problem in a specific setting.

In the second sense of applied communication research proposed earlier, investigators may engage in research as a means of explicitly testing one or more theories as they *apply* to a particular problem or situation. Another example may clarify this sense of applied research. Some years ago Seibold and Roper (1979) were interested in the comparative utility of two theories of behavioral intention for aiding in the construction of messages designed to persuade women to be more health conscious with regard to cancer detection.

Because the research funder, the National Cancer Institute, sought recommendations concerning the design of national message campaigns encouraging cervical cancer examinations, it was imperative to comparatively test the two theories (and their communication-related implications) in the specific domain of factors motivating women's intentions to obtain Pap tests. What resulted in the Seibold and Roper citation, and in another paper explicating a practical statistical procedure (Seibold & McPhee, 1979), was a quasi-experimental test of the two theories and methods for identifying their predictive powers. But what made this "applied research" was the restrictiveness of the applied realm in which the study was undertaken. Furthermore, the impetus for the study, the participants involved in it, and the practical implications drawn from it all were occasioned by the policy agenda and message campaign problems of the national health agency that commissioned it.

The two examples described indicate that applied communication research may serve two functions: (a) responding to applied agendas with communication theory and methods but with little immediate concern for whether important theoretical questions within the discipline are being answered, and/or (b) responding to the discipline's theoretical agendas but primarily as they apply to a specific problem domain. In some cases, as with the two examples given, these are very different emphases, and reports of the research may feature one aspect or the other. Often, however, both functions are served in the same project. Two sorts of research studies may emanate from such an investigation: those which report on theoretical matters studied in the course of the project, and those which merely utilize the tools of theory and method to illuminate and solve the problem. If another personal example will be forgiven, consider a project in which a team sought to identify for administrators and health educators in a regional health information center the effectiveness of their widely disseminated newsletter. As it happened there was adequate time to design the evaluation, a rarity in much applied research and many program assessments (see Brickman, 1981). The opportunity was used to survey relevant mass and health communication research on information-seeking and utilization. This research framework enabled the authors to interpret their findings for program personnel in more informative terms, and to couch these results within a conceptual framework that health practitioners routinely use (Seibold, Meyers, & Willihnganz, 1984). But this preparation also led to theoretical questions in marketing communication research and in program evaluation literature that could be answered with a more careful design of the study. Thus, the same project enabled the authors to address those theoretical issues as well, with the results appearing in applied research articles in the *Journal of Applied Communication Research* (Meyers, Seibold, & Willihnganz, 1983) and in the *Southern Speech Communication Journal* (Meyers & Seibold, 1985).

Since it is possible to conduct research that both extends theory by testing it in a restricted domain and utilizes theory as a means to an applied end, it might be noted that the twofold conception of applied communication research proposed here rests squarely between those described by Miller and Sunnafrank (1984) on one hand and by Eadie (1990) on the other. Miller and Sunnafrank, first, eschewed studies in which practitioners merely apply social science methods without regard to "solidly based theoretical notions of what to look for or how to interpret what is eventually found" (p. 255), a position with which I concur. These projects cannot be considered "research" merely because they are applied. But Miller and Sunnafrank also resisted a second approach in which investigators "elect to apply the results of basic communication research or the propositions of communication theory to the situation with minimal concern for producing theoretical or empirical contributions to the scholarly community" (p. 256). This method is the first sense I have proposed concerning what can and should be called applied communication research. Rather, Miller and Sunnafrank granted legitimacy to a third approach, namely only those studies in which applied researchers "draw upon the best scientific resources available, reasoning from clearly articulated and supported theories and using methods designed to test these theories as unequivocally as possible" (p. 256).

While this is the second sense identified in this essay in which communication research might be termed "applied," to restrict our conception of applied communication research *only* to "pure research carried out in applied settings" (p. 256) is limiting. It ignores the contributions that studies in the first sense make in furthering the field's dual missions of building theory *and* informing practice, and limits applied research in the second sense to theory advancement in particular contexts, too often without concern for efficacy.

Miller and Sunnafrank's conception denigrated theory-based applied studies in favor of theory-building applied research, whereas Eadie (1990) emphasized theory-based application but excluded theory-building investigations, even those in applied settings. Specifically, Eadie proposed three criteria for determining what is applied communication research (which were to be used by *JACR* associate editors in assessing papers' suitability for that journal during his editorship). First, the research should provide thorough exploration of a communication problem or situation, or yield results which are immediately applicable to such situations. Second, results should reveal information of substance about the problem or situation, and readers should feel confident about their validity. Third, "the research is securely based in theory but its purpose is not immediate theory building" (p. 3).

Taken together, these three criteria elegantly set forth the first sense of applied communication research I have proposed: research that draws upon the discipline's theories and methods as means to applied ends of problem scrutiny and problem solving. But Eadie's third criterion, theory-based but not theory-building, parts company with Miller and Sunnafrank and, by extension, with my second sense of applied research. In fairness, Eadie agreed that theory-building research can and should be done in applied settings. But he encouraged directing such studies to journals whose principal "criterion for publication is contribution to theory" rather than *JACR*'s primary emphasis on the "significance of contribution to the problem or situation being studied" (1990, p. 7). To my mind, excluding theory-building papers by encouraging their publication in journals other than *JACR* unnecessarily bifurcates applied research (which we have seen is capable of being both theory-based and theory-building), unduly restricts *JACR*'s scope, and may reinforce the misconception that applied research is limited to practice with little to contribute to the field's theory-building mission.

The discussion thus far has centered on two issues: (a) assumptions concerning the role of applied research in communication including the relationships among theory, research, and practice, and (b) a working definition of applied communication research that acknowledges its potential to be theory-based, theory-building or both, as well as resultant distinctions between this conception and more restrictive perspectives currently prominent in our discipline. The remainder of this chapter treats two other matters central to setting an agenda for applied communication research as we near the millennium: (c) which social problems and issues should applied communication research address?, and (d) what quantitative *methods* will be most useful for applied communication research? These questions are answered, in turn, in the following sections.

FOCI FOR APPLIED COMMUNICATION RESEARCH

Nearly two decades ago, Coleman (1980) offered an insightful treatment of the development of applied social research during the 20th century. His thesis was that trends in social research, including the emergence and decline of prominent "schools" of social research, were directly related to broader changes in society, especially changes in social structures. The Chicago School, for example, with its focus on the city, immigrants and their adaptation, marginal persons and subcultures, and qualitative methods of interviewing and participant observation, was associated with a very specific period in America: the transformation from a rural to an urban society, accompanied by teeming immigration, disorder and marginality, and local philanthropists funding local studies of local problems. Hence, Coleman contended, the social research this school performed which catapulted it into scholarly and policy prominence, was largely a reflection of the social fabric of the time.

In turn, just as the decline of the Chicago School in the 1930s and 1940s also mirrored the decline of the types of social problems and social structures that it had documented, the ascendancy of the Columbia School not coincidentally corresponded with new changes in the structure of social interaction. Coleman proposed that the emergence of a greater national awareness, national mass media, national manufacturing firms, and attendant problems of national markets/audiences/constituents, created an environment in which new questions and methods predominated: namely, policy research; mass communication effects studies; contract research for a different class of national sponsors; and the development of commensurate large-scale quantitative methods including survey research, national random samples, standardized questionnaires, and statistical analyses.

If Coleman's analysis is correct (and it should be noted that Delia, 1987, offered a strikingly parallel assessment of the history of communication research in general, and Putnam and Cheney, 1985, similarly linked specific developments in organizational communication research to societal dynamics since the 1920s), then two implications follow for applied communication research in the next century. First, the question of what applied researchers should study misses a more fundamental matter. Rather, changes in social structures and practices in 21st century America will necessarily give rise to certain types of applied studies across the social sciences, including communication, as researchers quite naturally strive to apply theory to the pervasive changes that envelop society (and themselves as societal members). Much as current applied researchers struggle to understand and to positively affect societal practices related to social issues such as AIDS, advanced interactive technologies in the workplace, videotaped testimony in the courtroom, and federal laws mandating educational practices with previously disenfranchised groups, future applied researchers will use communication theory and research methods and/or test theory in domains emerging from developments in the next century. By extension, second, projections concerning the foci of applied communication research in the next century must first anticipate what changes we are likely to face as a society. Since potential demographic, environmental, legal, intercultural, political, and technological changes are too numerous to address in this chapter, especially when other authors in this volume possess expertise in several of these areas, I restrict myself to changes likely to be felt at the group/organizational level in a variety of institutions, especially commerce and industry.

Johnston and Packer (1987) discussed a variety of market, technological, economic, demographic, cultural, and international forces shaping American organizations and their workforces as we approach the year 2000. They identified key trends likely to affect work and workers in the last years of this century: growth in the U.S. economy despite brief periods of recession; a decrease in manufacturing's share of the economy and a commensurate increase in the role of service industries (which will create 90% of new jobs);

and higher skill levels to be required for new jobs, especially those in service industries.

Particularly noteworthy are projections concerning the composition of organizational workforces in the year 2000. Johnston and Packer proposed that only 15% of new entrants to the labor force will be native White males, compared to 47% in that category before the 1990s. More women will enter the workforce. Almost 66% of new entrants will be women, and 61% of working-age women are expected to have jobs by the year 2000. They will enter professional and technical fields more rapidly than ever before, stimulate further growth of convenience industries, and prompt restructuring of work schedules and work locations as many also press for part-time, flexible and stay-at-home jobs. Non-Whites will make up 29% of new entrants into the labor force by the year 2000, twice their share of the workforce during the 1980s. Immigrants will represent the largest share of increases in the workforce since World War I. Even with more restrictive immigration laws, more than 66% of the annual 600,000 immigrants to the United States are likely to join the labor force. Finally, the average age of the population and the workforce will rise, and the pool of young workers entering organizations early in the next century will shrink. The average age of the workforce will climb from 36 in the 1980s to nearly 40 by the year 2000, and the number of young workers between 16 and 24 years of age will drop by almost 2 million, or 8%. Johnston and Packer (1987) summarized:

> In combination, these demographic changes will mean that the new workers entering the workforce . . . will be much different from those who people it today. Non-whites, women, and immigrants will make up more than five-sixths of the net additions to the workforce between now and the year 2000, . . . Juxtaposed with these changes in the composition of the workforce will be rapid changes in the nature of the job market. The fastest growing jobs will be in the professional, technical, and sales fields requiring the highest education and skill levels. Of the fastest growing job categories all but one, service occupations, require more than the median level of education for all jobs. Of those growing more slowly than average, not one requires more than the median education. (pp. xx–xxi)

These changes in the fabric of work and the weave of workers in the workplace will not only give rise to new textures in 21st century organizations but, following Coleman's (1980) analysis, will just as likely condition the foci of applied research on the character and effects of these new social structures. How will applied communication research in the 21st century reflect these changes?

On one hand, many traditional organizational communication concerns and perspectives will be even more salient. Interaction processes reflecting vocational/organizational socialization and assimilation (Jablin, 1987a), impression management (Giacalone & Rosenfeld, 1989), emergent communication networks (Monge & Eisenberg, 1987), structure/integration (Dansereau & Markham, 1987; Jablin 1987b), and traditional organizational outcomes (Downs, Clampitt, & Pfeiffer, 1988) will be of continued interest, and perhaps increased importance. Given the more pluralistic organizations of the next century, applied research on members' interpretive and coordinative problems will continue to be informed by subjectivist (Euske & Roberts, 1987) theories and concepts of enactment and improvisation (Weick, 1979; 1989) and sense-making (Eisenberg & Riley, 1988; Gioia & Ford, 1991). And if current trends in decentralization of responsibility and decision-making continue into the next century, applied researchers doubtlessly will continue to study participative processes (Monge & Miller, 1988) in now more diverse organizations.

At the same time, applied research on group/organizational communication processes will likely be transformed intellectually by the very changes researchers document and struggle to understand. Research on problems associated with diversity and multiculturalism in organizations likely will also draw upon theoretical perspectives salient in intercultural (Gudykunst & Nishida, 1988), intergenerational (Giles et al., 1990), and intergroup (Tajfel, 1982; Turner, 1987) areas of our discipline and others. Too, organizational/ group researchers confronting problems of power, politics, and influence (Frost, 1987) increasingly may turn to well-established language and communication perspectives in those areas (cf. Giles, Coupland, & Coupland, 1991). Finally, as organizations are changed by advances in information/ communication technology (Fulk & Steinfield, 1990), applied research in the next century is likely to assimilate established and emerging perspectives on technology and new media (cf. Poole & DeSanctis, 1990).

In summary, applied communication research in the 21st century will be conditioned by larger societal changes, and will reflect applied researchers' efforts to document and understand changes that are intellectually challenging, practically important, and in which they themselves are immersed as societal members. More restrictively, if organizations in the next century evidence projected diversification, decentralization, and technological transformation, applied communication research will similarly reflect intergroup, intergenerational, intercultural, participatory, media, and adaptive foci. In some respects this will represent a continuation of current applied group/organizational communication research. But it also will mark important expansion of the area to incorporate concepts, theories, and findings (even investigators) from other areas of the discipline. This pluralism in research orientations should enable organizational researchers to more adequately capture the multiple perspectives of organizational members while continuing to emphasize message content and processes (Putnam & Cheney, 1985).

APPLIED COMMUNICATION RESEARCH METHODS

Applied communication research was earlier defined as both quantitative and qualitative empirical work pursuing theory-based means to application specific ends and/or applied means to theorybuilding ends. A variety of empirical methods are suitable, especially when applied researchers' aims are not to rigorously test theory in applied contexts but to illuminate social problems through appropriation of communication research methods and application of communication theory. Many quantitative and qualitative methods will continue to be available: case analyses, survey protocols, experimental design and statistical analyses, comparative-historical analyses, program evaluation methods, ethnographic techniques, content and interaction analyses, metaanalysis of previous findings, economic and comparative analyses, metaphor and fantasy theme analyses, focus group and other interview procedures, narrative assessment, and archival research among others.

Many of these methods are employed or advocated by researchers interested in the group/organizational sphere parceled in the preceding section: root metaphor analysis (Smith & Eisenberg, 1987), case studies (Frey, 1994), analysis of organizational narratives (Mumby, 1987), meta-analysis (Steel & Ovalle, 1984), facilitation interventions (Frey, 1995), network analysis (Monge, 1987; Wigand, 1988), longitudinal designs and time series analyses (Monge et al., 1984, 1991), experimental designs and tests of between-group differences (reviewed by Gordon, Slade, & Schmitt, 1986), questionnaires (Podsakoff & Dalton, 1987), content and interaction analyses (Putnam & Jones, 1982), audits (see review in Greenbaun, Hellweg, & Falcione, 1988), and scale development (Putnam & Wilson, 1982), among many others. Poole, Seibold, and McPhee (1985) have urged and Canary, Brossmann, and Seibold (1987) have incorporated *both qualitative and quantitative methods,* and other contributors to this volume who specialize in qualitative methods address the potential of those tools. Within the organizational arena identified above, I discuss only implications for quantitative methods in applied communication research during the 21st century in concluding this chapter. In focusing upon only quantitative methods in closing, I do not imply that quantitative approaches should be accorded primacy over qualitative methods. Furthermore, as Smith (1991) emphasized, choice of method is ultimately dependent upon the nature of the inquiry.

Podsakoff and Dalton (1987) analyzed the research methods of all 1985 publications "in five largely empirical journals dedicated almost exclusively to organizational studies" (p. 420). Based on the most frequently used methods in each category coded, the authors proposed that a hypothetical typical study would be based on:

> 1. a survey relying on a questionnaire that solicits data from a single sample, or a laboratory study relying on student subjects; 2. conducted at the individ-

ual level of analysis; 3. with a sample size of some 372 subjects from the private sector of the economy who are professional/managerial/technical personnel if conducted in the field, or 115 college students if conducted in the lab; 4. there will be more than one dependent variable and those variables will be attitudinal and/or perceptual; 5. these data will be cross-sectional and analyzed by regression techniques or ANOVA; 6. there will be no provision for crossvalidation or any hold-out procedures; and 7. the construct validity of the metrics, scales, or measures relied on in this study will not be shared with the reader. (p. 420)

Mazen, Graf, Kellogg, and Hemmasi (1987) would add that consideration of statistical power issues "was almost nonexistent" (p. 376). The reviewers' survey included neither communication journals nor organizational communication research. However, with the possible exception of better validation of measurement scales like those routinely summarized in *Management Communication Quarterly*, it is doubtful that quantitative group/organizational *communication* studies, especially published applied research, reflect a discernably different methods profile. Given the costs, time, labor and number of groups and organizations required to do behavioral, longitudinal, and cross-validated research (and the recent proliferation of outlets that make possible publication of nearly any study), it is not surprising to see the frequency with which less rigorous methods are reported. And, for the same reasons, it is doubtful that methods in applied communication research published early in the next century will look appreciably different. Still, refinements in methods and their adoption in more basic research, developments in applied research in other disciplines, and calls for increased rigor by funders, editors, and researchers themselves suggest that the following changes in quantitative applied communication research are possible in the 21st century.

Projections concerning training in the quantitative applied research for the year 2000 are plausible and are already becoming evident based on Smith's (1991) assessment of current methodologies that will carry into the next century. Desktop computers and software will be available to graphically plot and interpret data, including simulation of dynamic processes (Contractor & Seibold, 1993). Data collection methods will be enhanced as research from cognitive psychology is incorporated into survey techniques so as to minimize response sets, as computer-assisted interviewing data elicitation techniques become routine in telephone surveys and computer-mediated group meetings, as computerized data collection and storage become more routine in organizational life and afford baseline measures against which to judge changes in interaction processes. Advances in data reduction, especially classification, clustering and scaling techniques, could yield correlative improvements in network techniques which rest on clustering algorithms. Field research designs also may become more rigorous, with randomized experiments becoming embedded within sample surveys as they have been in other disciplines for years (Berk & Rossi, 1977). Following demonstration by Gordon, Slade, and Schmitt (1986) of significant between-group differences in studies using both student and nonstudent samples, future applied research involving tasks more appropriate for nonstudent populations may no longer be able to utilize convenient samples of easily accessible students (see the Guion, 1983, editorial on this requirement elsewhere). Particularly in applied research with theory-testing aims, including enhancing our understanding of how groups adopt and organize themselves around new technologies like those discussed above (e.g., Contractor, Seibold, & Heller, 1992; Seibold, Heller, & Contractor, 1994), dynamic process analysis and longitudinal research will become necessary (Monge, 1991). Too, statistical analyses will likely include more causal analysis techniques. Operations research techniques, which rest on powerful mathematical procedures and enable projections, could be used profitably in applied research. Before completing a study of whether health organizations are processing information inquiries from patients efficiently, various models of how health information services might operate in principle, if certain criteria were optimized, could be constructed. Meta-analyses, already used frequently (Light & Pillemer, 1984), will become even more prevalent if applied communication researchers become as involved in policy analyses as are applied researchers in sociology, political science, and psychology. Finally, since communication researchers are likely to be involved in studies of communication training, development, and education interventions, evaluations of these change efforts hopefully will be more sophisticated than past change studies—especially in dealing with the small sample sizes, nonequivalent control groups, and response-shift biases that plague intervention assessments (Arvey & Cole, 1989; Seibold, Kudsi, & Rude, 1993).

Underlying these projections concerning the nature of applied communication quantitative methods of research in the 21st century has been a presumption that should be made explicit in closing. Many communication students, who are tomorrow's researchers, are being trained in yesterday's less rigorous quantitative methods. If quantitative methods like those described previously are not incorporated into graduate program curricula, the next generation of quantitative applied research will be limited, and applied communication research will appear weak in comparison with quantitative applied research in other disciplines. This should not be construed as a call for a return to laboratory research, as the limitations of utilizing only those methods in applied research have been noted (see Locke, 1986). Rather, it is a call for training in more rigorous quantitative data collection, reduction, and analysis techniques suitable for the settings in which applied research typically will be conducted, as outlined in the preceding section. Nor should this assumption be taken as a reflex call for more "basic" social science research. Instead it is an acknowledgment that, without the descriptions afforded by rigorous but appropriate quantitative methods, applied communication researchers can neither fulfill their mandate to be accurate and practically useful (Alderfer, 1990; Patton, 1982) nor the mission of practicality that, we began by noting, is inherent in the discipline of communication. Furthermore and finally, Argyris and Schön (1991) summarily note the challenge facing all applied researchers in academe:

> In our view, social scientists are faced with a fundamental choice that hinges on a dilemma of rigor or relevance. If social scientists tilt toward the rigor of normal science that currently dominates departments of social science in American universities, they risk becoming irrelevant to practitioners' demands for usable knowledge. If they tilt toward the relevance of action research, they risk falling short of prevailing disciplinary standards of rigor. . . . The challenge is to define and meet standards of *appropriate* rigor without sacrificing relevance. (p. 85)

REFERENCES

Alderfer, C. P. (1990). Editor's comments on the *Journal of Applied Behavioral Science*. *Academy of Management OD Newsletter,* Summer, 7–9.

Argyris, C., & Schön, D. A. (1991). Participatory action research and action science compared: A commentary. In W. F. Whyte (Ed.), *Participatory action research*. Newbury Park, CA: Sage.

Arvey, R. D., & Cole, D. A. (1989). Evaluating change due to training. In I. Goldstein & Associates (Eds.), *Training and development in organizations* (pp. 89–117). San Francisco: Jossey-Bass.

Berk, R. A., & Rossi, P. H. (1977). *Prison reform and state elite.* Boston: Ballinger.

Berteotti, C. R., & Seibold, D. R. (1994). Coordination and role definition problems in health care teams: A hospice case study. In L. R. Frey (Ed.), *Communication in context: Studies of naturalistic groups* (pp. 107–131). Hillsdale, NJ: Lawrence Erlbaum Associates.

Brief, A. P., & Duckerich, J. M. (1991). Theory in organizational behavior: Can it be useful? *Research in Organizatioal Behavior, 13,* 327–352.

Brickman, L. (1981). Some distinctions between basic and applied approaches. In L. Brickman (Ed.), *Applied social psychology annual* (Vol. 2, pp. 23–44). Beverly Hills, CA: Sage.

Canary, D. J., Brossmann, B. G., & Seibold, D. R. (1987). Argument structures in decision making groups. *Southern Speech Communication Journal, 53,* 18–37.

Coleman, J. S. (1980). The structure of society and the nature of social research. *Knowledge: Creation, Diffusion, Utilization, 1,* 332–350.

Contractor, N. S., & Seibold, D. R. (1993). Theoretical frameworks for the study of structuring processes in group decision support systems: Comparison of Adaptive Structuration Theory and Self-Organizing Systems Theory. *Human Communication Research, 19,* 528–563.

Contractor, N. S., Seibold, D. R., & Heller, M. A. (1992, May). *Interactional influences in the structuring of media use in groups.* Paper presented at the annual conference of the International Communication Association, Miami.

Craig, R. T. (1988). Communication as a practical discipline. In B. Dervin, L. Grossberg, B. O'Keefe, & E. Wartella (Eds.), *Paradigm dialogues in communication* (Vol. 1, pp. 97–122). Newbury Park, CA: Sage.

Dansereau, F., & Markham, S. E. (1987). Superior-subordinate communication: Multiple level analysis. In F. M. Jablin, L. L. Putnam, K. H. Roberts, & L. W. Porter (Ed.), *Handbook of organizational communication: An interdisciplinary perspective* (pp. 343–388). Newbury Park, CA: Sage.

Delia, J. G. (1987). Communication research: A history. In C. R. Berger & S. H. Chafee (Eds.), *Handbook of communication science* (pp. 20–98). Newbury Park, CA: Sage.

Downs, C. W., Clampitt, P. G., & Pfeiffer, A. L. (1988). Communication and organizational outcomes. In G. M. Goldhaber & G. A. Barnett (Eds.), *Handbook of organizational communication* (pp. 171–211). Norwood, NJ: Ablex.

Eadie, W. F. (1990, November). Being applied: Communication research comes of age. *Journal of Applied Communication Research,* Special Issue, 1–6.

Eisenberg, E. M., & Riley, P. (1988). Organizational symbols and sense-making. In G. M. Goldhaber & G. A. Barnett (Eds.), *Handbook of organizational communication* (pp. 131–150). Norwood, NJ: Ablex.

Euske, N. A., & Roberts, K. H. (1987). Evolving perspectives in organization theory: Communication implications. In F. M. Jablin, L. L. Putnam, K. H. Roberts, & L. W. Porter (Eds.), *Handbook of organizational communication: An interdisciplinary perspective* (pp. 41–69). Newbury Park, CA: Sage.

Frey, L. R. (Ed.). (1994). *Group communication in context: Studies of natural groups.* Hillsdale, NJ: Lawrence Erlbaum Associates.

Frey, L. R. (Ed.). (1995). *Innovations in group facilitation: Applications in natural settings.* Cresskill, NJ: Hampton Press.

Frost, P. J., (1987). Power, politics, and influence. In F. M. Jablin, L. L. Putnam, K. H. Roberts, & C. W. Porter (Eds.), *Handbook of organizational communication: An interdisciplinary perspective* (pp. 503–548). Newbury Park, CA: Sage.

Fulk, J., & Steinfield, C. (Eds.). (1990). *Organizations and communication technology.* Newbury Park, CA: Sage.

Giacalone, R. A., & Rosenfeld, P. (Eds.). (1989). *Impression management in the organization.* Hillsdale, NJ: Lawrence Erlbaum Associates.

Giles, H., Coupland, N., Henwood, K., Harriman, J., & Coupland, J. (1990). The social meaning of RP: An intergenerational perspective. In S. Ramsaran (Ed.), *Studies in the pronunciation of English: A commemorative volume in honor of A. C. Grimson.* London: Routledge.

Giles, H., Coupland, N., & Coupland, J. (1991). Accommodation theory: Communication, contexts and consequence. In H. Giles, N. Coupland, & J. Coupland (Eds.), *Contexts of accommodation: Developments in applied sociolinguistics.* Cambridge: Cambridge University Press.

Gioia, D. A. & Ford, C. M. (1991). Organizational sensemaking. In L. Thayer (Ed.), *Organizational communication: Emerging perspectives, III.* Norwood, NJ: Ablex.

Gordon, M.E., Slade, L. A., & Schmitt, N. (1986). The "science of the sophomore" revisited: From conjecture to empiricism. *Academy of Management Review, 11,* 191–207.

Greenbaum, H. H., Hellweg, S. A., & Falcione, R. L. (1988). Organizational communication evaluation: An overview 1950–1981. In G. M. Goldhaber & G. A. Barnett (Eds.), *Handbook of organizational communication* (pp. 275–317). Norwood, NJ: Ablex.

Gudykunst, W. B., & Nishida, T. (1988). Theoretical perspectives for studying intercultural communication. In M. K. Asante & W. B. Gudykunst (Eds.), *Handbook of international and intercultural communication.* Newbury Park, CA: Sage.

Guion, R. M. (1983). Editorial: Comments from the new editor. *Journal of Applied Psychology, 68,* 547–551.

Jablin, F. M. (1987a). Formal organization structure. In F. M. Jablin, L. L. Putnam, K. H. Roberts, & L. W. Porter (Eds.), *Handbook of organizational communication: An interdisciplinary perspective* (pp. 389–419). Newbury Park, CA: Sage.

Jablin, F. M. (1987b). Organizational entry, assimilation, and exit. In F. M. Jablin, L. L. Putnam, K. H. Roberts, & L. W. Porter (Eds.), *Handbook of organizational communication: An interdisciplinary perspective* (pp. 679–740). Newbury Park, CA: Sage.

Johnston, W. B., & Packer, A. E. (1987). *Workforce 2000: Work and workers for the twenty-first century.* Indianapolis, IN: Hudson Institute.

Kytle, J., & Millman, E. J. (1986). Confessions of two applied researchers in search of principles. *Evaluation and Planning, 9,* 167–177.

Light, R. U., & Pillemer, D. B. (1984). *Summing up: The science of reviewing research.* Cambridge, MA: Harvard University Press.

Locke, E. A. (1986). Generalizing from laboratory to field: Ecological validity or abstraction of essential elements. In E. A. Locke (Ed.), *Generalizing from laboratory to field settings* (pp. 3–9). Lexington, MA: Lexington Books.

Mazen, A. M., Graf, L. A., Kellogg, C. E., & Hemmasi, M. (1987). Statistical power in contemporary management research. *Academy of Management Journal, 30,* 369–380.

Meyers, R. A., & Seibold, D. R. (1985). Consumer involvement as a segmentation approach for studying utilization of health organization services. *Southern Speech Communication Journal, 50,* 327–347.

Meyers, R. A., Seibold, D. R., & Willihnganz, S. C. (1983). Using an integrative model of health organization as a framework for program assessment. *Journal of Applied Communication Research, 11,* 28–44.

Miller, G. R., & Sunnafrank, M. J. (1984). Theoretical dimensions of applied communication research. *Quarterly Journal of Speech, 70,* 255–263.

Monge, P. R. (1987). The network level of analysis. In P. R. Berger & S. H. Chafee (Eds.), *Handbook of communication science* (pp. 239–270). Newbury Park, CA: Sage.

Monge, P. R. (1991). Theoretical and analytical issues in studying organizational processes. *Organization Science, 1,* 406–430.

Monge, P. R., Cozzens, M. D., & Contractor, N. S. (1991). Communication and motivational predictors of the dynamics of organization innovation. *Organization Science, 3,* 250–274.

Monge, P.R., & Eisenberg, E. M. (1987). Emergent communication networks. In F. M. Jablin, C. L. Putnam, K. H. Roberts, & L. W. Porter (Eds.), *Handbook of organizational communication: An interdisciplinary perspective* (pp. 304–342). Newbury Park, CA: Sage.

Monge, P. R., Farace, R. V., Eisenberg, E. M., Miller, K. I., & White, L. L. (1984). The process of studying process in organizational communication. *Journal of Communication, 34,* 22–43.

Monge, P. R., & Miller, K. I. (1988). Participative processes in organizations. In G. M. Goldhaber & G. A. Barnett (Eds.), *Handbook of organizational communication* (pp. 213–229). Norwood, NJ: Ablex.

Mumby, D. K. (1987). The political function of narrative in organizations. *Communication Monographs, 54,* 113–127.

Osborne, M. M. (1990). A defense of our discipline. *Spectra,* September.

Patton, M. Q. (1982). *Practical evaluation.* Beverly Hills, CA: Sage.

Podsakoff, P. M., & Dalton, D. R. (1987). Research methodology in organizational studies. *Journal of Management, 13,* 419–441.

Poole, M. S., & DeSanctis, G. (1990). Understanding the use of group decision support systems: The theory of adaptive structuration. In J. Fulk & C. Steinfield (Eds.), *Organization and communication technology* (pp. 175–195). Newbury Park, CA: Sage.

Poole, M. S., & DeSanctis, G. (1992). Microlevel structuration in computer support group decision making. *Human Communication Research, 19,* 5–49.

Poole, M. S., Seibold, D. R., & McPhee, R. D. (1985). Group decision-making as a structurational process. *Quarterly Journal of Speech, 71,* 74–102.

Putnam, L. L., & Cheney, G. (1985). Organizational communication: Historical development and future directions. In T. W. Benson (Ed.), *Speech communication in the twentieth century* (pp. 130–156). Carbondale, IL: Southern Illinois University Press.

Putnam, L. L., & Jones, T. S. (1982). Reciprocity in negotiations: An analysis of bargaining interaction. *Communication Monographs, 49*, 171–191.

Putnam, L. L., & Wilson, C. E. (1982). Communicative strategies in organizational conflicts: Reliability and validity of a measurement scale. In M. Burgoon (Ed.), *Communication Yearbook 6* (pp. 629–652). Beverly Hills, CA: Sage.

Rossi, P. H. (1980). The presidential address: The challenge and opportunities of social research. *American Sociological Review, 45*, 889–904.

Seibold, D. R., Heller, M. & Contractor, N. (1994). Group decision support systems (GDSS): Review, taxonomy and research. In B. Kovacic (Ed.), *New approaches to organizational communication* (pp. 143–166). Albany, NY: SUNY Press.

Seibold, D. R., Kudsi, O. S., & Rude, M. W. (1993). Does communication training make a difference? Evidence for the effectiveness of a presentation skills program. *Journal of Applied Communication Research, 21*, 111–131.

Seibold, D. R., & McPhee, R. D. (1979). Commonality analysis: A method for decomposing explained variance in multiple regression analyses. *Human Communication Research, 5*, 355–365.

Seibold, D. R., Meyers, R. A., & Willihnganz, S. C. (1984). Communicating health information to the public: Effectiveness of a newsletter. *Health Education Quarterly, 10*, 263–286.

Seibold, D. R., & Roper, R. E. (1979). Psychosocial determinants of health care intentions: Test of the Triandis and Fishbein models. In D. Nimmo (Ed.), *Communication Yearbook 3* (pp. 625–643). New Brunswick, NJ: Transaction/ICA.

Seibold, D. R., Rossi, S. M., Berteotti, C. R., Soprych, S. L., & McQuillan, L. P. (1987). Volunteer involvement in a hospice care program. *American Journal of Hospice Care, 4*, 43–55.

Smith, J. (1991). A methodology for twenty-first century sociology. *Social Forces, 70*, 1–17.

Smith, R. C., & Eisenberg, E. M. (1987). Conflict at Disneyland: A root-metaphor analysis. *Communication Monographs, 54*, 367–380.

Steel, R. P., & Ovalle, N. K. (1984). A review and meta-analysis of research on the relationship between behavioral intentions and employee turnover. *Journal of Applied Psychology, 69*, 673–686.

Tajfel, H. (1982). *Social identity and intergroup relations.* Cambridge: Cambridge University Press.

Thomas, F. A. (1983). The scholar and social needs. *American Council of Learned Societies Newsletter, 34*(1–2), 16–25.

Turner, T. C. (1987). *Rediscovering the social group.* Oxford: Blackwell.

Weick, K. E. (1979). *The social psychology of organizing* (2nd ed.). Reading, MA: Addison-Wesley.

Weick, K. (1989). Organized improvisation: 20 years of organizing. *Communication Studies, 40*, 241–248.

Wigand, R. T. (1988). Communication network analysis: History and overview. In G. M. Goldhaber & G. A. Barnett (Eds.), *Handbook of organizational communication* (pp. 319–360). Norwood, NJ: Ablex.

Work, W., & Jeffrey, R. C. (1989). Historical notes: The Speech Communication Association, 1965–1989. In W. Work & R. C. Jeffrey (Eds.), *The past is prologue: A 75th anniversary publication of the Speech Communication Association* (pp. 24–37). Annandale, VA: Speech Communication Association.

Response to Seibold:
Applied Health Communication Research

Vicki S. Freimuth
University of Maryland

Because all of my applied communication research experience has been in the health area, this chapter addresses the following questions from the perspective of health communication: (a) Which social problems and issues should applied communication research address? (b) What methods will be most useful for applied communication research? (c) How can applied communication research contribute to public policy and social change?

WHICH SOCIAL PROBLEMS SHOULD BE ADDRESSED?

As the field of public health shifted its focus from infectious diseases to chronic ones such as heart disease and cancer, prevention became the goal and communication became an important tool. The emphasis in most prevention programs is on the individual, that is, what one can do for one's own health and well-being. A wealth of scientific research reveals that the key to a person's health can be found in several simple personal habits: reduced smoking and drinking, diet, adequate sleep and exercise, observing speed laws, wearing seat belts, and practicing safer sex. Each year hundreds of thousands of people in the United States die of or suffer from various diseases despite existing information on ways to prevent and detect these diseases early to reduce their impact. Cancer is one of the best examples of this needless loss and suffering. The American Cancer Society (ACS) estimates that 170,000 people die each year who might have been saved with earlier diagnosis and prompt treatment (American Cancer Society, 1987). Similarly, the National Cancer Institute (NCI) targeted a 50% reduction in cancer deaths by the year 2000 with better application of existing knowledge and technology (National Cancer Institute, 1986).

Before members of the public can use the prevention, detection and treatment information available, they must know what should be done and how to take action. The sheer volume of scientific information being produced as well as the complexity and contradictory nature of much of the information about health issues can overwhelm consumers as they strive to take a more active role in their own health care.

The challenge became how to effectively disseminate health information to the public and how to motivate individuals to use this information and change their health behaviors. Communication channels became a favored strategy. That trend was accelerated by the AIDS epidemic. The public health community was faced with a deadly disease to combat for which the only weapon was prevention through public education and persuasion.

Even though communication became an important strategy, the communication discipline was not necessarily consulted for advice. In fact, many public health experts were unaware of this discipline and preceded to reinvent the field, describing the communication process in quite simplistic terms. The communication field, during this period, did respond to the applied concerns of public health with the development of health communication interest groups, first in the International Communication Association (ICA) and later in the Speech Communication Association (SCA). Most of the communication scholars in these groups, however, were studying the health professional/client relationship rather than the role of communication in the health behavior change process. This focus probably emerged because many of these scholars were trained as interpersonal researchers and became interested in health communication from their experiences teaching interpersonal communication skills to medical students.

Even though considerable opportunities exist for communication scholars to do applied research in public health, few have responded. At least two federal agencies, the National Cancer Institute and the Center for Substance Abuse Prevention have released Requests for Applications (RFAs) for communication-oriented grants during the last 5 years. Only a few communication researchers wrote proposals. Only one of the five cancer communication grants awarded had a principal investigator who was a communication scholar and only one other included a communication researcher. In addition, a panel of five leaders of the most active health communication programs in the federal government at the Dublin ICA conference failed to attract more than a handful of ICA members.

Many challenging communication issues need to be addressed with research studies including:

- How do people seek information about health issues?
- How do people process information from different sources and arrive at a decision to take action?
- Where does communication fit into a process of behavior change?
- What persuasive appeals motivate different types of people to make behavior changes?
- What sources are most credible for different health messages targeted to different audiences?

WHAT CAN APPLIED RESEARCH IN PUBLIC HEALTH CONTRIBUTE TO OUR FIELD?

Seibold (this volume, chapter 2) suggests that applied communication research may serve two functions: (a) responding to applied agendas with communication and methods but with little immediate concern for whether important theoretical questions within the discipline are being answered, and (b) responding to the discipline's theoretical agenda, but only insofar as they apply to a specific problem domain. In serving the latter function, applied communication research can contribute significantly to the field.

Burke, Becker, Arbogast, and Naughton (1987) learned about the inadequacies of many social scientific theories when they turned to them for guidance in developing a program to reduce adolescent smoking behavior. Because they found no single theory or discipline capable of explaining why adolescents smoke and suggesting strategies for reducing their use of tobacco, the authors integrated a variety of theories from several disciplines, including theories of reasoned action, social learning, differential association, inoculation, consistency, social bonding, the spiral of silence, and diffusion. They discovered that most of these theories had limitations even when their use was confined to very specific applications. Noelle-Neumann's spiral of silence theory (1973), for example, suggested that both the frequency and the consistency of public messages play an important role in influencing public opinion. Her work, however, was based on issues in which media coverage was essentially one-sided, and did not suggest ways to shift the balance of media coverage. Even a recognition of these weaknesses in theory can be a catalyst to theory development.

Hammond (1990) also discovered the inadequacies of a theoretical model previously tested only in laboratory environments. Her study was the first test of Petty and Cacioppo's (1981) elaboration likelihood model outside the laboratory and found little support for the model's predictions for the processing of environmental risk communication messages. Pohl and Freimuth (1983) tried to use diffusion theory to explain the dissemination of messages

through a supermarket nutrition program and found the theory deficient because of its failure to consider the multiple layers of organizations that exist
in our society. The study modified the theory's original conceptualizations of
centralized and decentralized diffusion to include a hybrid model which was
a better fit with a more developed society.

WHAT METHODOLOGICAL STRATEGIES
ARE MOST USEFUL?

Just as basic research is usually considered superior to applied, quantitative
empirical methods are valued more highly than qualitative ones. Many times,
however, the close-ended questions designed to collect data do not provide
much understanding of the behaviors studied. For example, research participants are frequently asked to identify the sources from which they receive health information or to remember where they first heard about a specific issue. These measures are not consistent with the reality of information
seeking.

Graber (1988), writing about political decision-making, developed a measurement technique much more isomorphic with actual behavior. She carefully selected a small sample of representative voters, interviewed them pe-
riodically over one year, and asked them to keep information diaries during
that time. I plan to conduct a study of newly diagnosed cancer patients' information seeking using similar methodology. Yet these more qualitative
techniques are frequently criticized because of the small samples and subjectivity involved in interpreting the data. In the public health field, the classic clinical trials paradigm is the prevailing standard; it is quite difficult to
gain legitimacy for more qualitative methods. Perhaps the new SAGE journal, *Qualitative Health Research,* is evidence of growing acceptability of
these methods.

Applied research in the health area forces investigators to be more creative in their measurement strategies. Many of the behaviors we try to affect
and thus need to measure are not easily observable, for example, breast self-
examination and safer sex practices. Yet relying on self-report measures is
especially unsatisfactory because of the social desirability factor. That is, because we know we "should" be engaging in a "healthy" behavior we often
over-report our actual behavior. These measurement challenges have stimulated some innovative solutions. Some AIDS researchers, for example, mea-
sured increased condom use by counting used condoms in the local sewage
system before and after a planned intervention.

Another strength of applied communication research in public health is
the necessity of using adult subjects rather than college students. Most of our
theories in communication have been developed and tested only on White,

middle-class college students. Many health issues are not relevant to this population, and researchers must use a more diverse group of participants. The concomitant disadvantage, however, is that external funding usually is essential to recruit such participants.

HOW CAN APPLIED RESEARCH MAKE A DIFFERENCE IN PUBLIC POLICY AND SOCIAL CHANGE?

Most importantly, the academic community must be willing to listen to practitioners and be responsive to their needs. I participated in a small conference in Washington, DC that was sponsored by several government health agencies and a social marketing firm. The goal of the conference was to provide guidance on the use of fear appeals in health communication campaigns. Several academic researchers (including one from communication) were asked to discuss their research findings about the use of fear appeals. Almost all of the researchers were unwilling to provide any guidance to the practitioners to assist them in deciding whether to use fear in their messages or how to use this appeal effectively. The practitioners were quite frustrated by this experience and are unlikely to turn again to the academic community for advice.

In contrast, when selected papers from the first AIDS Conference sponsored by ICA's Health Communication Division were published in the journal *AIDS and Public Policy,* each article included a discussion of policy implications of the research.

As experienced researchers, we know that few studies or even programs of research generate unequivocal conclusions. Yet, to have an impact on public policy and social change, those engaged in research must be willing to make tentative recommendations based on findings and conclusions.

To have an impact on public policy and social change, communication research must be disseminated in nontraditional ways. Practitioners cannot be expected to come looking for research results in academic journals, especially those with limited readerships. In the public health field, having an article published in *Public Health Reports* may not impress a tenure and promotion committee but it does have the potential of reaching thousands of practitioners.

Another nontraditional strategy for disseminating research is through conferences that bring together academicians and practitioners. A conference sponsored by several federal agencies convened experts from the fields of journalism, advertising, entertainment, communication science, public policy, medical science, and public health. Participants included practitioners, academic scholars, and representatives from government agencies and advocacy groups. The conference produced several products targeted toward different audiences, including the SAGE book, *Mass Communication and Public Health,* which was published primarily for the academic audience. A 25-minute videotape was produced to accompany the book. Another publication from the conference, *Mass Media and Health: Opportunities for Improving the Nation's Health* (U.S. Department of Health and Human Services, 1991), was designed for health communication practitioners.

Another way to disseminate communication research to policymakers is to change the nature of professional associations. The American Public Health Association (APHA) is a model of a professional association quite unlike our own academically dominated organizations. The APHA has nearly 31,000 members consisting of academics and practitioners. The divisions are structured around shared interests (like ICA) rather than around institutional affiliation such as SCA. The organization also sees itself as an advocacy group quite willing to take stands on policy issues and to lobby vigorously for issues relevant to its interests. Clearly it is an organization that does influence public policy and social change. Both of the major professional organizations in communications, ICA and SCA, have attempted to reach out to the nonacademic practitioners but to date have failed to sustain their interest.

Clearly, we would have to restructure our organizations to make them appealing to practitioners. For example, some public health practitioners might be interested in the health communication division of ICA but are uninterested in other aspects of the organization. Because their membership is with the entire organization and does not even include the one specialized journal in health communication, it is difficult to convince them that the benefits outweigh the costs of membership. Our membership drives produce some of these new members each year but few are retained over time.

Finally, more scholars in our discipline should actively seek funding from external sources. Only then will we have the opportunity to do the kind of applied research that addresses significant issues. In the health area, funding agencies show a growing recognition of our discipline. In the last few years, for example, the National Cancer Institute has issued an RFA for cancer communication system research, the Center for Substance Abuse has requested proposals for communication projects to prevent drug and alcohol abuse in high risk youth, and the National Institute on Alcohol and Alcohol Abuse sought proposals to investigate alcohol labeling laws.

Many of the funding opportunities require interdisciplinary teams. The large-scale heart disease prevention programs, for example, include physicians, psychologists, epidemiologists, communication scholars, and community developers. We need to reach out to these other disciplines on our own campuses and nationally to let them know who we are and what we can contribute.

SUMMARY

The health field offers the communication researcher many challenging research agendas that potentially can yield important theoretical advances and can enhance and, in some cases, even save people's lives. As the public health community emphasizes prevention of chronic disease, communication has gained legitimacy as an effective tool. Applying our theories in the real world can be quite productive. We can learn whether they are applicable to anyone other than White, middle-class college students under controlled conditions. Our creativity can also be stimulated by the difficult measurement issues faced in applied research. Finally we may be able to persuade others of the usefulness of qualitative methods by demonstrating the valuable insights gained from their use.

Because I have spent 15 years doing applied research in health communication, I know first hand of the bias from the academic community which suggests that if research has practical application it cannot be theoretically significant, and the bias of the practitioners who assume that an academician cannot relate to their real-world problems. Even though straddling that gap is often quite uncomfortable, the rewards for bridging it are quite satisfying.

REFERENCES

American Cancer Society. (1987). *1987 cancer facts and figures*. New York: Author.

Burke, J. A., Becker, S. L., Arbogast, R. A., & Naughton, M. J. (1987). Problems and prospects of applied research: The development of an adolescent smoking prevention program. *Journal of Applied Communication Research, 15*, 1–18.

Graber, D. A. (1988). *Processing the news: How people tame the information tide*. New York: Longman.

Hammond, S. L. (1990). *Issue involvement and the elaboration-likelihood model: A field experiment using environment risk messages*. Doctoral dissertation, University of Maryland.

National Cancer Institute. (1986). *Cancer control objectives for the nation: 1985 to 2000* (NIH Publication No. 86–2880). Bethesda, MD: Author.

Noelle-Neumann, E. (1973). Return to the concept of powerful mass media. In H. Eguchi & K. Sata (Eds.), *Studies of broadcasting: An international annual of broadcasting science* (pp. 657–678). Beverly Hills, CA: Sage.

Petty, R. C., & Cacioppo, J. T. (1981). *Attitudes and persuasion: Classic and contemporary approaches*. Dubuque, IA: Wm. C. Brown.

Pohl, S. N., & Freimuth, V. S. (1983). Foods for health: Involving organizations in planned change. *Journal of Applied Communication Research, 13*, 17–27.

U.S. Department of Health and Human Services, Public Health Service, Office of Disease Prevention and Health Promotion. (1991, Spring). *Monograph Series: Mass media and health opportunities for improving the nation's health.*

3

"I Think My Schizophrenia Is Better Today," Said the Communication Researcher Unanimously: Some Thoughts on the Dysfunctional Dichotomy Between Pure and Applied Communication Research

Gerald R. Miller
Michigan State University

As the Tom Swifty takeoff in my title implies, I believe that communication researchers have traditionally struck a schizophrenic, dysfunctional posture regarding the terms *pure* and *applied* research and their supposed relationship. In the unapologetically opinionated and argumentative remarks that follow, I sketch my grounds for this claim and suggest what I consider to be a more defensible stance for communication researchers to take. During the course of this journey, I touch upon the three questions I have been charged to address.

One confessional note is in order, lest I am accused of misleadingly casting stones from my own scholarly glass house. As a (somewhat) socialized member of the community of communication scholars, I have been guilty in the past of the conceptual and definitional sins I am here seeking to renounce. Having slowly discerned the error of my ways, I am driven to atone in the sunny climes of Tampa, for an Izod shirt and L.L. Bean chinos are much more comfortable attire than sackcloth and ashes when setting one's scholarly soul straight.

The traditional perceptions of the terms *pure* and *applied* research held by most communication researchers can, I think, be fairly contrasted as follows:

Pure research is scientific (at least for researchers characterizing themselves as scientists), theoretical, procedurally and methodologically rigorous, driven by an untainted motive of intellectual curiosity, and perhaps most importantly, intellectually and professionally respectable.

Applied research is atheoretical, "dust bowl" empiricism, procedurally and methodologically "loose" or "fuzzy," driven at best by a mundane concern with some "practical" communicative problem or at worst by an unseemly lust for agency or foundation dollars, and perhaps most importantly, intellectually and professionally suspect.

The vigor with which this dichotomy is asserted has softened over the years. When I entered the field in the early 1960s, it was not unusual to hear communication researchers proclaim their disdain for any concern with the practical, social implications of their research, a bizarre attitude I shall briefly return to later. However, I think that, if queried, the majority of contemporary communication researchers would express at least some elements of the contrast I have just outlined.

Note that there is considerably more connotation than denotation in the contrasting expressions. Indeed, neither specifies a crisp denotative distinction between the terms pure and applied research; rather, emphasis is placed on the differing *goals* of pure and applied researchers and the divergent scientific *quality* of the research outcomes realized from the two kinds of research. Such emphases serve primarily to communicate an attitude about the relative merits of pure and applied communication research, an attitude that clearly places pure research in the scholarly catbird's seat.

If the notion that applied communication research "means" narrow, atheoretical concern with an immediate social, political, or economic problem is allowed to stand unchallenged (with often the parenthetical implication that this concern is likely to yield substantial economic and status advantages for the researcher), hearty endorsement of the superiority of pure research is easily understood and perfunctorily justified. I believe that this notion represents a parochial, impoverished vision of applied research. Communication is a social process; it is both a means and an end toward being human, and it is precisely because of its crucial role in humanity's everyday activities and aspirations that communication perennially remains a keen object of curiosity (Miller, 1979). Thus if we conceive of the applied component of communication research as embracing the utility, or at a minimum, the potential utility of research outcomes for understanding some everyday, real world communicative process, whether antecedent or consequent, we are inexorably compelled to become advocates of a position of either hard or soft application: Hard application argues that all communication research is intrinsically applied research; soft application contends that all nontrivial communication research reflects a clear component of immediate or potential social utility. Because virtually every communication scholar with whom I am acquainted subscribes to the above-mentioned conception of communication as a vital social process, it follows that the inevitability of subscribing to either a position of hard or soft application holds for scientist and humanist alike—although as these two schools of inquiry are traditionally distinguished, the issues I address herein are probably more germane to the scientist than to the humanist.

Lest I am misunderstood, the conception of applied research I have endorsed does not compel researchers to be able to articulate precisely when and in what arenas their research findings will become pregnant with social import. Such a demand would place an unfair constraint on scholarly inquiry, while also ignoring that some facets of applied significance are virtually certain to elude a priori detection. What my conception does threaten is the attitude of indifference concerning applied significance mentioned earlier, for to deny any interest in, or notion of the practical, social implications of a communication research undertaking would constitute admission that the work is of trivial import. Consequently, researchers would be forced to think carefully about the potential generalizability or ecological validity (Brunswik, 1947) of their studies, which in turn would ensure more attention to issues such as the nature of the research population to be sampled and the potential verisimilitude of research environments to their real world counterparts. I will discuss these issues later.

Some skeptics may feel that my position not only obliterates any useful distinction between pure and applied research but also destroys any chance of placing social/behavioral sciences such as communication on an equal status with the physical and biological sciences. Any such consternation, of course, could be dismissed by contending that the purpose of scholarly inquiry is not, or at least should not, be the establishment of professional pecking orders but rather the advancement of understanding about the phenomena of interest. Beyond that rebuttal, however, a case can also be made for an inherent applied component to physical and biological research products. Although classical mechanics does not mandate building bridges nor quantum theory demand production of nuclear weapons, most contemporary accounts of the goals of science include control along with the traditional staples of prediction and explanation. Because control implies a desire to regulate aspects of the physical, biological, and/or social environment to improve humanity's lot (even the development of nuclear and biological weapons is typically rationalized by an appeal, no matter how fallacious and pernicious, to increased personal and collective security), a reasonable argument can be made for the claim that all research involves at minimum an element of soft application.

The preceding discussion, then, supports the conclusion that the frequently invoked distinction between pure and applied research is more an intellectual and professional liability than an asset. All nontrivial communication research addresses social problems and issues; it is misleading at best and illogical at worst to curry the belief that some research is applied and some is not. To be sure, much lively debate will continue to center on which social problems and issues most urgently demand attention, but this debate will rest on issues of competing value judgments and policy priorities, not on any intrinsic logical differences between varying kinds of scholarly inquiry as is typically wrongheadedly implied in arguments about the relative merits of pure and applied research. Usually, collective agreements about priorities can be forged without too much disagreement; for example, improving the effectiveness of doctor–patient communication about AIDS or cancer is virtually certain to take precedence over improved communication about the common cold or psoriasis, and persuading youthful citizens to "just say 'No!' to drugs" is likely to be regarded as more important than convincing them to lower their intake of fat-saturated fast foods. Even here, two qualifiers should be mentioned. First, collective harmony may vanish when trying to prioritize human and economic resource allocations to competing, highly valued issues and problems; for instance, should more resources be allocated to improving doctor–patient communication about AIDS or to enhancing the effectiveness of antidrug messages? Second, for individuals suffering from psoriasis or for the significant others of teenagers gorging on fat-saturated diets, greater understanding about the relevance of communication processes and outcomes to these problems will undoubtedly be perceived as crucial, even though the collective priority assigned to them is low. This is merely another way of saying that no problems are insignificant to their victims, and subsequently I will suggest how heightened attention to certain aspects of theory development could ensure a closer fit between diverging collective and individual concerns as well as producing more economical, prudent uses of resources.

To contend that all communication research should address applied issues does not, of course, imply that all research undertakings achieve this aim with equal social and scientific effectiveness. On the contrary, I would argue that most communication research fails markedly in coming to grips with its applied objectives and responsibilities, and I next outline what I consider to be two important reasons for this failure. Although I have little dramatic, insightful news to add to previous reports (Miller, 1979; Miller & Fontes, 1979; Miller, Fontes, Boster, & Sunnafrank, 1983; Miller & Sunnafrank, 1984), I am convinced that focusing a keener eye on these two areas would result in a greater impact of communication research on public policy and social change. Because of my conviction, I am not hesitant to revisit them.

LEWIN WAS RIGHT: ON THE APPLIED IMPORT OF THEORY

Some years ago we interviewed a candidate for a faculty position at Michigan State University whose dissertation research involved intensive study of the television viewing behavior of 10 children. As discussion of her research progressed, several faculty members queried the interviewee about the potential generalizability of her research findings. Each time the question arose, the candidate denied any interest in generalizing, indicating that the 10 children studied were her sole concern.

Midway through the questioning period of the candidate's colloquium, I noticed the quiet departure of one of our graduate students. When our paths crossed later in the hall, I asked the reason for his early exodus. He responded, "Well, Dr. Miller, I sat there listening to the conversation and it suddenly hit me that I would probably never meet any of those 10 kids in my life so there was no need to stick around any longer."

To avoid misunderstanding, I must note that this anecdote is not meant to sully the legitimacy of the candidate's research posture; intensive scrutiny of a population of 10 youthful television viewers may yield numerous interesting outcomes even if the researcher has no interest in arguing for generalization to other viewers. What the anecdote does underscore is that the candidate's stated motive renders the study scientifically trivial, for generalization is a key objective of scientific inquiry. Elsewhere I have stated this point somewhat differently, positing that scientific inquiry in communication centers on "observation of communication phenomena primarily for the purpose of making factual generalizations about similar phenomena not encompassed by the observations that have been made" (Miller, 1975, p. 232).

Theory is an invaluable ally in performing these inductive leaps; it is for this reason that the heading of this section applauds Lewin's wisdom in proclaiming "there is nothing so practical as a good theory" (1951, p. 169). Although the virtues of theory-driven research are usually discussed in abstract, intellectualized terms (here again it is as if it would be poor form to couch dialogue in terms of actual communicative settings), the crucial point for my present remarks is that theory based findings enhance the value and richness of the applied component of research by providing a set of generalizations which permit deduction of numerous specific communicative outcomes. In terms of an earlier mentioned social problem, improving communication between one cancer patient and his or her oncologist, although personally beneficial, is of minimal applied import; improving communication between many cancer patients and their oncologists represents a substantial applied step forward, and improving communication between many patients suffering from various medical problems and their physicians moves us yet closer to the best of all possible applied worlds. Theory driven research is not a sufficient condition to ensure successful ascent of this ladder of abstraction, but there are solid grounds for assuming it is a necessary condition.

Little would be served by an extended tirade about the atheoretical nature of much communication research. It is generally recognized that the field must continue to improve in this regard. A substantial segment of our prior research merits the epithet "dust bowl empiricism," and even much of our best theoretically oriented work is derivative, relying on theories developed in other disciplines. Nevertheless, as my previous paragraph implies, recent years have witnessed a heightened concern with theory building, and there is reason to be optimistic that this trend will continue. Hence, I will content myself with a few remarks about one theoretical problem that is particularly evident in the applied arena.

Approaching the problem inductively, let us consider the substantial research literatures dealing with viewers' responses to varying types of media content. Spurred by legitimate social concerns, researchers have invested vast amounts of energy in scrutinizing the effects of violent media content, pornographic media content, certain kinds of advertising and public service content (e.g., alcohol commercials, seat-belt campaigns, antismoking messages), and so on. Unfortunately, proportionately little energy has been devoted to developing more general theories of media viewing and effects, although researchers dealing with various content areas do share a tendency to invoke elements of theories drawn from other disciplines, such as social learning theory, to guide their work.

Rather than continuing along this path, some theoretical reformulation aimed at achieving at least a level of middle-range theorizing (Merton, 1957) is in order. This move would be particularly useful for ascending from rung two to rung three on the abstraction ladder constructed earlier. To continue the present example, such middle-range theories would permit predictions about the ways many viewers would respond to various types of media content instead of limiting generalization to singular types of media content. Progress on this front would, in turn, ensure a closer fit between diverging collective and individual concerns. For example, although improving communication between psoriasis patients and their physicians might not be collectively considered worthy of extensive resources, a more general theory of patient–physician communication could have as one benefit such an improvement and would eliminate costly duplication of effort across various social problems and issues.

Nothing in this section seeks to suggest that all research must be theory-driven if it is to make an applied contribution. Many descriptive questions about communication processes and outcomes remain mysteries, and until they are solved, communication research is unlikely to realize its fullest applied potential. Nevertheless, without careful attention to the theoretical matters discussed above, our ability to deal with the application of research findings is likely to remain in a relatively primitive state.

MAKING THE WORLD A STATE: VERISIMILITUDE IN COMMUNICATION RESEARCH

If asked to nominate a candidate for the chief threat to the applied power of communication research, I would unhesitatingly pick the extremely low verisimilitude that exists between our research and the real world communicative phenomena we seek to understand. Indeed, only the most impetuous, panglossian communication researcher could look at the conditions embodied in most research and argue earnestly for its probable ecological validity. As Sunnafrank and I have emphasized:

> Communication researchers working with limited resources must often make practical concessions when conducting their research. These concessions often result in research environments which bear relatively little semblance to the actual communicative settings of interest. Moreover, depending upon the seriousness of the concessions, the end result may retard theoretical development by culminating in results which, at best, can only support theoretical scope conditions of a highly limited range. As some researchers admit, and others imply in the "Discussion" section of their research reports, research settings often fall far short of optimal verisimilitude. (Miller & Sunnafrank, 1984, p. 259)

Most communication researchers first encounter the verisimilitude issue when queried about the lack of correspondence between the human component of research and of real world environments. The "college sophomore" issue has earned a place in the folklore of communication research. To what extent, it is commonly queried, can a research literature resting on a participant foundation of battle-scarred, suspicious college undergraduates be generalized to other parent populations of interest? Although most seasoned researchers invent jargon-laden, impressive-sounding responses to obfuscate and to deflect this query, only the most naive or cynical could fail to find the question disquieting.

To illustrate the gravity of this issue, consider the substantial body of research dealing with communication in legal settings such as the courtroom. The vast majority of these studies rely on samples of college undergraduates asked to role-play a courtroom role such as a juror. Clearly, these samples deviate from many of the demographic characteristics associated with typical panels of actual venirepersons. Students are younger, of higher socioeconomic status, and better educated, to mention but three relevant characteristics. In work conducted by my colleagues and me during a 4-year research program dealing with juror responses to videotaped trial materials, we discovered that when compared to members of actual juries, members of role-playing student juries retained significantly more trial-related information and returned significantly more verdicts favoring defendants, the latter finding suggesting a more liberal bias on the part of student jurors (Miller & Fontes, 1979). Differences such as these underscore the perils of generalizing research findings to actual trial settings, particularly since college students are seldom represented on actual juries.

Even if one chooses to shrug off demographic differences, the fact remains that there is a marked difference between role-playing a juror and being one. In the latter instance, the decisions reached and the recommendations offered have a genuine, and frequently dramatic effect on others' lives; in the former case, no such consequences are entailed by the role player's actions. This same problem exists for a variety of settings and roles; for example, does it seem reasonable to equate the emotional and cognitive states of actual AIDS or cancer patients with students asked to role-play these victims? Certainly, a strong case can be made for the claim that generalizations from the college classroom or laboratory to the doctor's office are fraught with peril.

Although differences between research and real world populations are sufficient to cast doubt on the ecological validity of most communication research, the problem does not end there. Often, the research settings and communicative protocols employed are shallow, inadequate imitations of real world locales and interactions. Short written summaries of items of inadmissible material or of the testimony of a particular witness cannot capture the quantity and richness of information or the face-to-face verbal and nonverbal exchanges found in actual trials. College classrooms have little in common with courtrooms, either in terms of architecture or symbolism. In short, confident generalization of communication findings demands research settings that capture informational and presentational conditions closely approximating the real world settings of interest. Moreover, such settings would doubtless heighten the influence of communication research on public policy, for professionals in other areas are inherently suspicious of findings generated in research environments bearing little resemblance to their real world counterparts.

As suggested earlier, much research probably lacks verisimilitude because of inadequate investigational resources; researchers simply lack the economic wherewithal to employ non-student populations and to produce realistic research simulations. To accept this explanation as both a necessary and sufficient cause for the verisimilitude problem, however, lets researchers off the hook too easily; some inadequate work occurs because it is easier and can be carried out more quickly. Granted, researchers face professional pressures to publish prolifically, but in order to enhance the applied significance of research outcomes, rapid output must be subordinated to the procedural goal of verisimilitude. As Miller et al. (1983) point out, "unlike a rose, a simulation is *not* a simulation is *not* a simulation; instead, some simulations surpass others in their potential for providing ecologically valid research findings" (p. 34).

A CONCLUDING COMMENT

In questioning the traditional distinction drawn between pure and applied research, I have sought to suggest that, at least, the distinction is muddled and wrongheaded, and at most, it is vacuous and unnecessary. Although I have stressed the goal of buttressing the applied power of communication research, the priorities I have underscored—increased theoretical sophistication and more realistic research procedures—are not hallmarks solely of applied communication research, but rather hallmarks of all communication research grounded in a behavioral science perspective. "Scientifically viable communication research . . . must be at least potentially capable of shedding light on real-world communication transactions" (Miller & Sunnafrank, 1984, p. 262).

REFERENCES

Brunswik, E. (1947). *Systematic and representative design of psychological experiments with results in physical and social perception.* Berkeley: University of California Press.

Lewin, K. (1951). *Field theory in social science: Selected theoretical papers* (D. Cartwright, Ed.). New York: Harper & Row.

Merton, R. K. (1957). *Social theory and social structure.* Glencoe, IL: Free Press.

Miller, G. R. (1975). Humanistic and scientific approaches to speech communication inquiry: Rivalry, redundancy, or rapprochement. *Western Speech Communication, 39,* 230–239.

Miller, G. R. (1979). On rediscovering the apple: Some issues in evaluating the social significance of communication research. *Central States Speech Journal, 30,* 14–24.

Miller, G. R., & Fontes, N. E. (1979). *Videotape on trial: A view from the jury box.* Newbury Park, CA: Sage Publications.

Miller, G. R., Fontes, N. E., Boster, F. J., & Sunnafrank, M. J. (1983). Methodological issues in legal communication research: What can trial simulations tell us? *Communication Monographs, 50,* 33–46.

Miller, G. R., & Sunnafrank, M. J. (1984). Theoretical dimensions of applied communication research. *Quarterly Journal of Speech, 70,* 255–263.

Response to Miller:
Sexing His Text for Plurals

H. L. Goodall, Jr.
Clemson University

I had considered calling this discussion:

A Post-Positivist Response to Gerald R. Miller's
Inscription of the Dysfunctional Dichotomy
Between Pure and Applied Communication Research; or:

We find ourselves considering the metaphors of sex or love
in Kansas, but perhaps these are not just metaphors
and this isn't Kansas; or:

Two doctors come into a room. They examine a body of knowledge
for clues to the future. One doctor, an empiricist,
prescribes a better version of more of the same.
The other doctor, a radical empiricist, disagrees.
Perhaps nothing changes. Perhaps everything does.

But I didn't. Instead, I'll tell it this way.

THE UNANIMOUS ORIGINS
OF TWO DIFFERENT RESPONSES

My task is to provide a reply to the chapter by Gerald R. Miller on the dysfunctional dichotomy between pure and applied communication research. It is a task I was pleased to complete but one that induced in me two very different sorts of responses.

The primary source of induced response is one of gratitude. I feel professionally honored by this request because Professor Miller has long been one of my personal intellectual heroes in the discipline. He is a scholar whose works I regularly offer to my students as exemplars of reason and science. His own research contributions and stances on a variety of issues have, for me, always been a source of pride and inspiration despite the fact that my own works tend to diverge considerably from his positions.

This induces a secondary source of response. I am made uneasy by the text I have been asked to review and evaluate. My uneasiness is born of a desire to affirm Miller's distinctive scholarly voice, complete with its attendant clear arguments and good supporting reasons for a view of applied communication that elevates the status of that which I do to the respectable level of "pure" research. At the same time, I am in virtually complete disagreement with how that status is to be attained and with his clear positioning of applied research as just another object of scientific method and scrutiny.

Resolving these disparate sources of affirmation and resistance is no easy task. For some time I labored to construct an essay that accomplished both purposes, only to fill various waste baskets with the resultant products. Wishing for a transcendent noetic vision and having to date received none, I have instead decided to commit to print the true nature of my dichotomous state: an affirmation of Miller's argument that dissolves into a language-based critique of that argument. Perhaps this is precisely as it must be, for the position I ultimately will advocate is one of a postpositivist scholarly pluralism in which all theories are true somewhere (Eisenberg & Phillips, 1991), differences are the sources of scholarly articulation (Goodall, 1991) and distinctly different voices are encouraged to participate in the dialogue (Rorty, 1979).

THE LANGUAGE OF ARGUMENT IN OUR DISCIPLINARY KANSAS, OR: *CERTES, TOTO, SENTIO NOS IN KANSATE NON LAM ADESSE*

In the recorded history of our discipline, a history I hasten to add that is mostly limited to the written words found in our professional literatures, there has never been consensus about what it is that we are committed to studying or the methods we should use to study it. Ours has always been a responsive, at times reactionary group, from the original split the teachers of speech made from the teachers of English to those scholars who derive sources of legitimacy and purpose from scientific or rhetorical (later, humanistic) models.

This is to say that our shared disciplinary passage through the 20th century has been a passage over contested scholarly terrain. We have disagreed over just about everything from the name of that which we claim as ours to the methods we sponsor when we do our work to what, exactly, our work should be. We have debated these positions openly and in public at conventions as well as privately in late night caucuses held in various hotel rooms. There has been strength in our argumentative disunity, creativity in our lack of consensus, and a healthy spirit of competitiveness heard in the various rooms of our common, if untidy, scholarly house.

I begin this way because I think it is important to situate our arguments about applied communication research historically, to see them as extensions of issues and debates that preceded us as well as resources for future endeavors. In a way, our home has always been a disciplinary Kansas, a border state, a place at the heart of a scholarly nation that is often thought of by its scholarly neighbors as just another roadside attraction midway between various elsewheres, best gotten through on the available speed of its main arteries. For others of us and other scholarly neighbors, Kansas has been a wide place for the free exercising of the imagination, a head space rather than a place of the heart, a kind of seeding ground for the tall wheat of wild notions, a space where wizards roam and bright children seek their narratives, a field of dreams made up largely of dreamers.

Gerald R. Miller has, for the better part of the last half of our common century, been a consistent reminder to us that productive fields need doers as well as dreamers. He has advocated the centrality of his disciplinary Kansas to the interests of the neighboring social sciences. At the same time he has urged us away from the rhetorical spells of various wizards and gotten us to reaffirm our faith in the virtues of hard work, professionalism, and the primacy of the language of argument in productive scientific inquiry. His Kansas is not so much a border state as an ordered state, a disciplined place for disciplined scholars to make productive contributions—in the language of argument—to the science of communication.

At least this is who he has been to me. So it is within this interpretive biographical framework that I read his work on applied communication research for the 21st century, positioning him as a leading voice of scientific reason speaking in a commonly understood language of argument within our contested field. What he offers in the preceding chapter is, therefore, neither particularly unexpected nor particularly new. In a brief summary, here is the language of his argument, read from my point of view.

The adjectives *pure* and *applied* when used to modify the noun *research* have unfortunately privileged the work of those in pure research to the detriment of those doing applied studies. This need not be so. To rectify this unfortunate situation, applied communication researchers need to distinguish themselves by tackling real world problems with scientific rigor.

The real world problems that we should tackle with scientific rigor are those that have true social import; examples include improving the effectiveness of doctor–patient communication, legal communication, communication designed to turn children and adolescents away from drugs, fast food, and random unsafe sexual activities, and (although this one is a bit vague) research about the influences of mass media on everyday habits and attitudes.

To accomplish these tasks Miller suggests we need to (a) adopt Kurt Lewin's (1951) stance on the relevance of theory to research practices (thus avoiding the "pure" and "applied" dichotomy), and (b) strive for greater verisimilitude between our research contexts and the contexts of everyday life (read: avoid role-playing and simulations) in which the fruits of our research are supposed to have social import if not impact.

If we do these things, and do them well, applied communication research will inevitably transcend its nonscientific status and make substantive contributions to our discipline, to other disciplines, and most importantly, to the world.

This is a fine argument. It is reasonable, it offers to solve a problem about disciplinary status as well as worldly contributions, and it makes laudable and productive use of the dominant argumentative form of the English language. I come away from the experience of reading it convinced that if everyone in our discipline who did scientific research wrote as well and as convincingly as Miller, we would at least understand each other a lot better.

On the surface, I have no disagreements with any of these arguments. I could quibble over some areas of the discipline being excluded from his list of examples—organizational communication, for instance—but that would be a small quibble borne of my own interests rather than with what I see as the intent of his overall position. It is a neat, fully-rendered account that seeks through the conventions of its argumentative language and form to position applied communication research squarely in the mainstream of communication studies, which is to say squarely in the middle of our disciplinary Kansas.

My problem with the essay begins when I sense that we, or at least some of us, are, as a discipline, in fact *not* in Kansas anymore. By this I mean that for some of us, simply put, the world has changed and is no longer easily accounted for by or in a scholarly language of argument rendered under the privileged influence of a strict scientific framework. We have found ourselves situated not in a modern world but in a postmodern one in which the modern has not been replaced but instead continues to exist in an awkward and unequal side-by-side relationship with its newer explanatory competitor. Finding ourselves no longer at home in our ordered disciplinary Kansas, not only do we discover that the world we seek to describe and explain is different, but that the language skills and methodological competencies we learned for the accomplishment of those scholarly tasks are woefully inadequate.

We could, like a properly modernist Dorothy, simply click our heels together three times, chant the scientific method, and confine our applied research activities to the already well-ordered domains known locally as

Kansas. Or we could, like Dorothy gone postmodern, go out and mingle in the strange experiential mysteries that call into question scholarly goals and disciplinary borders, that reveals in the language of scientific argument sources of privilege and domination, and that begins—as all good existential journeys do—with noticing that something that would otherwise seem absolutely ordinary (such as the language of scientific argument) seems now somehow, well, different and troubling.

So it is here that my alternative reading of Miller's chapter begins.

TERMINISTIC MALAISE, OR: TWO DOCTORS SEE THE SAME SYMPTOMS, BUT DIAGNOSE DIFFERENT SOURCES OF DIS-EASE AND TREATMENT

Let us begin with the language we have inherited for articulating our problem. The term *applied communication* is redundant. So is the label *speech communication*. Both terms are, unfortunately, indigenous to the discipline Miller and I share. Both are causes of our common concern and one of them, the term *applied communication,* is not only our concern, but is the organizing principle for the Tampa Conference on Applied Communication, a conference designed to articulate appropriate resources for scholarly treatment of this particular dis-ease.

Using the medical metaphor of diagnosis, what we see displayed in the discussion before us is a corpus, a living body at whose outward extremities lie the rough outlines of empirical knowledge, a body whose human limbs reach out to a universe of mysteries, a body inscribed by academic and professional cultures responsible for its naming and parsing, a body that—when approached as a problem—is given the promise of miraculous new technologies that soon may be used to overcome the problems, reverse the dread, wipe away the damage caused by years of a relatively good life lived around the edges of bad habits.

This is quite clearly the body in question. It is a body of knowledge that presents us with an empirical nature and diverse cultural values. It is a body, that, because of our local participation in its very everydayness, reproduces in us a dis-ease in the ways we conduct our research into what is essentially our own lives. It is a body of questions that clearly presents us with far more than common symptoms; it presents us with a dramatic irony of paradigmatic proportions. And that dramatic irony is, finally, the source of our dis-ease, a dis-ease that in its terministic formulations uneasily speaks to a deeper existential and terministic malaise.

These words also could be spoken over the corpus labeled speech communication. But because I have been asked to respond to Miller's diagnosis for the body of applied communication and not to present my views on the silly, offputting, awkward, and ultimately unpoetic name attached to our discipline, I shall limit the scope of my analysis to precisely the duty I was asked to perform. Before I do that, however, allow me a little playful space here to worry over the medical diagnostic metaphor we seem to have chosen to frame this discussion.

One objection might be that perhaps we should not look for illness when the patient seems, at least by the fact if not by the spirited discussions held at the conference leading to this book, to be quite well and thriving. Is not, one might argue, one major sign of subdisciplinary health the recent elevation in status of the *Journal of Applied Communication Research?* Is not the empirical presence of a scholar with the stature of Gerald R. Miller renouncing the errors of his previous ways a testimony to far more than his desire to clothe himself in chinos and Izods while basking in the Florida sun?

Another objection might be to the narrow and perhaps colonizing influences that necessarily come with the baggage of Western medical science as a metaphorical model, a model that tends to privilege scientific diagnosis and treatment over more holistic and decidedly less behavioral medical models (Davis, 1986). Should we perhaps expand our notion of medicine to include other currently marginalized but apparently useful ways of understanding and dealing with the symptoms and causes of our dis-ease?

And finally, there are those who would inevitably suggest that a conference of academics talking about applied communication is practically equivalent to a Tipper Gore collectivity of White middle-class politicos talking about the language of African-American rap music: Our innocent and well-meaning efforts at direction for research and writing in the 21st century may, in fact, only further implicate us in sponsoring a privileged agenda that effectively functions as scholarly and methodological censorship, rather than encouraging a healthy spirit of democratic inquiry and pluralistic inclusion.

My point here is that metaphors are never innocent. As instruments of our own metaphorical and cultural making they reveal our worldly concerns just as surely as they reveal our personal and professional politics (Said, 1983). Ours is not a perfect language despite its perfecting impulse; its users are necessarily its abusers; what constitutes progress for the interests of one group more than likely constitutes marginalization for the interests of other groups (Burke, 1945/1969).

What we must take great care to guard against is not only the politics of metaphorical framing, but the tendency in every argument from metaphor to privilege its center at the expense of what lives at its margins. Paradigms do shift, but never from the center outward. In our discussions here I hope we remember that productive change—scientific, artistic, or political—has always occurred precisely the other way around, from the outside in. With this caveat firmly in place, I now address and deconstruct the terms of Miller's diagnosis.

THE SEXUAL POLITICS OF TEXTUAL PRACTICES

Miller began his diagnosis with a definitional argument within which he carefully embedded a brilliant and disquieting sexual metaphor. Reduced to the naked political aggression of its oppositional adjectives, "pure" research is characterized as dominant, scientific, theoretical, rigorous, innocent, and respectable; while "applied" research is characterized as dominated, nonscientific, atheoretical, loose, fuzzy, practical, capitalist, and suspect. Miller suggested that these modifiers are largely attitudinal and parochial; neither definitional set specifies crisp denotative distinctions and therefore offers an impoverished vision of applied communication research.

What this definitional argument accomplishes, it accomplishes simultaneously at the level of claim and embedded metaphor, thus at once forcing upon us both what we are buying into as well as what that purchase really costs us. At the level of argument, it is easy for those of us who share a commitment to applied research to agree with his claim that dichotomous distinctions between pure and applied categories offer an impoverished view of applied communication research. But the terms that lead up to our agreement suggest, slyly, precisely what this agreement assumes.

Miller layered his argument stance with the deeply embedded language of sexual conquest, a latent sexual orientation (perhaps a fantasy theme) that structurally positioned the respectable scientist above the loose, suspect, easy-to-rent body of the applied researcher for purposes that become clear in his demand that "research findings will become pregnant with social import" (p. 49). All that was missing in this parochial and obviously male depiction was the presumably large, thrusting penis, an absence of a presence perhaps intentionally engendered by the oppositional elegance of his next series of modifiers, the "hard" or "soft" application.

Within these designations Miller forced us to encounter the myth that if you are a scientist it is easy to be hard, a condition apparently not as easily achieved by the repressed soft researchers among us who labor vainly in the hope that our work will potentially achieve social utility. If this is not enough to awaken our sensitivities to the language structure being used to construct his argument, Miller then surgically performed the final cut in this definitional operation: social utility, having already been equated with the condition of pregnancy, produced an offspring—a scientifically-produced "finding"—who was, after the birth, abandoned by the scientist (who, we assume, must be off for newer lusty conquests), and the seeds of his scientific research practices (in his own mind) were left to come to fruition naturally while lovingly but distantly placed in the care of a presumably welcoming crowd of terminally soft practitioners.

Miller, ever the rhetorician under his scientific skin, then thoroughly denounced the attitude embedded within this depiction, an "attitude of indif-

ference concerning applied significance . . . to deny any interest in, or notion of the practical, social implications of . . . communication research" (p.
49). Not only was the oppositional positioning that brought forth the offspring called into question, but professional repugnance at the attitude of indifference toward practical and social implications—the offspring—was pas-
sionately expressed. Bravo, Doctor Miller! So far I am not only with you, but
my reading of your intentions certainly has been weighted in your favor; at
last the scientist and the postpositivist stand together, side by side.

This moment of congratulatory unity vanished, however, in the next
breath of Miller's diagnosis with the statement, "researchers would [I read:
should] be forced to think carefully about the potential generalizability, or
ecological validity of their studies, which in turn would ensure more attention to issues such as the nature of the research population to be sampled
and the potential verisimilitude of research environments to their real world
counterparts" (p. 49).

What I object to here—and to continue this discussion within the framework of Miller's sexual metaphor—is that what he is really advocating is little more than practicing science in the streets armed with a cheap condom.
Somehow the same old privileged positioning of the researcher to the subject researched, the same old depiction of the inherent validity of traditional
scientific research activities, and the truly random attitudes that Miller had,
I thought, previously argued against, *are all still here!*

The only difference is that the scientist is encouraged to don a shield: The
old original sinful colonizing act with its privileged positioning of science
over the welcoming body of the applied is materially condoned so long as the
offspring is planned for, and in the planning, controlled. From a traditional
view of social science, this may be sound ecology, but when research validity is solely equated with generalizable results, this argument opens itself to
another kind of ecological critique—specifically, the politics of the expressed
ecology.

Granted, science can and does produce generalizable results. Biological
science, for example, leads to medical technologies that cure most of the people most of the time. It is true, of course, that some people suffer unantici-
pated side effects as a result of those generalizable conclusions and that still
others are simply not cured, despite scientific reasoning to the contrary
about what ought to happen. It is also true that engineering and computer
science produce weapons of astonishing accuracy and space vehicles that
move to the dance of physics among the poetry of the stars, even though
sometimes missiles, rockets, and space craft crash or do not perform according to the logics of generalization that produced them.

I could argue here that what does not work or what gets hurt is valuable
for study in its own right. While this is certainly true it is the not the source
of my ultimate complaint about validity in applied research being equated

with generalizable findings. There are differences, however, between the aims of science in the applied arenas of medical technology, engineering, or computer science, and the aims of science in the arenas of *in vivo* humans communicating (Goodall, 1989).

To continue in the language of the embedded sexual metaphor, the aim of science in the arena of technology may be to produce the perfect condom or a cure for sexually transmitted diseases; in the arena of learning about humans communicating, the same aims for a science valid by generalizable results are akin to establishing an approved program of prescribed sex: We can have sex if, and only if, the researcher is a priori guaranteed of producing not only multiple children, but children who are all exactly alike, and who are destined to enter the world to accomplish only their Father's purposes.

MEDICAL AND THEORETICAL MATTERS IN A POSTMODERN, POSTPOSITIVIST WORLD READ AS FRAGMENTS WITHIN LARGER CULTURAL TEXTS

Every scientific argument has to provide evidence of warrantable assent to its claim. Miller's warrant for the dis-ease he has named as the domain of applied communication research seeks to link social and scientific effectiveness while relying heavily on Lewin's (1951) familiar dictum: "There is nothing so practical as a good theory" (p. 169). Under the broad, happy canopy of this academic truism we are invited to agree that (a) "effectiveness" in the social realm is the true measure of applied research, (b) that "heightened attention to certain aspects of theory development could ensure a closer 'fit' between diverging collective and individual concerns" (p. 50), and, finally, that (c) the failure of communication research to link theory with effectiveness is due to the atheoretical nature of a substantial body of our work.

I would like to agree with each one of these claims, but to read their meanings differently. To do that, I rely on certain tenets of postpositivist critical and cultural theories that I firmly believe have utility here. Reduced to their basic outline, these tenets suggest:

The World We Live In and Through Is Complex, Diverse, Dialogic, and Existential. A walk down any street will indicate that contemporary literary theory to the contrary, the postmodern has not replaced the modern, it exists in a variety of side-by-side relationships with it. This is true in architecture, art, fashion, music, speech, and behavior (Connor, 1990; Harvey, 1990). Hence, there is no true single-minded, single-behaviored collectivity within reach of scientific generalization unless one strips away individual differences in favor of a less complete account of what it means to be human.

That this happens, happens regularly within the sacred territory of our scholarly literatures, and that it is apparently endorsed by social scientists strongly suggests that the politics of scientific inquiry and publication are, in fact, not value free and self-correcting, but instead thoroughly hegemonic, singularly reductionist, and blatantly capitalist. Under these political conditions, what is practiced in the name of useful science can and probably should be read as a cultural subtext in support of a general theme of the destruction of the individual through elitist marginalization of difference.

The purpose of this political act is to create a rather narrow, passive, rule bound, culturally uninformed, and elite audience for scientific discourse, a homogeneous body of isolated language users who move (rather than dance), lockstep, to the same boring Muzak. One result of this trend over the past 50 years or so is the steadily increasing distance between academic discourse and a public audience for that discourse; another is the collusion of methodolatry and image making as a dominant social form (Ewen, 1989). I do not believe that a closer fit between theory and research practices is the answer, merely an answer for those practitioners of modernist social science whose theories admittedly apply somewhere, but certainly not everywhere.

Furthermore, individual differences still seem to matter to the individual, which is semantically similar to Miller's claim that "no problems are insignificant to their victims" (p. 50). However semantically similar our observations, we reach very different conclusions. For me, the individual is both a social agent and an existential actor; failure to account for her or his performances, motives, and activities with explanations that deny—or claim not to be able to account for—these sources of everyday, applied complexity are in my view of our postmodern, postpositivist world, unwarrantable.

When the World Changes, So Do the Questions. I am here most intrigued by the stale breath of "effectiveness," a thoroughly modernist term that carries with it a decidedly political odor. In the recorded history of communication theory, this term is associated with an effects model, or, if I am to be somewhat fairer, a mediated effects model. Its root metaphor, mediated or not, is causation.

In Miller's view, effectiveness should be the measure of the social utility of our work, and his examples included finding "effective" ways to link theory and research, finding "effective" ways of communicating to the fat teenager the disadvantages of fast foods, finding "effective" ways to communicate to the real or potential drug user the negative effects of drug use, and finding "effective" ways of communicating to an AIDS or cancer patient . . . something of value. The meaning of life, I suppose, viewed from an effectiveness perspective, is located somewhere in the magic bullet of an undeniable message, and if only we can find it, what a wonderful world this would be!

I do not know what constitutes having or living a life in East Lansing, but in the places I have lived I have yet to meet an overweight person who did not know he or she was overweight and the effects of fast food on the problem; nor have I ever met a real or potential drug user who could not explain to me in some detail the negative effects (as well as the positive ones) of substance abuse. As for AIDS or cancer patients, I have known and communicated with both, and none of the individuals in either group were at all interested in my assessment of the causes of their illness nor of some prescription for daily coping that they could already easily recite. What they wanted, and what they desperately needed, was some way to talk meaningfully about their life experiences, to connect their small dot with the larger mysteries, to learn how to "be" rather than to "do."

The idea for meaningful postpositivist social research, or for any research question, is to render a perceived problem problematic. This means, essentially, to complicate it, not to reduce its complexity. Viewed this way, issues of effectiveness are by and large unproblematic. As a research agenda, offering the obvious to the those who already have access to the messages seems trivial. Do we expect to change the content of a medical prescription, or perhaps just its style? I believe that the world that we and our subjects live in deserves better treatment. What we need are research questions that get at the experiences of being human, the meanings we attach to purposes and moments in life, and a general reframing of our methods toward aspects of life as a mystery rather than as a problem.

It is this final observation that encourages me to take serious issue with the example cited in Miller's chapter about the graduate student who left a colloquium because he would "never meet any of those 10 kids . . . so there was no need to stick around any longer" (p. 51). Miller used this bit of petty narcissism to endorse his claim that generalizability is the true and proper aim of scientific research. He went on to add: "improving communication between one cancer patient and his or her oncologist, although personally beneficial, is of minimal applied import; improving communication between many cancer patients and their oncologists represents a substantial applied step forward, and improving communication between many patients suffering from various medical problems and their physicians moves us yet closer to the best of all possible applied worlds" (p. 51).

The idea of applied "progress" seems to be at work here. I am tempted to extend this argument to say that "if all people and their physicians just had cancer, what a marvelous sample population that would be!" But that would probably spoil the theory-driven fun. To that graduate student who left a lecture because he wouldn't meet any of its subjects, I wonder if the reverse situation were true how easily he would apply to his own life the same logic and conclusion: If no one in the general reading public is likely to ever meet him, why should they continue to pay taxes that support his research program?

Finally, I suggest to Miller that he remember that Lewin's theories were sponsored by a government that wanted to invoke science as "proof" that democratic forms of leadership were best. That there is "nothing so practical as a good theory" is indeed true somewhere, and probably especially useful for a leadership study done in 1939 at the doorstep of a World War. Perhaps his "good theory" had little to do with good research practices or with leadership, and far more to do with survival.

Survival is an interesting term. Linked to democracy as a form of governance and leadership, it would seem to suggest that that government survives best that includes many voices, many perspectives, and as I say, many research agendas. I may well disagree with Miller's diagnosis so far, but in the best interests of my discipline I would never suggest that he cease his research agenda and adopt my own. Nor would I deny him access to journal space by refusing to read accounts that were not rendered in interesting prose narratives with decidedly existential characters engaged in mystery. My interest, and our joint interest, is in applied scholarly pluralism, not pure scholarly unity. That we find fault with each other's research values should be expected; that we read each other's research carefully and with an open mind should be our goal. This is perhaps the only valid generalization that I can safely sponsor.

VERISIMILITUDE AS A JOINT VENTURE

The next argument given by Miller is for a treatment program for applied communication research. It begins with the idea that "the chief threat to the applied power of communication research . . . [is] the extremely low verisimilitude that exists between our research and the real world communicative phenomena we seek to understand" (p. 52). On this point Miller and I are in total agreement.

We do differ, however, in our means of achieving verisimilitude. Here again Miller's solution is basically to go—as he poetically phrased it over a decade ago—"down where the iguanas live" (1978, p. 1). So far, so good. But what he wants to do when he gets there is where he and I are still divided. In Miller's world of scientific privilege the idea is to apply to the iguanas laboratory-tested theories using academically sound research methods. The end result is a translation of the voice of the iguana into academic cant, and, I might add, a thorough colonization of the iguana's world.

My approach is to go down where the iguanas live, crawl around with them, learn their ways and their language codes (as much as that goal is ever achieved), and use their voices in the co-construction of my text. The idea is to avoid privileging my world over theirs by engaging their world on—as much as this is ever possible—its own terms.

Do I claim that this is not a colonizing act? No, unfortunately, I cannot. I have used the world of my particular iguanas to build my scholarly career, so no, I am neither innocent nor pure. On the other hand, my iguana texts do strive for precisely the sort of verisimilitude that is warranted, and I do so by writing of their culture and communication in the form and style of its occurrence—again, as much as that is ever possible. My accounts do not read like research reports, but they are research reports. They are not theory-driven but theory-seeking; they are not motivated to find a technology but they are highly motivated to understand the meanings of individuals in various situations working out the complexities of their lives within the intricate webs of an array of technologies.

And there is one other difference between Miller's approach and my own. My research reports are capable of being read by the general public as well as by our academic colleagues. If there is a greater testimony about the ability of a researcher to address real world issues and write about them in a way that has the potential for true social impact, I cannot name it. To be read is to be listened to; to be read by persons who do not share the rarified intellectual breeding of academics or academic values is to be listened to by persons who are rarely given even so much as lip service by academic researchers but whose tax dollars and votes tend to support us. Most importantly, it is to give access to what communication research can do in the world that lies beyond the academy.

POST-STRUCTURALISM, RADICAL EMPIRICISM, AND APPLIED COMMUNICATION RESEARCH: AN ALTERNATIVE DIAGNOSIS

Now that I have addressed the issues in Miller's chapter, I offer an alternative vision for applied communication research. My objective here is not to suggest that Miller's diagnosis and favored treatment be replaced with mine, merely that both visions be encouraged to co-exist—probably never very peacefully, which is all right—within the framework of the same academic discipline. What Miller and I share is a commitment to excellence and to a future in which our research has social import; where we differ is on the choice of paths we take to get there.

Having already tread on his path, allow me to outline the path I have chosen. For me, there are important differences between a philosophy of empiricism and a philosophy of radical empiricism. Because a philosophy of empiricism is deeply embedded in Miller's approach to bringing science to bear on the world of the applied, I assume no further explication of it is needed here. Instead, I devote some space to the philosophy of radical empiricism, a philosophy that, according to the anthropologist Michael Jackson, "seeks to grasp the ways in which ideas and words are wedded to the world in which we live, how they are grounded in the mundane events and experiences of everyday life (1989; pp. 5–6).

The essential arena for radical empiricism is the lived experience of situated individuals. Lived experience "encompasses both the 'rage for order' *and* the impulse that drives us to unsettle or confound the fixed order of things" (p. 2) and as such "accommodates our shifting sense of ourselves as subjects and as objects, as acting upon and being acted upon by the world, of living with and without certainty, of belonging and being estranged . . . and remains skeptical of all efforts to reduce the diversity of experience to timeless categories and determinate theorems, to force life to be at the disposal of ideas" (p. 2).

As a way of approaching a research context, radical empiricism "is, first and foremost a philosophy of the experience of objects and actions in which the subject itself is a participant. . . . Unlike traditional empiricism, which draws a definite boundary between observer and observed, between method and object, radical empiricism denies the validity of such cuts and makes the interplay between these domains the focus of its interest" (p. 3). But what is "lived experience" to count as when it is defined ambiguously as an interplay of influences that emerge from a situated context of Self and Other(s)? Jackson puts it this way:

> Experience, in this sense, becomes a mode of experimentation, of testing and exploring the ways in which our experiences conjoin or connect us with others, rather than the ways they set us apart. In this process we put ourselves on the line; we run the risk of having our sense of ourselves as different and distanced from the people we study dissolve, and with it all our pretensions to a supraempirical position, a knowledge that gets us above and beyond the temporality of human existence. As for our comparative method, it becomes less a matter of finding "objective" similarities and differences between other cultures than of exploring similarities and differences between our own experience and the experience of others. (p. 4)

EMPIRICISM VERSUS RADICAL EMPIRICISM 1: STRUCTURAL VERSUS POSTSTRUCTURAL NOTIONS OF SELF AND OTHER(S)

Earlier in this chapter I labeled Miller a "structuralist." This is not some alternative form of name calling so much as an important starting point for the divergence of methods we have elected, the paths we have chosen. Allow me to explain.

Miller's empiricism is firmly rooted in structural opposition and strict categorical adherence to differences. My radical empiricism blurs those distinctions and focuses on the resultant lived experience of both the researcher and those researched. This distinction allows me to situate Miller's arguments within a philosophical and pragmatic framework of structuralism that privileges the voice of the Self (in his case, the Scientist-Self) over the voice(s) of the Other (in his case the Object-Others in a research program) while allowing me to offer a poststructuralist alternative. In a philosophy of radical empiricism Self and Other(s) are dialogically positioned as co-constructors of the lived experience under scrutiny. No voice is privileged, no one set of explanations are sanctioned.

For me, the concepts of Self, Other, and Context are the irreducible problematics in any theory of communication and are always rendered problematically in any applied research program and resultant text (Goodall, 1991). Hence, the research report is a text of experience—the lived experience of Self within a Context populated by Others—and communication consists primarily of the various ways in which negotiations among those constructions are made, interpreted, understood, and misunderstood (Bakhtin, 1981).

By contrast, the study of lived experience is neither the focus nor the intent of structural empiricism. Inherent to structural empiricist arguments is the expressed need for oppositional categories—what Miller characterized as "useful conceptual distinctions"—that are fixed boundaries marked by the territorial imperatives of words. These boundaries separate Self and Others and define "communication" as an object-state of specific behaviors rather than as a fluid state of negotiated meanings rendered meaningful through lived experience.

From a structuralist perspective, the boundaries must remain intact if categorical distinctions are to be made and knowledge of the contents of those categories attained. From a poststructuralist perspective, categories and boundaries are suspect. Communication is not about putting knowledge contents into some categorical container, but instead is about the experience of living through signs, symbols, and other representational traffic as if that representational traffic was in itself meaningful (see Goodall, 1995).

From a radical empiricist, poststructural construction of social life, if we are to study communication as a social process, which is Miller's belief and mine as well, we must necessarily add the dimension of doing that research within fluid contexts—what Miller rightly refers to as "verisimilitude"—rather than in fixed rooms with observational windows.

RADICAL EMPIRICISM VERSUS EMPIRICISM II: THE ROLE OF THE SENSES IN THE CONSTRUCTION OF KNOWLEDGE

While we are on the topic of observational windows, let me further suggest that social life in the everyday is lived through at least five senses and that applied research worthy of wearing the verisimilitude label should also reflect total sensual immersion in the research context (Jackson, 1989; Stoller, 1990). It is interesting to note here an important difference between the philosophies of empiricism and radical empiricism that play into this formulation.

Empiricism values detaching the observer from those observed, the Self from the Others, but that detachment is designed to service an epistemology that privileges sight over and often to the exclusion of other senses. As Jackson has it:

> It is thus fascinating and pertinent to note how the separation of subject and object in traditional empiricism is in large measure a function of the sensory mode and metaphor it privileges: vision. . . . Thus the plethora of terms in our Western epistemological vocabulary which evoke the notion of knowledge as seeing (eidos, eidetic, idea, ideation, intuition, theory, theorize) or refer to optics as a metaphor of understanding (reflect, speculate, focus, view, inspect, insight, outlook, perspective). (p. 6)

As John Dewey rightly realized some years ago, the result of privileging the optical metaphor provides us with at best a "spectator theory of knowledge" (cited in Jackson, p. 6). This spectator view of knowledge, in turn, reproduces itself by granting privilege to the study of humans communicating as a science of behavior. This science, of course, leaves out, ignores or marginalizes alternative conceptions of what it means to communicate, and what it means when humans communicate. Furthermore, why privilege sight and an emphasis on behavior when Being-in-the-world establishes influential lines of communication to all of our senses in a variety of modes?

EMPIRICISM VERSUS RADICAL EMPIRICISM III: THE ROLE OF THE AUTHOR IN A TEXT OF EXPERIENCE

Similar to the argument about empiricism privileging sight over the other senses is the argument that the scholar's voice should dominate the research text. By contrast, if that research text is a text of lived experience it should be a free interplay of narratives. Questions about who owns the rights to speak in a discipline committed to the democratic values of freedom of speech for all are questions that we ought not need to ask, but clearly we find that such a need exists.

Empiricism sponsors the scientist as the active agent of all knowing. The Other(s) is silenced, or perhaps more generously, reduced to behavioral-object status, subjected to and by the researcher's "gaze." This is in perfect accord with the philosophy that supports an objective rendering of distanced behavioral knowledge, but is diametrically opposite to a philosophy of radical empiricism that views this research move, as George Devereaux puts it, "as a stratagem for alleviating anxiety, not a rule of scientific method" (cited in Jackson, p. 4).

As you can see, the shift of paradigms here has direct impact on how research texts can be written, and on how the territory of a research project can be fairly represented in a textual format. Here again we confront a crisis in our own discipline. What our research literature privileges is a fairly limited view of empirical scholarship, a formula narrative bound by rules that constrain both what counts as "knowledge" as well as what ultimately gets known.

Admittedly these alternative scholarly visions for radical empiricism as a method for doing applied communication research tend to be dangerous. They induce an existential and terministic malaise among those trained to respect structural and scientific rules for conducting empirical research and fitting in to the dominant scientific culture of our academic communities.

The malaise is induced partly because these alternative visions challenge our received view of both the rightness and righteousness of research practices, and partly because when we ask these questions about communication as lived experience we suddenly discover that we have also left behind the familiar academic landscape we were reared to love. We have left behind, for example, a verbal, categorical geography of fixed boundaries and attendant logics of observation-based, single-voiced science; we have now entered a new territory that pragmatically renders the traditional goals and methods of structuralist science incongruent with the goals and methods of postpositivist applied communication research.

Generalizations, like theory-driven research programs, in a radical empiricist, postpositivist, poststructuralist world are reduced to little more than, as the novelist Barry Hannah (1978) puts it, "fun in the air." You can enjoy talking about them, but they really don't matter very much. Finding ourselves in a world that values most what matters most to situated individuals, that values differences and personal meanings that defy easy categorizations or generalizations, and that actively sponsors sources of cultural diversity, we learn very quickly that we are no longer at home with our colonizing academic talents. Furthermore, when radical empiricism is taken out into the world and practiced, it is the Self, not the Other, that is the truest stranger.

POSTPOSITIVIST, POSTSTRUCTURAL, RADICAL EMPIRICISM INVADES THE APPLIED RESEARCH PRACTICES OF RHETORICAL CRITICISM, TOO

Of course this is unsettling to those who have learned well how to practice their science or art, and certainly their theory-building agendas, within the bounded rationality of modern structuralism. But unsettling it must be. For all of us the world has changed—not just for those of us who talk about it as having changed—and, as I pointed out earlier, so too should our questions.

This world change that brings with it the demand for a paradigm shift is not any easier for the bona fide humanist than it is for the bona fide scientist. For example, McGee (1990) pointed out that in a poststructural, post-modern world rhetoricians can no longer assume that there is a text, nor that their time honored methods of analyzing texts make any real contributions to knowledge. Instead, McGee argued, the dictates of a poststructural world suggest that the task of the critic is to assemble a text out of fragments of culture and to implicate him or herself in the critique. When this transfor-mation of purpose occurs, new methods must be found to deal with these new, fluid critical contexts and the social responsibility that morally and eth-ically comes with assuming the role of the critic in the world.

McGee called for criticism to move out of its early 20th century mod-ernism and its structural irrelevancy and to embrace the news of the world at this end of the 20th century. Imagine being a rhetorician and facing the prospect of a world without any texts. Imagine being a rhetorician and real-izing, with McGee, that who and what you are is no longer nobody's business when you practice your critical activities, but a necessary fragment in the text you are creating; in fact, who and what you are is not only a necessary part of the text but its true subject; your Being, not your Knowing, is the real work of applied rhetorical criticism in a postmodern world. Surprise!

I believe applied communication researchers, both scientific and rhetori-cal, must learn to be similarly surprised. We also must learn to read and em-brace the scholarly news at the end of the 20th century prior to making our scholarly appearance in the 21st.

SEXUAL METAPHORS AND
TEXTUAL PRACTICES REVISITED

To return to Miller's original metaphor privileging the potent thrust of pure research above the receptive cries and whispers of the applied researcher, what is far more useful than merely applying a real world condom to scien-tific research practices—metaphorical or not—is to fully embrace the mean-ings of human sexuality with an eye toward re-evaluating the politics as well as the practices embedded within the sexual metaphor. Our goal, I should think, should be to learn how to make better love rather than just how to en-gage in sexual intercourse.

By analogy, the goals of human communication research (which by my definition necessarily occurs *in vivo* and therefore is always "applied") should move away from the dominating gaze of sensually limited scientific observation and anally compulsive laboratory control to a conscious realiza-tion that unless we study communication in its naturally occurring contexts (verisimilitude) and learn how to implicate ourselves directly in our research processes and findings (postpositivist critique), we will succeed in doing little more for applied work than to reaffirm the trivial in the name of science for the advancement of our careers.

Toward what is clearly a revisionist agenda for applied communication research, I therefore suggest a far different kind of diagnosis and treatment for our patient. In my view the corpus before us is alive—thoroughly so—and comes fully equipped with a life. The purpose of research is not simply to describe the outward appearance of that body or to assess its attitudes through questionnaires, or to attempt to control its urgencies, but instead to engage that human life as lived experience fully and on its own terms.

Hence, my revisionist, poststructural, postmodern, postpositivist diagnosis begins posthaste with the need to blur distinctions among all categories of research as well as among genres for reporting research. To blur these distinctions, oppositional categories such as "pure" and "applied," "hard" and "soft" and more importantly, to place all considerations of communication research activities within specific situated rather than contrived contexts, is to liberate science from a received medium. This medium privileges the observer over the persons and things observed and calls into serious question the unholy trinity of explanation, prediction, and control which, after all, seeks its own political ecstasy at the colonizing expense of the complexity and humanity of the Other.

Such a diagnosis also recognizes that the research report is not a sacred text, but a secular one. Privileging formulaic scientific method over other forms of writing is merely to privilege the methodolatry of the contrived at the expense of the empirically experimental and lived. Perhaps more relevant to Miller's open but nuanced concerns for the the status of communication research in the academic pecking order, it should be pointed out that to condemn communication scholars to the logical and deductive model of science is to ignore major events in anthropology, history, literary studies, philosophy, and even artificial intelligence research in favor of merely repeating the methods and goals of the modern scientific past.

This last comment is worth belaboring a little longer. To commit the future to the goals of the past is to buy into another kind of dysfunctional activity—one I call the Jay Gatsby Syndrome—or, if you will, the disabling belief that the past can and should be repeated. In that book, you may recall, Jay Gatsby dies—vaingloriously and wrongly perhaps—but dies nonetheless because what he stands for is crucified by a larger truth.

CONCLUDING COMMENT:
KANSAS IS AND IS NOT KANSAS, MAYBE

What I am arguing for is simple, but not easy to attain. I believe in an applied communication research future that does not solely privilege the scientific and behavioral (the predictable and controlled and generalizable) and includes a more democratic and pluralistic vision. This disciplinary pluralism would include space for both Miller's diagnosis and favored treatment and my own. It would sponsor both the empirical and scientific as well as what Jackson and I are labeling a radical empiricism. This radical empiricism invites applied communication research into situated contexts of lived experience and produces an experimental text of multivocal, multitextual dimensions of Being to stand alongside the dominant, if solo voice and routinized text of a mathematics of empirical Knowing.

We know how to accomplish Miller's vision. It represents the best of the mainstream of our disciplinary Kansas, fine work done by able scholars whose contributions are informed by modern(ist) science. There are no ready formulas or procedures to follow for what I am advocating. There are no proven generalizations and few exemplars to pick up along the way, and, perhaps most damning of all, no final research destination—these are life mysteries of situated communication we engage rather than attempt to solve. Our Kansas is not Kansas anymore.

To become a scholar of an alternative Kansas—an applied communication scholar of the radical empirical sort that I am describing—is not procedurally as easy nor as methodologically tight as its scientific counterpart. It is surely an alternative voice, a voice of resistance, experimentation, and pluralism, whose promise will only be proven if research done in its spirit is found to be meaningful within our scholarly communities.

It is not yet a proven path, but one that must be cleared as it is made. But it is a path whose challenges are very appealing.

REFERENCES

Bakhtin, M. (1981). *The dialogic imagination.* Austin: University of Texas Press.
Burke, K. (1969). *A grammar of motives.* Berkeley: University of California Press. (Original work published 1945)
Connor, S. (1990). *Postmodern culture: An introduction to theories of the contemporary.* New York: Basil Blackwell.
Davis, W. (1986). *The serpent and the rainbow.* New York: Simon & Shuster.
Eisenberg, E. M., & Phillips, S. R. (1991). Miscommunication in organizations. In N. Coupland, H. Giles, & J. M. Weimann (Eds.), *Miscommunication and problematic talk* (pp. 244–258). Newbury Park, CA: Sage.
Ewen, S. (1989). *All-consuming images.* York: Basic Books.
Goodall, H. L. (1989). *Casing a promised land: The autobiography of an organizational detective as cultural ethnographer.* Carbondale: Southern Illinois University Press.
Goodall, H. L. (1991). *Living in the rock n roll mystery: Reading context, self, and others as clues.* Carbondale: Southern Illinois University Press.
Goodall, H. L. (1995). *Divine Signs: Connecting spirit to community.* Carbondale: Southern Illinois University Press.
Hannah, B. (1978). *Airships.* New York: Knopf.
Harvey, D. (1990). *The conditions of postmodernity.* New York: Oxford University Press.
Jackson, M. (1989). *Paths toward a clearing: Radical empiricism and ethnographic inquiry.* Bloomington: Indiana University Press.

Lewin, K. (1951). *Field theory in social science: Selected theoretical papers* (D. Cartwright, Ed.). New York: Harper & Row.

McGee, M. C. (1990). Text, context, and fragmentation of contemporary culture. *Western Journal of Speech Communication, 54,* 274–89.

Miller, G. R. (1978). *Down where the iguanas live: Issues in applying communication research.* Unpublished manuscript, Michigan State University, East Lansing.

Rorty, R. (1979). *Philosophy and the mirror of nature.* Princeton, NJ: Princeton University Press.

Said, E. W. (1983). *The world, the text, and the critic.* Cambridge, MA: Harvard University Press.

Stoller, P. (1990). *The taste of ethnographic things.* Philadelphia: University of Pennsylvania Press.

4

Between Rigor and Relevance: Rethinking Applied Communication

Dwight Conquergood
Northwestern University

Those who pose the issue as a choice between pure, value-free research and applied or "relevant" social science employ a false set of opposites. The real question is relevance on whose side?   —Schoepf, 1979, p. 330

A professor of communication studies working on public policy issues shared the following story with a small but appreciative audience of colleagues gathered around a table to write a grant proposal and, incidentally, to swap narratives about the "ivory tower" and "real world" tensions of academic life: "And then the [university] president said to me, 'I don't like any of your applied stuff' [dramatic pause] 'because it contaminates theory!'" After repeating to his astonished audience that the president, indeed, did say those exact words—"because it *contaminates theory!"*—the narrator elaborated, "He [the president] is an econometrician. He prides himself on searching for data sets that will have *absolutely no use.* He said that once he selected the price of tomatoes in Milwaukee as a data set. He chose the price of tomatoes in Milwaukee because he was sure that this was a data set that would have *absolutely no use* or application."

This occupational narrative is ethnographically interesting on many levels. As relational currency it signals solidarity among colleagues through their collaborative critique of the administrator's wrongheaded remarks. Storyteller and audience bond through their reinterpretation of the president's example, "the price of tomatoes in Milwaukee," as a *reductio ad absurdum,* instead of a triumph, of his position. The collusion is strengthened because

the interpretation is tacit, and because the interpretive alignments corre-
spond to the hierarchical tensions within academic institutions, that is, those
between adminstration and faculty. Like all narratives, the meaning of this
story is in its telling.

True to its function as a cultural narrative, this story also expresses and me-
diates deep tensions, contradictions, and oppositions within university life.
No doubt many versions and variants of this tale circulate within the oral traditions of academia. One of the grand oppositions of the academy expressed
in this tale is the division between "theory" and "applied" research. This descriptive polarity becomes charged with moral force through the verb "contaminated." In this case, syntax mirrors semantics: the phrase "it contaminates theory" casts applied research as the active subject (the contaminator)
and theory as the passive object (the contaminated). The fundamental binary
opposition, then, is between "applied" and "pure" on the semantic level, and
"active" and "passive" (or "subjective" and "objective") on the syntactical
level.

The important question to ask of all binary oppositions is this: What is excluded or suppressed here? Binary oppositions function according to a di-
vide-and-conquer logic. One term is privileged by virtue of its domination
over the other term. This hierarchy of values is stabilized through affiliative
connections with a chain of other binarisms. The associative dichotomies can
be set forth thus:

applied—pure
practice—theory
derivative—basic
subjective—objective
commitment—distance
experience—reason
biased—neutral
engaged—disinterested
centrifugal—centripetal
politics—epistemology
social responsibility—conceptual coherence
action—abstraction
participation—explanation
humanistic—scientific
utility—objectivity
relevance—rigor

These dualisms reinforce and rest on a deeper set of cultural oppositions:

body—mind
emotional—rational
feminine—masculine

homosexual—heterosexual
Third World—First World
Non-European—European
nature—culture
low—high
Other—Self

Clearly the terms on the left are devalued relationally by the terms on the right. Applied research is situated disadvantageously within an academic discursive formation that organizes value and power through excluding the "practical" from the "theoretical" and opposing "utility" to "objectivity," and "agency" to "truth."

Within departments of communication the pure-applied hierarchy corresponds to the higher status of courses that teach theory over practice. In the quest for intellectual respectability, communication departments have moved away from production courses—this is as true for speech communication, media, and journalism as it is for English, film, and theater—distancing themselves from skills courses as one moves up the curriculum from freshman to graduate levels of instruction. Scholes (1985) insightfully notes that academic departments "privilege consumption over production, just as the larger culture privileges the consuming class over the producing class" (p. 5).

By displaying and dismantling these binary oppositions we can unmask their ideological underpinnings. The applied versus pure polarization of research is, quite literally, a Burkean act of "purification" through the pollution and victimage of applied research-cum-scapegoat. Applied research becomes polluted through association with research that is partisan, partial, opportunistic, unprincipled, compromised, for hire, or what Sanjek (1987) debunked as "have-gun-will-travel social science mercenaries" (p. 168). The vivid description of applied research as "prostituted science" and "pure" research as "unadulterated" draws on patriarchal metaphors for its polluting force. The purification of research through the purge of applied work is an exclusionary move that evacuates many things along with egregious mercenary motives. The major accomplishment of this exclusionary move is the evacuation of politics from research. To disconnect research from the useful and the applied is to disengage research from the world, and from human relevance. This retreat to laboratory and ivory tower decontextualizes, dehistoricizes, and ultimately conceptually impoverishes all research, particularly inquiries into the complexities of human communication.

Instead of defending and apologizing for applied research—an infinitely co-optable move that only recycles the oppressive binary constructions—I have used this chapter as an opportunity to rethink applied communication research in a more radical and emancipatory way. The first move is to desegregate research, undermine the pure-applied hierarchy, and expose this dichotomy for what it is: a rhetorical sleight of hand for conjuring the fiction of "pure" research. My basic point is that pure research sustains its pristine identity, indeed defines its purity, in a hostile relationship to the transgressive Other of "applied" research: affirmation by negation, scholarly antisepsis. The shaky claims to pure research are stabilized by the displacement of applied research. If one side of the ratio is branded worldly, then it is easier for the opposite side to pose as innocent (see Douglas, 1966; Stallybrass & White, 1986). But just as Whites as well as people of color are racialized subjects (Dyer, 1988; hooks, 1992), and the experience of men as well as that of women is gendered (Boone & Cadden, 1990; Gilmore, 1990), so pure like applied research is useful. The question is, useful for what and whom? What interests does it serve? Whose voice does it authorize and amplify? Whose experience does it marginalize, silence, or erase? What political-economic forces does it accommodate or contest? How does it mask, naturalize, enable, or expose and oppose domination? How does it inspire, or foreclose, social struggle and transformation?

In *The World, the Text, and the Critic*, Said (1983) provided a trenchant and sobering answer: "intellectuals are eminently useful in making hegemony work" (p. 15). Depoliticized knowledge supports the status quo and serves the interests of those in power, the dominant class. The apolitical stance, therefore, is aligned with establishment structures, conventional wisdom, and conservative politics—in a phrase, business as usual. In his monumental book *Orientalism*, Said (1979) questioned the fake dichotomy between pure and political knowledge: "the general liberal consensus that 'true' knowledge is fundamentally nonpolitical (and conversely, that overtly political knowledge is not 'true' knowledge) obscures the highly if obscurely organized political circumstances obtaining when knowledge is produced" (p. 20).

Said argued that the discipline of Orientalism developed beside and was shaped by colonialism but masked its complicity with imperialism behind scholarly detachment and professional discourse. Although Orientalist scholarship provides a particularly compelling example of how the production of knowledge is staked in political interests, Said (1989) insisted that all research is situated in history and politics: "there is no discipline, no structure of knowledge, no institution or epistemology that can or has ever stood free of the various sociocultural, historical, and political formations that give epochs their peculiar individuality" (p. 211; see also Said, 1993, 1994). In his address to the Society for Applied Anthropology, Stavenhagen (1971) made the point succinctly: "It is not a matter of science versus politics, but of one kind of science-in-politics versus another" (p. 343).

One of the important lessons to be drawn from Said's critique of Orientalist scholarship is that the university does not provide any high moral ground for the purity claims of researchers. Indeed, it is particularly the role of educator as well as researcher that embeds the academic in politics. Williams (1973) de-mythologized the romantic image of the ivory tower as a privileged space apart or free from worldly politics:

> The educational institutions are usually the main agencies of the transmission of an effective dominant culture, and this is now a major economic as well as cultural activity; indeed it is both in the same moment. . . . The processes of education; the processes of a much wider social training within institutions like the family; the practical definitions and organisation of work; the selective tradition at an intellectual and theoretical level: all these forces are involved in a continual making and remaking of an effective dominant culture. (p. 9)

It is the academic researcher's contributions to the production of an intellectual-cultural "selective tradition" that most enables domination. Williams (1973) explained what he meant by "selective tradition":

> that which, within the terms of an effective dominant culture, is always passed off as "the tradition," "the significant past." But always the selectivity is the point; the way in which from a whole possible area of past and present, certain meanings and practices are chosen for emphasis, certain other meanings and practices are neglected and excluded. Even more crucially, some of these meanings and practices are reinterpreted, diluted, or put into forms which support or at least do not contradict other elements within the effective dominant culture. (p. 9)

Said's work on Orientalist scholarship provided a detailed and inside view of the production of a politically consequential selective tradition about non-Western cultures.

And for anyone who wishes to neutralize the force of Said's critique by saying that his example, Orientalist scholarship, after all, was not a science, and therefore says more about the pitfalls of humanistic scholarship than scientific method, then the work of Foucault is discomfiting. Foucault (1980) argued that the rigor of scientific method is aggressively political precisely because of its apolitical and value free posturing:

> What types of knowledge do you want to disqualify in the very instant of your demand: "Is it a science?" Which speaking, discoursing subjects—which subjects of experience and knowledge—do you then want to "diminish" when you say: "I who conduct this discourse am conducting a scientific discourse, and I am a scientist"? (p. 85)

No one has argued more forcefully than Foucault (1980) for the enmeshed and enabling linkages among power, knowledge, and communication practices (discourse):

> What I mean is this: in a society such as ours, but basically in any society, there are manifold relations of power which permeate, characterise and constitute the social body, and these relations of power cannot themselves be established,

consolidated nor implemented without the production, accumulation, circulation and functioning of a discourse. There can be no possible exercise of power
without a certain economy of discourses of truth which operates through and
on the basis of this association. We are subjected to the production of truth
through power and *we cannot exercise power except through the production
of truth.* (p. 93, italics added)

Foucault's and Said's theorizing about the mutually sustaining co-articulation
of knowledge and politics has inspired thoughtful case studies and meta-
disciplinary critiques of specific scholarly fields implicated in domination,
notably Haraway (1989), Miller (1985), Mudimbe (1988), and Starn (1992).
Within the discipline of communication, Bochner (1985, 1994), drawing on
Rorty as well as Foucault, has argued against prevailing notions of disinterested, value-free research.

Even without the theorizing of Foucault, Said, and others, our everyday
language signals the link between knowledge and power. Academics should
be sobered, it seems to me, by the fact that this country's major spy organization is named the Central Intelligence Agency (CIA). The slipperiness
between the production of knowledge and domination is revealed in the
euphemism for espionage, *intelligence gathering,* a term that is uncomfort-
ably close to describing the activity of academic researchers. A domestic
counterpart to the CIA is named the Federal Bureau of *Investigation,* and
leaders of scientific research teams are called PIs, abbreviation for Principal
Investigators, but the acronym PI also stands for Private Investigator (as in
the popular television show *Magnum, PI*). Further, the term *informant* is deployed by the CIA, the police, and social scientists. In Southeast Asian
refugee camps administered by the military, and in the Gaza Strip under military occupation—two intensely politicized zones of control and contest
where I have done fieldwork—military informants also are called *collabora-
tors,* a term that highlights the aligned nature of all intelligence. In order to
avoid the unfortunate resonance with espionage, ethnographers have begun
substituting *consultant* for informant, but the new term carries overtones of
corporate capitalism. All these slippages of the terms *intelligence, investigation, informant,* and *consultant* in the arenas of scholarship, surveillance,
and capitalism should at least alert academics to the ethico-political complexities and entanglements of all inquiry. According to Eleanor Leacock
(1987), "The ostrich pose, head in sand, may protect the would-be purist
temporarily from self-criticism, but the ethical problems will not disappear"
(p. 321).

Let me hasten to add that the consequence of facing up to the hard truth
that as university researchers we are always already appropriated should not
be a hand-wringing guilt or cynical nihilism. Guilt is debilitating because it
breeds inertia. Guilt and innocence are flip sides of the same coin: Both states
of mind lead to "the passive kind of conservatism called quietism" (Lentric-

chia, 1983, p. 51). Humility and vigilance about the vulnerability of our work to worldly co-optation should encourage us towards more thoughtful struggle. Even if complete freedom from worldly constraints is not possible, resistance is. One of the great lessons I have learned from field research with poor and displaced people in Thai refugee camps, the Gaza Strip, and inner-city Chicago, is that even though socially marginal people are acutely vulnerable, they are not passive (see Conquergood 1985, 1988, 1990, 1992a, 1992b, 1992c, 1994; Conquergood & Thao, 1989). Within the most forbidding structures of domination people in myriad and creative ways carve out space for resisting, contesting, subverting authority, and refurbishing their own identity and dignity. Academics certainly have as much to learn from ordinary people living under extraordinary oppression as they do from Derrida (see Scott, 1990).

The choice is no longer between pure and applied research. Instead, we must choose between research that is "engaged" or "complicit." By engaged I mean a clear-eyed, self-critical awareness that research does not proceed in epistemological purity or moral innocence: There is no immaculate perception. Engaged intellectuals take responsibility for how the knowledge they produce is used instead of hiding behind pretenses and protestations of innocence. In a post-colonial, late capitalist world, marked by sexism, racism, homophobia, and class bias, we understand, with Said (1989), that "Innocence is now out of the question of course" (p. 213). As communication scholars who traffic in symbols, images, representations, rhetorical strategies, signifying practices, the media, and the social work of talk, we should understand better than anyone else that our disciplinary practice is *in* the world. As engaged intellectuals we understand that we are entangled within world systems of oppression and exploitation. We need to attend to the complex way macro-structures of power and consolidation penetrate and shape even the micro-textures of communicative interactions and intimacies. Our choice is to stand alongside or against domination, but not outside, above, or beyond it. Our dual challenge is to forego innocence and to keep cynicism at bay.

The scholarly commitment of the engaged intellectual is to praxis, not detachment. By praxis I mean a combination of analytical rigor, participatory practice, critical reflection, and political struggle. One thing I do not mean is a purist, dispassionate stance in which the intellectual holds him or herself apart from the people. Gramsci (1971) critiqued intellectuals about their aloofness:

> The intellectual's error consists in believing that one can know without understanding and even more without feeling and being impassioned (not only for knowledge itself but for the object of knowledge): in other words that the intellectual can be an intellectual (and not a pure pedant) if distinct and separate from the people-nation, that is, without feeling the elementary passions of

the people, understanding them and therefore explaining and justifying them in the particular historical situation. . . . One cannot make politics-history without this passion. . . . (p. 418)

Proximity to and vulnerability with the people are epistemologically necessary as well as politically and ethically desirable for the researcher (see Strine, 1991).

Praxis is fundamentally about placement, about taking a stand, marking (not masking) the self, positioning one's research ethically, politically, as well as conceptually. It is about willingness to connect, instead of the will to control. Haraway (1991) explained:

> I am arguing for politics and epistemologies of location, positioning, and situating, where partiality and not universality is the condition of being heard to make rational knowledge claims. These are claims on people's lives; the *view from a body,* always a complex, contradictory, structuring and structured body, versus the [scientific] *view from above,* from nowhere, from simplicity. (p. 195; italics added)

Like Gramsci, Haraway (1991) urged researchers towards embodied, passionate, complicated ways of knowing that acknowledge their partial and partisan perspectives but also include the potential for connection, the ability "to join with another, to see together without claiming to be another" (p. 193). Many researchers will be reluctant to substitute the vulnerable "view from a body" for the omniscient "view from above." "Location," Haraway (1991) reminded us, "is about vulnerability" (p. 196), in contrast to the universal (the opposite of local, that which cannot be located), which is about authority.

Engaged research committed to *praxis* is situated between two axes of tension. These axes can be schematized horizontally as the tension between Relevance and Rigor, and vertically, as the tension between Discipline and Solidarity (see Fig. 4.1). The "Relevance-Rigor" horizontal axis delineates the opposition between centrifugal and centripetal forces, outside and inside, connectedness and closure. This axis traverses a boundary tension between social responsibility (outreach) and professional integrity (consolidation). The "Discipline-Solidarity" vertical axis negotiates the tension between introspection and involvement, individual and community, private and public. This axis marks the pull between thoughtfulness (identity) and action (affinity). These intersecting axes form quadrants on which we can map dimensions of the research process.

The upper right B quadrant bounded by Discipline and Rigor corresponds with so-called "pure" research. It is the quadrant where introspection is privileged. Its diagonal opposite, the D quadrant, bounded by Relevance and Solidarity, corresponds with so-called "applied" research. This quadrant provides a space for advocacy and political action. Political Struggle is the space

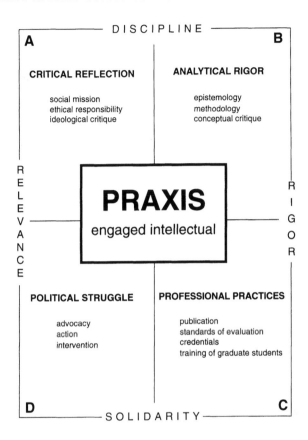

FIG. 4.1.   Mapping the space of praxis.

where knowledge is brought to bear on the outside world in struggles for social change. It is the space of *kinesis* (movement) instead of *stasis* (consolidation). The B-D diagonal axis delineates the tension between the academy
and the world, represented in popular discourse as the "ivory tower" and the
"real world." This diagonal axis is complemented and counterbalanced by
the quadrants it borders but does not traverse. "Professional Practices" (C)
is the space where "Analytical Rigor" gets institutionalized and reproduced.
"Critical Reflection" (A) is the mediating space where worldly (political) concerns are brought into productive tension with the more introspective and
endogamous nature of disciplines and their professional associations, the
space where epistemology meets ethics.

In a *praxis* model of the engaged intellectual, all four quadrants interact dialogically, instead of existing discretely. Any one of the quadrants disconnected and isolated from the others is a distortion of the *praxis* model. For purposes of explanation I have laid out the quadrants as two-dimensional contiguous planes. However, I see all four sites—Analytical Rigor, Professional Practices, Political Struggle, and Critical Reflection—as dynamically interdependent, criss-crossing, superimposed practices of the engaged intellectual. Instead of a map with quartered sections, I see *praxis* as a palimpsest, or, even better, a braided wreath or cable. My favorite definition of *praxis* comes from Frank (1991): "Thus 'praxis,' which has become a hollow word in its overgeneralization, takes on new meaning as *the embodiment of theory in communal performance*" (p. 83, italics added).

CULTURAL DIVERSITY IN THE 21ST CENTURY

Cultural diversity is an especially fertile and urgent site of research for *praxis*-oriented communication scholars. When all the statistics of the 1990 U.S. Census are available they will reveal a stunning shift in the demographic portrait of the country. Immigration plays an increasingly important role in population growth. Currently, immigration accounts for one third of population growth, but by the year 2019 it is projected to outweigh natural increase (births minus deaths) as a source of population growth ("What Lies Ahead," 1989). There has been a significant change in the immigration pattern that the 1980 Census only had begun to capture. The immigrants who came to this country in successive waves during the 19th and early part of the 20th century were by and large of European stock. Because of quotas imposed on immigration in legislation passed in 1924, it became difficult for anyone who was not northern European to immigrate to this country.

During the last decade most of the immigration has shifted from Europe to the south and the east, or what is called the Third World. This shift was enabled by two key acts of legislation. The 1965 Immigration Act amendments that repealed many of the racist quotas, and the 1980 Refugee Act that facilitated entry into this country of large numbers of Southeast Asian refugees from the Vietnam War. During the 1980s approximately 500,000 people annually, including refugees, have entered the country legally. This number is bolstered by an estimated 100,000–200,000 undocumented people entering the country annually from Latin America. This underground immigration is one of the consequences of having the major country of the First World sharing a border with an economically strapped Third World country (Lamphere, 1992; Reimers, 1992).

Currently one in three U.S. residents is a minority but by the year 2010 it is projected that the majority of residents will be of non-European descent

(Sanjek, 1990)). Many states, like California, already are approaching a "majority minority" status. Most of the people of color, including the new immigrants, are concentrated in the country's largest cities.

This pluralizing of the ethnic and racial composition of the country, co-articulated with social movements that have raised consciousness about the status of women, gays and lesbians, and people with disabilities have put "cultural diversity" on the national agenda for the 21st century. How diversity gets constructed—rhetorically defined, communicatively negotiated, managed, and contested—should be of enormous interest to engaged intellectuals in communication studies. *Cultural diversity* already is a keyword in public discourse and it will become increasingly a contested site of struggle for meaning and conflict of interpretations with social, ethical, political, and legal implications (Williams, 1983).

The construction of American identity in the 21st century will be an ongoing negotiated site of exchange between established residents of European descent and the new immigrants and people of color. Identities are not given, they are made and remade within arenas of adaptation and struggle. Competing conceptions of American identity and American life are tactics and tools for assimilation or resistance within the encounter between large numbers of new immigrants from Asia, South Asia, Southeast Asia, the Middle East, Mexico, and Central and South America whose cultural practices differ from those of Whites and African Americans. Currently, there are two competing views of identity deployed in the political debate about what it means to be "American." The conservative position views identity as monolithic, dominant, and assimiliative of difference. This position is defended by appeals to order and common, core values in opposition to anarchy and societal disintegration, the so-called "fraying of the cultural fabric." The progressive position views identity as porous, processual, and enriched by difference. This position is supported by appeals to pluralism and liberty in opposition to totalitarianism and sterile homogeneity. The courtroom, particularly with the emergence of the "cultural defense" in cases involving new immigrants in trouble with the law, has become a crucible of public argument where competing conceptions of American identity are tested and reconstructed (see Conquergood, 1991b).

Moreover, the crossing of borders and displacement and resettlement of vast numbers of people is now a global phenomenon. Refugees, exiles, expatriates, as well as internal ethnic uprisings, are now visible parts of the social landscape all over the world, as for example in Germany, Eastern Europe and the Balkans, the former Soviet Union, and Africa. Said (1990) characterized the current period as "the age of the refugee, the displaced person, mass immigration" (p. 357). Cultural zones of contest, margins, boundaries, borderlands, syncretism, and creolization should become resonant themes for communication researchers committed to *praxis* and social change.

CONCEPTUAL ISSUES

Research on cultural diversity entails newly developing epistemological concepts and methodological strategies. Many ethnographers, perhaps because
they are in the vanguard of work on cultural diversity, are rethinking basic
definitions such as "culture" and "identity" in less static and more processual and performative ways (Conquergood, 1991a). In *Culture and Truth:
The Remaking of Social Analysis,* Rosaldo (1989), drawing on his own
ironic positionality as a Latino academic who studies "the Other," recon-
ceptualized basic tenets of social analysis:

> Human cultures are neither necessarily coherent nor always homogenous.
> More often than we usually care to think, our everyday lives are crisscrossed
> by border zone eruptions of all kinds. . . . Along with "our" supposedly trans-
> parent cultural selves, such borderlands should be regarded not as analytically
> empty transitional zones but as sites of creative cultural production that require
> investigation. . . . All of us inhabit an interdependent late-twentieth-century
> world marked by borrowing and lending across porous national and cultural
> boundaries that are saturated with inequality, power, and domination. (pp.
> 207–208, 217)

Clifford (1988) likewise argued that identities are characterized more by
contradiction, predicament, and paradox, than by pattern, continuity, or coherence:

> Twentieth-century identities no longer presuppose continuous cultures or tra-
> ditions. Everywhere individuals and groups improvise local performances from
> (re)collected pasts, drawing on foreign media, symbols, and languages . . . or-
> ganic culture reconceived as inventive process or creolized "interculture." The
> roots of culture are cut and retied, collective symbols appropriated from ex-
> ternal influences . . . culture and identity are inventive and mobile. (pp. 14–15)

Said (1989), drawing on his personal experience as a Palestinian exile teaching at Columbia University, supported this new ethnographic theorizing of
culture because of its liberatory potential:

> If we no longer think of the relationship between cultures and their adherents
> as perfectly contiguous, totally synchronous, wholly correspondent, and if we
> think of cultures as permeable and, on the whole, defensive boundaries be-
> tween polities, a more promising situation appears. Thus to see Others not as
> ontologically given but as historically constituted would be to erode the exclu-
> sive biases we so often ascribe to cultures, our own not least. Cultures may then
> be represented as zones of control or of abandonment, of recollection and of
> forgetting, of force or of dependence, of exclusiveness or of sharing, all taking
> place in the global history that is our element. (p. 225)

Trinh (1989) succinctly articulated this epistemological response to the empirical experience of border-crossings, migrations, and global circulation and

transmutation of images, ideas, and messages: "Despite our desparate, eternal attempt to separate, contain, and mend, categories always leak" (p. 94).

Scholars of feminist cultural studies have joined ethnographers to promote the emancipatory potential of rethinking identity in the dialogic rather than monologic mode (Bakhtin, 1981). Anzaldua (1987) argued that in our postcolonial world the blurred zones of the borderlands have displaced the capitol, and viewpoints from the margins vie with those from the metropolis:

> The new *mestiza* [person of mixed ancestry] copes by developing a tolerance for contradictions, a tolerance for ambiguity. She learns to be Indian in Mexican culture, to be Mexican from an Anglo point of view. She learns to juggle cultures. She has a plural personality, she operates in a pluralistic mode. . . . Not only does she sustain contradictions, she turns the ambivalence into something else. (p. 79)

Trinh (1989) carefully rethought and linked the epistemological with the political:

> The differences made *between* entities comprehended as absolute presences— hence the notions of *pure origins* and *true* self—are an outgrowth of a dualistic system of thought peculiar to the Occident. . . . They should be distinguished from the differences grasped *both between* and *within* entities, each of these being understood as multiple presence. Not One, not two either. "I" is, therefore, not a unified subject, a fixed identity, or that solid mass covered with layers of superficialities one has gradually to peel off before one can see its true face. "I" is, itself, *infinite layers*. (pp. 90, 94)

An intervention in everyday language use correlates with academic theorizing about the hyphenated nature of identities. Jesse Jackson urged a shift from Black to African American as the progressive signifier for Americans with lineage from Africa and the African diaspora. He advocated this renaming because it emphasized cultural heritage instead of race or color. "African American" positions a person within a dynamic chronotope of historical and geographic dislocation, violence, and reforged connectedness, whereas "Black" totalizes and conflates the complexities of identity. The politics of signification turn on the axis of African American being a both/and connector, and Black being a term of differentiation. Further, African American takes its signifying place alongside Mexican American, Korean American, Polish American, Italian American, Greek American, Vietnamese American, Lao American, and other intercultural identities.

By integrating, or intersecting, identity with cultural heritage, the conception of American identity becomes one of multiple and shifting sites within the borderlands among cultures rather than a stable, assimilated, and homogeneous entity. The idea of the person shifts from that of a static, autonomous, individuated self to a polysemic site of articulation for multiple, mingling, and overlapping identities, perspectives, and voices. The methodological extension of this reconceptualizing is to open up and pluralize research *praxis*. The line between knower and known, observer and observed, representer and represented, blurs and wobbles. Engaged intellectuals working on cultural diversity will follow the lead of contemporary ethnographers who dialogize their research (see Clifford & Marcus, 1986; Fabian, 1983, 1990; Lavie, 1990; Marcus & Fischer, 1986). Studies *of* or *about* "others" will become research *with* them. *Praxis*-oriented communication scholars will explore more participatory, cooperative, and collaborative methods with the subjects of their research (see Bochner, 1995).

EFFECTING SOCIAL CHANGE

I agree with Lentricchia (1983) that the important site for intellectuals working for social change is in their teaching and research practices as much as on the ramparts: "Our potentially most powerful political work . . . must be carried out in what we do" (p. 7). Although I certainly have nothing against participating in demonstrations, testifying in courtrooms, and engaging in overtly political work, academics, particularly communication scholars working directly with meanings and representations, are situated importantly on a strategic front: the symbolic register. The magnificent oeuvre of Kenneth Burke is devoted to the importance of the symbolic register as the fundamental infrastructure for social and political action, "equipment for living." For Burke, all research on language, rhetoric, and communication is inescapably "applied." According to Lentricchia (1983), "the real force of his [Burke's] thinking is to lay bare, more candidly than any writer I know who works in theory, the socially and politically enmeshed character of the intellectual" (p. 38). Universities and educational institutions are enormously important political arenas. At every level, from what and how we teach and research (or do not teach or research), to the recruitment and mentoring of students and professional colleagues, knowledge workers are enmeshed in cultural politics.

In a seminal essay published two decades ago, Hymes (1972) described three relationships that researchers could have to their work: "that of critic and scholar within . . . the academic world; that of working for communities, movements, operational institutions; that of direct action as a member of a community or movement" (p. 56). Sanjek (1987) named these three research goals "academic, applied, and advocacy." I agree with Hymes that the role of the scholar and critic is indispensable, but I want to emphasize and call for engaged research that braids together all three of these roles into a multitextured weave of research practices. My major point is that the identity of the researcher, like that of Anzaldua's (1987) *mestiza* (the researched), also needs to be pluralized and reconceived as an ensemble of identities, an intersection of criss-crossing goals, a repertoire of multiple relationships. I most admire researchers who juggle simultaneously the roles of academic scholar, community consultant, and activist. The kind of research to which I aspire is that which continuously shifts and slides between critical theorizing, work in the community, and political action. The interaction and overlap between and among critical scholarship, applied work, and political advocacy strengthen each strand: The interacting ensemble becomes greater than the sum of the parts.

Let me illustrate with an example. Harrell-Bond (1986) conducted remarkable ethnographic field research in refugee camps in Africa. In the hands of a less brilliant and politically engaged fieldworker, such a project would have been ripe for "applied research" in the limited sense of that term: to offer recommendations to the humanitarian agencies about ways they could improve their delivery of assistance programs to the starving refugees. Instead, Harrell-Bond incisively critiqued political-economic forces and the "ideology of compassion" that underwrite humanitarian assistance programs and inadvertently contribute to the dehumanization and suffering of refugees: "The fault lies with the ideology of compassion, the unconscious paternalism, superiority, and monopoly of moral virtue which is built into it" (p. 353).

Harrell-Bond's research is a radiant exemplar of the productive mingling of scholarly critique, applied work, and political advocacy. Because she actually lived and worked inside the refugee camps—distributing food, helping to select sites for settlements, conducting censuses—she acquired an embodied, experiential understanding of the refugee condition that deepened insight and enlivened her scholarly critique of structures of assistance that rob refugees of agency and induce dependency. And because her scholarly critique was so careful and theoretically informed, her political interventions were more effective and authoritative. Although her research laid bare the injury wreaked on refugees by do-gooder humanitarian assistance programs, and she couched her critique in strong language, including the terms "imposing aid" and "monsters of concern" (p. 362), she followed up deconstruction with reconstruction. She organized a symposium, "Assistance to Refugees in Africa: Alternative Viewpoints," at Oxford University, her home institution, where a number of radical resolutions and recommendations were adopted:

> That they were passed by consensus by a group of refugees, government officials, and humanitarian workers reveals just how much *can* be accomplished by discourse. One might sum up the lesson of that meeting by saying there need to be *more* opportunities for outsiders to crawl out of their Mercedes and down off their pedestals to listen. (p. 365)

Moreover, her role as political activist fed back into her role as academic researcher and encouraged her to develop creative, cooperative, and dialogic methods of data collection and analysis: "I employed a team of researchers and together we were consciously acting as agents of social change by reporting our findings to the refugees and discussing the implications with them" (p. 21).

To would-be purists, Harrell-Bond's research program must appear hopelessly messy. My overarching argument, however, is to rethink applied communication as a "blurred genre" (Geertz, 1983), a refraction of all significant communication research. My major strategy has been to link the applied or useful dimension of research with cultural politics—not the consultation fees of the researcher. As long as applied communication is thought about and discussed mainly in terms of corporate consulting and supplementary income or alternative career paths for researchers, then it will remain a convenient straw man for professional conservatives to knock down, and thereby expel the political implications of all communication research. We must first "decolonialize" applied communication and then reappropriate the worldliness of applied communication for research that is committed to social change (Stavenhagen, 1971). By taking up this challenge, we can build compelling conceptual frameworks that embrace social justice and struggle. Applied communication, reconceived along these lines, can exercise and develop, not contaminate theory.

REFERENCES

Anzaldua, G. (1987). *Borderlands/la frontera: The new mestiza.* San Francisco: Spinsters.

Bakhtin, M. (1981). *The dialogic imagination* (M. Holquist & C. Emerson, Ed. & Trans.). Austin: University of Texas Press.

Bochner, A. (1985). Perspectives on inquiry: Representation, conversation, and reflection. In M. Knapp & G. R. Miller (Eds.), *The handbook of interpersonal communication* (pp. 27–58). Newbury Park: Sage.

Bochner, A. (1994). Perspectives on inquiry II: Theories and stories. In M. Knapp & G. R. Miller (Eds.), *The handbook of interpersonal communication* (pp. 21–41). Newbury Park: Sage.

Bochner, A. (1995). Talking-with as a model for writing-about: Implications of Rortyan pragmatism. In L. Langsdorf & A. R. Smith (Eds.), *Recovering pragmatism's voice: The classical tradition, Rorty, and the philosophy of communication* (pp. 211–233). Albany: State University of New York Press.

Boone, J., & Cadden, M. (Eds.). (1990). *Engendering men.* New York: Routledge.

Clifford, J. (1988). *The predicament of culture.* Cambridge: Harvard University Press.

Clifford, J., & Marcus, G. (Eds.). (1986). *Writing culture: The poetics and politics of ethnography.* Berkeley: University of California Press.

Conquergood, D. (1985). *Between two worlds: The Hmong shaman in America* [videodocumentary]. Chicago: Siegel Productions.

Conquergood, D. (1988). Health theatre in a Hmong refugee camp: Performance, communication, and culture. *The Drama Review, 32*(3), 174–208.

Conquergood, D. (1990). *The heart broken in half* [videodocumentary]. Chicago: Siegel Productions.

Conquergood, D. (1991a). Rethinking ethnography: Towards a critical cultural politics. *Communication Monographs, 58,* 179–194.

Conquergood, D. (1991b). Roosters, blood, and interpretations: Domination and resistance in the courtroom. In E. Slembek (Ed.), *Culture and communication* (pp. 149–160). Frankfurt: Verlag fur Interkulturelle Kommunikation.

Conquergood, D. (1992a). Fabricating culture: The textile art of Hmong refugee women. In E. Fine & J. Speer (Eds.), *Performance, culture, and identity* (pp. 206–248). Westport, CT: Praeger.

Conquergood, D. (1992b). Life in Big Red: Struggles and accommodations in a Chicago polyethnic tenement. In L. Lamphere (Ed.), *Structuring diversity: Ethnographic perspectives on the new immigration* (pp. 95–144). Chicago: University of Chicago Press.

Conquergood, D. (1992c). Performance theory, Hmong shamans, and cultural politics. In J. Reinelt & J. Roach (Eds.), *Critical theory and performance* (pp. 41–64). Ann Arbor: University of Michigan Press.

Conquergood, D. (1994). Homeboys and hoods: Gang communication and cultural space. In L. Frey (Ed.), *Group communication in context: Studies of natural groups* (pp. 23–55). Hillsdale, NJ: Lawrence Erlbaum Associates.

Conquergood, D., & Thao, P. (1989). *I am a shaman: A Hmong life story with ethnographic commentary*. Southeast Asian Refugee Studies Program (Occasional Papers, No. 8). Minneapolis: University of Minnesota, Center for Urban and Regional Affairs.

Douglas, M. (1966). *Purity and danger: An analysis of pollution and taboo*. London: Routledge & Kegan Paul.

Dyer, R. (1988). White. *Screen, 29*, 44–65.

Fabian, J. (1983). *Time and the other: How anthropology makes its object*. New York: Columbia University Press.

Fabian, J. (1990). *Power and performance*. Madison: University of Wisconsin Press.

Foucault, M. (1980). *Power/knowledge* (C. Gordon, L. Marshall, J. Mepham, & K. Soper, Trans.). New York: Pantheon.

Frank, A. (1991). For a sociology of the body: An analytical review. In M. Featherstone, M. Hepworth, & F. Turner (Eds.), *The body: Social process and cultural theory* (pp. 36–102). Newbury Park: Sage.

Geertz, C. (1983). Blurred genres: The refiguration of social thought. In *Local knowledge* (pp. 19–35). New York: Basic.

Gilmore, D. (1990). *Manhood in the making: Cultural concepts of masculinity*. New Haven: Yale University Press.

Gramsci, A. (1971). *Selections from the prison notebooks* (Q. Hoare & G. Smith, Eds. & Trans.). New York: International.

Haraway, D. (1989). *Primate visions: Gender, race, and nature in the world of modern science*. New York: Routledge.

Haraway, D. (1991). Situated knowledges. In *Simians, cyborgs, and women: The reinvention of nature* (pp. 183–202). New York: Routledge.

Harrell-Bond, B. (1986). *Imposing aid: Emergency assistance to refugees*. New York: Oxford University Press.

hooks, b. (1992). Representing whiteness in the Black imagination. In L. Grossberg, C. Nelson, & P. Treichler (Eds.), *Cultural studies* (pp. 338–346). New York: Routledge.

Hymes, D. (1972). The use of anthropology: Critical, political, personal. In D. Hymes (Ed.), *Reinventing anthropology* (pp. 3–79). New York: Pantheon.

Lamphere, L. (Ed.). (1992). *Structuring diversity: Ethnographic perspectives on the new immigration*. Chicago: University of Chicago Press.

Lavie, S. (1990). *The poetics of military occupation*. Berkeley: University of California Press.

Leacock, E. (1987). Theory and ethics in applied urban anthropology. In L. Mullings (Ed.), *Cities of the United States: Studies in urban anthropology*. New York: Columbia University Press.

Lentricchia, F. (1983). *Criticism and social change*. Chicago: University of Chicago Press.

Marcus, G., & Fischer, M. J. (1986). *Anthropology as cultural critique: An experimental moment in the human sciences*. Chicago: University of Chicago Press.

Miller, C. (1985). *Blank darkness: Africanist discourse in French*. Chicago: University of Chicago Press.

Mudimbe, V. Y. (1988). *The invention of Africa: Gnosis, philosophy, and the order of knowledge*. Bloomington: Indiana University Press.

Reimers, D. (1992). *Still the golden door: The third world comes to America* (2nd ed.). New York: Columbia University Press.

Rosaldo, R. (1989). *Culture and truth: The remaking of social analysis*. Boston: Beacon.

Said, E. (1979). *Orientalism*. New York: Vintage.

Said, E. (1983). *The world, the text, and the critic*. Cambridge: Harvard University Press.

Said, E. (1989). Representing the colonized: Anthropology's interlocutors. *Critical Inquiry, 15,* 205–225.

Said, E. (1990). Reflections on exile. In R. Ferguson, M. Gever, T. M. Trinh, & C. West (Eds.), *Out there: Marginalization and contemporary cultures* (pp. 357–366). Cambridge: MIT Press.

Said, E. (1993). *Culture and imperialism*. New York: Knopf.

Said, E. (1994). *Representations of the intellectual*. New York: Pantheon.

Sanjek, R. (1987). Anthropological work at a gray panther health clinic: Academic, applied, and advocacy goals. In L. Mullings (Ed.), *Cities of the United States: Studies in urban anthropology*. New York: Columbia University Press.

Sanjek, R. (1990). Urban anthropology in the 1980s: A world view. *Annual Reviews of Anthropology, 19,* 151–186.

Schoepf, B. G. (1979). Breaking through the looking glass: The view from below. In G. Huizer & B. Mannheim (Eds.), *The politics of anthropology* (pp. 325–432). The Hague: Mouton.

Scholes, R. (1985). *Textual power*. New Haven: Yale University Press.

Scott, J. C. (1990). *Domination and the arts of resistance*. New Haven: Yale University Press.

Stallybrass, P., & White, A. (1986). *The politics and poetics of transgression*. Ithaca, NY: Cornell University Press.

Starn, O. (1992). Missing the revolution: Anthropologists and the war in Peru. In G. Marcus (Ed.), *Rereading cultural anthropology*. Durham, NC: Duke University Press.

Stavenhagen, R. (1971). Decolonializing applied social sciences. *Human Organization, 30,* 333–344.

Strine, M. S. (1991). Critical theory and "organic" intellectuals: Reframing the work of cultural critique. *Communication Monographs, 58,* 195–201.

Trinh, M. (1989). *Woman, native, other: Writing postcoloniality and feminism*. Bloomington: Indiana University Press.

What lies ahead: Countdown to the 21st Century. (1989). Alexandria, VA: United Way of America.

Williams, R. (1973). Base and superstructure in Marxist cultural theory. *New Left Review, 82,* 3–16.

Williams, R. (1983). *Keywords: A vocabulary of culture and society* (rev. ed.). New York: Oxford University Press.

Response to Conquergood:
Don Quixotes in the Academy—
Are We Tilting at Windmills?

Samuel L. Becker
University of Iowa

Much of the discussion of applied research in the communication field evokes the image of Don Quixote, tilting at windmills. For a few moments, I assume the role of Sancho Panza (type casting, you are probably saying), an ignorant rustic unencumbered with sophistication about such weighty ideas as deconstruction, postmodernism, superstructure, and hegemony, and so able, I hope, to see ignorance where Quixote sees villainy, to see bluster where he sees power, and to find hope where he sees despair.

AN HISTORICAL CONTEXT FOR OUR VIEWS

This Sancho Panza tends to be an optimist. It is an optimism based on a rather long history in this field. I recall with amusement and some amazement my years in graduate school when the communication field was perceived by its leaders as so bereft of substance that, to make it "respectable," and to give it substance, doctoral candidates in communication studies (what was then called "speech") were required to take courses in phonetics, acoustics, and the anatomy of the vocal organs. Those areas were perceived to be the core of our discipline. To paraphrase one of those terrible cigarette ads, "We've come a long way, baby."

In those days, when the communication field's self-concept was so weak— and probably deservedly so—it is understandable that we shunned the thought that our scholarly work, like our souls, could be anything but pure and unadulterated by application. We were starved for acceptance and were certain that the route to that acceptance was the yellow brick road of science, and especially that science we could call basic research.

Much has changed in the past four or five decades, but far too many researchers in our field seem to be blind to those changes. One of the major changes has been in the nature and vastly improved quality of the scholarly work being done in communication research. In part because of that quality, and in part because of the obvious importance to our society of understanding and improving our communication, there is growing recognition of the centrality of this field to the academic enterprise. (Clearly this recognition has not yet made its way into the administrative quarters of all institutions, but it is getting there.)

Another factor that has changed in the academy is the value placed on research that has application. Every university in the country that I know of is searching for such research and for the scholars who do it. Now, admittedly, much of that interest is built on the hope that such research will attract bushels of dollars in grants from government agencies or foundations, or that it will lead to patents on products or processes that can bring returns to an institution of millions in royalties. Although those are the major spurs for change, they are not the only ones. Contemporary university administrators know the value of guiding, as well as reacting to, change. Thus, for example, there is great interest in having scholars on one's faculty doing policy research. In fact, in fields such as political science, geography, and communication, the demand for such scholars far exceeds the supply. I would also note that universities now pay engineering faculty a good bit more than they pay physics faculty, something that would have been unheard of a few decades ago when engineers were looked down on as mere technicians or users of science, not as true scientists.

Thus, I take exception to some of Conquergood's conclusions about which terms in his binary oppositions are more valued today in the academy. From the sample of institutions I have observed and the segments of those institutions that I could see, subjectivity, commitment, engagement, social responsibility, the feminine, Third World, nature, and the humanities are valued far more than he suggests. It is objectivity, distance, disinterestedness, social science, the Western world, and even masculinity that are on the defensive. (I do not mention "conceptual coherence" here because I do not understand in what sense it is a binary opposition to "social responsibility." The same for "rigor" and "relevance." Why can't relevant research be rigorous??? Sancho Panza is confused.)

REASONS FOR ANTIAPPLICATION PREJUDICES

By these quibbles, I do not mean to suggest that prejudice against applied research no longer exists. There are vestiges of it all around us. I would suggest six reasons for that prejudice, most of which reflect negatively on the opposer of applied research, rather than the proponent.

One reason for the negative attitude is the insecurity that continues to pervade our field. Our faculties have achieved a fair degree of success with non-applied research and they want to avoid anything that might jeopardize that success.

Another reason for denigrating applied research is the fear of that application. One of my colleagues, for example, opposed our hiring a scholar whose major line of research was aimed at discovering the ways groups could reach better decisions. My colleague argued that such research was potentially dangerous because the results could be used by government and industry to carry out their business more effectively—and he disapproved of their business.

This is the same sort of reasoning that has led many persons to oppose research on persuasion; they fear that the findings will be used by politicians and businesses to make their advertising more effective, thus making the public even more helpless than it already is. What these critics fail to realize is that government and, even more, business, do not need academics to tell them how to make their advertising or public relations more effective. (Neither Colin Powell nor Stormin' Norman Schwarzkopf needed help from any of us.) The primary gain from the persuasion research done in the academy to date has been to help give the rest of us this knowledge so that we could strengthen our defenses.

I do not mean to suggest here that we should not be concerned with the possible uses or consequences of our research, because I believe we must be, to the extent we are able to divine what those consequences might be, which is far from a simple task. This problem of possible uses has been brought to the fore by the research which led to the development of nuclear weapons and, perhaps closer to our kind of research, that by Shockley and others on differences in intellectual capacity between African American and White American children. The latter research has been used by many bigots to justify continued racial discrimination. These studies have led to a great debate in the scholarly community about whether certain areas of inquiry ought to be off limits, or to what extent academic freedom relieves scholars from the consequences of their work.

Some scholars believe, like John Stuart Mill, that even though some bad ideas surface, the good ideas will ultimately triumph. They claim the important thing should be that all ideas be subjected to open debate and criticism— that is, that we should have a free marketplace of ideas.

On the other hand, there are those who claim that knowledge is never pure and the marketplace is never free. According to these claimants, all ideas have consequences and so we cannot separate thought from action. Therefore, in effect, we must censor our own thoughts, as we do our own actions, if we are to be responsible scholars. This is an issue each of us must ponder and based on those thoughts, construct a personal mode of operation. I would only suggest that the fear of possible negative consequences should not inhibit us from doing research that might make a difference.

But back to reasons for the negative attitudes toward applied research that we continue to find in the academy. Probably the most defensible reason for these attitudes is the quality of most of such research that has been done in the past. In a word, it has been terrible. And I should note that I speak from experience; I did some of it. I think, for example, of the late 1950s and early 1960s when our country faced a crisis in the educational system. We had booming enrollments in schools and colleges, without a concomitant increase in the number of trained teachers available. This was just at the time that television was reaching its so-called "Golden Age"—the time when people thought this exciting medium could do anything, including substituting for or even replacing some classroom teachers. So, with the largess of the Ford Foundation and the U.S. Office of Education, we began experimenting with the use of television to bring teachers to classrooms without live teachers, or to classrooms with less expert teachers. All over the country we did the same sort of experiment, comparing the effectiveness of the teacher on television to the teacher in the classroom. There was virtually no thinking about why the mediation of television should make a difference for what kinds of students in what situations for what kinds of subject matter. That is, in the rush to solve a national problem, no one stopped to theorize that problem or this proposed solution. In retrospect, it is not surprising that the same conclusion echoed across the many research sites spread about the country: "no significant differences."

With this model of applied research, and the many similar models observable in the output of colleges of education, psychology departments, sociology departments, and, unfortunately, even communication studies departments, it is not surprising that there was great disdain in the past for applied communication research. However, it is surprising that this disdain continues to exist because contemporary applied research is as different from that old research as contemporary curricula in communication are from that which was the norm 30 and 40 years ago. Recent work on health communication by such people as Freimuth, research by Miller and others on communication and the law, and so forth have set a new standard for applied communication research.

The fourth reason for the disdain of applied research—in fact, for the disdain of much social scientific research, whether applied or not—is that it is not very interesting intellectually. Not only is the theory unimaginative, the writing of the results is worse. Most of us do not know how to tell our story in a way that is clear, interesting, and challenging. Reading many of the articles that appear in our journals, it is little wonder that some of our colleagues perceive our work as nonintellectual.

Another reason for the poor image many have of applied communication research is the large number of people in our field who have put themselves and their applied communication research skills up for hire—moonlighting, as it were. This practice has damaged the credibility of scholars in the field because it suggests we have given up on the struggle to approximate to the best of our ability that unattainable goal of objectivity.

The final reason I note at this point for the vestiges of anti-application attitudes that can still be found in the academy—and the reason I find most surprising—is that many, perhaps most, scholars in our field are unable to perceive the potential applications of their work. This came home to me quite vividly last year when I was reporting to our department's PhD Seminar on some of our research on ways to help people reduce or stop their tobacco use. The PhD Seminar is a weekly assembly of all of the faculty and doctoral students in our department where we listen to and argue about the research one of us is doing. One colleague, whom I shall call Mike, is a scholar of rhetoric. He is also a habitual smoker who is unable to break the habit, despite the fact that he suffers from severe emphysema. This ailment has left him with a deep anger against those who make and sell cigarettes. When I finished my preliminary comments, Mike immediately pounced on me. Why was I trying to discover ways to get those poor users to stop smoking or using smokeless tobacco? Instead, why didn't I find ways to get Congress to make the sale and manufacture of tobacco products illegal? Not once in his lengthy tirade did the irony of his suggestion seem to occur to Mike. There was no recognition that the field to which he, not I, had devoted his entire professional life—the study of rhetoric—which is, primarily, the study of persuasion, prepared him to theorize and test his theory by trying to carry out that task. I am still searching for an understanding of the reasons for that blindness or, perhaps, the reasons for his unwillingness to put his ideas and his knowledge to this rigorous test.

TESTING THEORY THE HARD WAY

There is a great deal of talk and writing these days about the "rhetoric of science," the "rhetoric of the human sciences," or the "rhetoric of inquiry." In fact, a new, exciting, interdisciplinary line of scholarship has developed on this topic—scholarship that examines and attempts to explain the way scholars in different disciplines argue. Some of the most avid of these scholars of inquiry take the position that the major work of the scholar is persuasion. They readily accept Kuhn's argument on the arbitrariness of proofs and extend it to the position that we prove by persuasion (Kuhn, 1970). Thus, the good scientist is the good arguer.

Although the position of these rhetoricians of inquiry is valid up to a point, we err if we accept persuasion as the end. We in communication, as well as in most, if not all, disciplines, must also be concerned about whether the theories about whose validity we try to persuade also work in practice. This is why I have talked about the importance of "testing theory the hard way." One of the great advantages in testing theory through application on a problem outside the laboratory or library is that it is the ultimate test.

That reminds me of another story, one that may be apocryphal. Whether apocryphal or not, though, it is relevant to the issue at hand. This story concerns a scholar whose field of expertise was communication and organizations. After many years of research in that field, he decided to try administration and obtained a job as dean of a college in a growing university. Well, one of the things he had found in his research on organizations, and one of the things he taught every term to his students, was that a good manager "walks and talks." That is, a good manager ought to spend as much time as possible walking around the organization, rubbing shoulders and talking with the workers so they know he is interested in their problems and their ideas.

Naturally, upon becoming a manager he decided that he had better follow that dictum. So he spent a great deal of time walking around the campus, dropping in on departments and talking with whomever was around. Before long, and much to his surprise, since his actions had been guided so carefully by theory, the faculty turned on him and had him forced out of the deanship. What had happened, according to my informants, is that all of his walking and talking did not lead the faculty to perceive him as interested in their problems and their ideas. Instead, what they perceived was that he was spying on them, and they did not want to be led by a spy. As far as I know, this was the first time this particular limitation was observed in the walk and talk theory of management. This was the first time we saw a need to refine this generalization. This was the first time this particular theory had been tested "the hard way."

I might add that our efforts to test the hard way some of the existing theories relevant to reducing tobacco use among adolescents and adults are turning up similar needs for theory refinement.

APPLIED RESEARCH FOR WHOM

Conquergood made many interesting and important points in his chapter. One of the most important was his reminder that the major question most of us face in our lives as scholars is not whether our research should be useful; it is, rather, what it should be useful for and for whom it should be useful.

I do not agree with his answers to those questions, though. Not only do I disagree with his conception of relevance and rigor as a dichotomy, I disagree that the answer to the utility problem is "humility and a decent modesty about the vulnerability of our work to world co-optation" along with "thoughtful struggle." Instead, or perhaps also, we should attack the problem of co-optation by doing everything possible to make the results of our learning available to all of the other Sancho Panzas of the world. Although advertisers may always be ready to grab the results of our persuasion research and use them to their ends, adequate communication of those results through our educational system and the popular media to the targets of those ads will foil that co-optation. As an example, I recall the first study I published when I was a beginning graduate student, enamored with statistics and happy to find something to pound with my newfound chi-square hammer. I analyzed the effect of order of speaking on the probability of winning oratorical contests and discovered, among other things, that those who spoke first in such contests were virtually eliminated from any chance of winning. Any contestants who tried to use that finding to their own ends, though, were doomed to failure. The next year's judges of the Northern Oratorical League contest, whose past contests had produced the data for this study, all were readers of the *Quarterly Journal of Speech,* in which the study appeared. That year, first place was awarded to the contestant who spoke first. The education of the people about whom we theorize may place our theories in jeopardy, but it is one of the ways to respond to the fear of co-optation.

I am also less concerned than Conquergood and others about the problem of our not being able to step outside our culture. In doing research applicable to another culture whether African American, Hispanic, Asian, or other, Sancho Panza's simple minded solution is:

1. Do the best we can, trying to do more good than harm.

2. Accept the fact that, although ours is only one of many possible cultural perspectives, it is generally as valid as any other. Panza sees no need for a hair shirt.

3. Although we probably cannot change who we are, we can affect the kinds of people doing research. Although Conquergood did not draw the conclusion, his analysis argued for increased efforts to educate more scholars with different ethnic and cultural backgrounds to do communication research. The more cultural perspectives from which we approach the problems that concern us, the more likely we are to find some theories that are fruitful for more than one culture.

RESEARCH FOR WHOM AND FOR WHAT ENDS

I would be remiss if, before ending these comments, I did not attempt to supplement Conquergood's response to the question of for whom we should be doing research and the ends toward which we aim. I briefly note just a few problems that I believe communication scholars can help to solve:

1. Probably the most serious and intractable problem our society faces is racism. It is one on which much research has been done but, so far, with only limited results. Past failures, though, must not deter us from continuing the struggle for solutions.

2. Great strides have been made in our society's attitudes toward and treatment of women, but we still have a way to go. We can even work on this without straying far from home. Some applied communication researcher might be able to make a contribution working on ways to eliminate the sexual harassment of female students by male college professors.

3. There are a great many policy issues in mass communication that are based on assumptions about effects. The FCC's Fairness Doctrine (Becker & Roberts, 1992), Equal Opportunity Provision (Becker & Roberts, 1992), and policies on children's programming are just three of many possible examples. We need better evidence than we have had so far to guide the policy makers. Much of this evidence is the sort that communication scholars can obtain.

4. And last, I would reinforce Freimuth's point in her response to Seibold in chapter 2 about the contributions communication scholars might make in the health area. When we note that the major causes of illness and early death today are people's behaviors, rather than viruses or bacteria, it is clear that we who study influences on behavior may have as much to contribute to the nation's health as the medical profession does.

In short, there is much important applied communication research to be done. We probably ought to stop talking about it and go out and do it. With Sancho Panza's clear eyes and Don Quixote's spirit, we might make a difference. As Cervantes (1900) wrote of Quixote, each of us "should become a knight-errant, and go throughout the world, with . . . horse and armour, to seek adventures, . . . revenging all kinds of injuries, and offering himself [or herself] to occasions and dangers, which, being once happily achieved, might gain him [or her] eternal renown" (pp. 1, 3).

REFERENCES

Becker, S. L., & Roberts, C. L. (1992). *Discovering mass communication* (3rd ed.). New York: HarperCollins.

Cervantes, M. de. (1900). *The history of the valorous & witty knight-errant, Don Quixote of the Mancha* (T. Shelton, Trans.) (Vols. 1–3). New York: Macmillan.

Kuhn, T. (1970). *The structure of scientific revolutions* (2nd ed.). Chicago: University of Chicago Press.

5

Adwatch: The Unblurring
of Political Genres

Kathleen Hall Jamieson
University of Pennsylvania

As many have argued, in 1988 the Republicans defined the campaign terrain for Dukakis, for the press, and for voters. Ads played an important role in the Republicans' ability to set this agenda. To the extent that the spots succeeded and their images were used in broadcast news as visual illustration of the power of the Bush appeals, ads were contextualizing news.

Ads also contextualized news in a second sense. After a viewer has seen the same ad many times, exposure to a small segment of it can evoke the whole ad. My work with focus groups across a 20-year period suggests that unless the verbal message is highly salient (e.g., the mention of your profession in the ad, reinforced by print on the screen, or repeatedly uttered in the ad), it is not until the third exposure to a typical production ad that the typical viewer is able to recall a substantial amount of the ad's spoken content.

But weeks after exposure to a single ad image, viewers can accurately recall whether or not they have seen it before. (The discussion of whether pictures dominate words or words pictures is confused by its assumptions that one invariably dominates the other, that music plays no role in cueing recall, and that the impact of each remains the same with repeated exposure.[1])

---

[1]This conclusion is consistent with scholarship about recall of advertising and of television (e.g., Hayes & Birnbaum, 1980; Hayes, Chemelaki, & Birnbaum, 1981; Hayes & Pingree, 1982; Pezdek & Hartman, 1983). However, the evidence does not suggest that the visual interferes with comprehension of the audio (Hoffner, Cantor, & Thorson, 1989; Rolandelli, 1989). There is evidence that the visual imagery of television changes the processing of audio (see Beagles-Roos & Gat, 1983). Some have argued that Iyengar and Kinder's (1987) research calls the im-

Ads have an additional recall advantage over news. Most ads are "bedded" in a sound track that invites emotions consistent with the ad's message. So, for example, the musical backtrack for an ad about a candidate's accomplishments is upbeat and often patriotic. Lee Greenwood's "I'm Proud to Be an American" hitchhiked into network news in 1984 when the Reagan ads incorporating it were clipped into broadcast news stories. Although network news opens and closes with theme music, the news segments themselves aren't musically scored. Therefore, when a segment of the ad airs in news, its soundtrack is usually preserved.

Moreover, the announcer's voice on the ad is usually more resonant than the reporter's. These factors increase the power of the embedded ad segment and dampen the corrective words spoken by the reporter.

Repeated exposure increases the likelihood that the words and pictures will be remembered. When a segment from a remembered ad is then shown on news, two things happen. First, if the segment is able to function synecdochically for the whole ad, the viewer will recall a larger part of the ad than that shown. Second, the audio that is likely to be remembered is not the reporter's words about the ad but rather some form of the audio from the ad itself.

If reporters are to focus on fairness and accuracy, they require visual and verbal means to enhance their message. When treating ads in stories, reporters should, at least, not give advantage to distortive ads. Yet this is precisely what occurred in 1988 when the most often aired ad image in news showed circling convicts as a print overlay reported "268 Escaped." This segment of the Bush furlough ad invited a false inference; the same occurred in 1990 when news coverage of "Woman in the Red Dress II" repeatedly carried to the nation the false Helms claim that "Harvey Gantt favors abortion in the final weeks of pregnancy."

THE PROBLEM

Unless the news viewer has had sufficient exposure to an ad to recall it from that context, an ad that is aired full screen in news without a disclaimer will be remembered as news rather than as an ad.

---

pact of vivid communication into question. Their summary of the existing scholarly literature states, "When vividness is defined as the contrast between personalized, case history information and abstract statistical information, the vividness hypothesis is supported every time" (p. 35). The structure of their chapter seems to suggest that they then take issue with this consensus. Yet they conclude, "Our results do not argue against vividness effects in general; they indicate only that dramatic vignettes of personal suffering do not enhance agenda setting" (p. 46). Additional information on verbal/visual processing can be found Buchholz and Smith (1991) and Edell and Keller (1989).

By airing ads in news, reporters increase the likelihood that they will: (a) inadvertently provide advantage to one candidate over another in a given race; (b) pass through an ad's unexamined misinformation in the credible environment of news.

After 3 years of study the Annenberg team offered reporters the following findings and recommendations: In adwatches: preview, distance, disclaim, displace, and recap:

1. *Preview.* A category of story should be created that carries the expectation that it will treat the accuracy of political ads. Give it a title, a logo, and a regular place in the news broadcast. The station's most credible reporter should have this as a regular beat.

2. *Distance.* In political ad stories, distance the audience from the manipulative advertising.

    a. Box the ad content in a television screen and either

        1) Squeeze zoom the screen to upper screen left; or

        2) Cant the screen, which will undercut some of the evocative power of such images as David Duke and the burning cross and the meld of Dukakis and Kerry in a Rappaport ad.

    b. Set the boxed ad distinctively off from its background so that it does not look like a regularly broadcast ad.

        1) Setting the boxed ad into a background with a horizon line is the clearest way of defining the ad as "not endorsed news content."

        2) The background should provide a clear contrast to the ad content.

    c. Some stations run the ad full screen before squeeze zooming to box it. Others begin by boxing it and then move to full screen. The former technique is effective because it lures the viewer into the ad and then distances. The latter distances and then heightens the ad's power by giving it full screen play.

    d. It is possible at the most manipulative points in an ad to increase the audience distance, that is, to move to squeeze zoom at first manipulative point, cant screen at second; run a red or yellow line from disclaimer through ad content at third.

3. *Disclaim* the content of the ad:

    a. By using contrasting print in a distinguishable font size and color (yellow or red test well against most content) to identify the ad specifically as both a political ad and one that is sponsored by a specified party, candidate, or political action committee (PAC; independent expenditure). Each should have its own identifying logo (e.g., "Bush (R) Advertisement," "Dem. Party Advertisement," or "$I. E. Conservatives for Victory (pro Bush)"). In addition, hold the identification (ID) in place throughout the entire ad segment. (Note: A pulsing disclaimer is very effective at reminding viewers that they are watching an ad. However, this visual also makes viewers angry as it is visually intrusive!)

   b. The ID or disclaimer should intersect the content of the ad. If the disclaimer does not intersect the boxed ad, viewers will perceive that it is part of the ad itself. An ID or disclaimer can be printed into the visual field of the ad by including a red line that runs from the disclaimer through the ad.

   c. The disclaimer should not be in a color of print used in the ad and should not be in font size or type style used in the ad.

   d. If the ad includes print, the disclaimer gains maximum persistent attention in upper screen right.

   e. If the ad does not include print, the disclaimer gains most persistent attention in upper screen left.

   f. Disclaimers at the bottom of the screen are easily ignored.

4. *Displace*

   a. Verbally

     1) By putting print corrections on screen, and by documenting the source of the corrections.

     2) By having the reporter speak the corrections as they are synopsized on screen. When the reporter uses words against ad print and pictures, the reporter's corrections are lost.

     3) Corrections should be simple and appear in single statements. We are not accustomed to reading television. Print corrections that are syntactically complex and/or contain multiple sentences are likely to be ignored.

     4) When two sentences or phrases are needed, separate them into two visual units.

   b. Visually

     1) by rolling the ad's image off the screen, or

     2) by wiping the ad's image, or

     3) by squeeze zooming the ad's image, or

     4) by putting the universal warning sign over the ad's image, or

     5) by displacing the ad's images with corrected images, or

     6) by showing the full context from which the distortive print or picture is drawn.

   c. Vocally

     1) Fade down the audio so that reporter can talk over it.

     2) Segment the ad into units broken by corrective print and words so that the ad's power can't build.

5. *Recap.* Audiences will see the manipulative ad many times; the cor-

rective news only once. Using a clearly recognized format, a clear forecast, a clearly structured presentation, and a clear recap will increase the likelihood that the news critique will inoculate against the distortive ad.

In December 1991, The John D. and Catherine T. MacArthur Foundation approved a grant of $95,000 to the Trustees of the University of Pennsylvania for use by The Annenberg School for Communication to test, produce, and distribute these guidelines to television news editors for use in analysis of political advertising.

In January 1992, the grant team met with producers for NBC in Philadelphia, for CBS in Washington, and for ABC in New York. Because CNN had helped us develop the computer graphics for the guidelines in November and was using the guidelines on air in January, we did not meet again with the CNN producers.

On February 13, 1992, The Annenberg School for Communication sponsored a Washington, DC press conference at the site of the Washington Annenberg Program. By this time, all three broadcast networks and CNN had adopted and were using the guidelines on-air. The conference, which was attended by 32 broadcast and print reporters from Washington, DC bureaus, was an attempt to draw the attention of stations around the country to the existence of the visual guidelines and to allay concerns about technical difficulties in adopting them. It was an attempt as well to certify that the guidelines had the blessing of the network producers.

The press conference, which was covered by C-SPAN, included a presentation by the author on the elements of the guidelines and three responding panels. The first panel identified the problems posed for journalists attempting to cover visually evocative political ads. It featured Richard Threlkeld who produced the first adwatch of 1988 for ABC. The second panel included network reporters Lisa Myers of NBC and Brooks Jackson of CNN and CBS political affairs director Marty Plissner. That panel explored the legal, reportorial, and technical problems associated with adwatches. The final panel presented three local reporters/producers who had prepared adwatches in 1988 and planned to do so again in 1992.

Those attending the press conference were given a copy of a print guide summarized earlier. The AP wire announcement of the press conference indicated that station managers could obtain a copy by calling either the Annenberg Washington Program or the Annenberg School. Within 48 hours of the airing of the press conference on C-SPAN, the authors received 112 requests, from stations (79), political consultants (12!), students (16), and scholars (5).

An unexpected byproduct of the conference occurred when an NPR producer who attended the conference asked how the guidelines, which are primarily visual, could be adapted to radio. Subsequently, audio equivalents of the television guidelines were experimented with and the following recommendations made to Andy Bowers of NPR who had been assigned to cover the broadcast ads of 1992:

1. Listeners have a sense that there is "foreground" and "background" on radio. The reporter is foreground; what the reporter covers is background. One is supposed to be in the front of the "picture" in analogic terms; one is framing, the other framed.

2. The problem is that ads in radio news sound more like foreground than background. The announcer's voice often sounds like the voice of the reporter.

    a. The audio quality of the ad is usually higher not lower than that of the reporter (one quality of the things covered is that they are not audio equals—the phone interview, for example, puts the interviewee in a weaker audio environment).

    b. The content of ads occasionally simulates a news form—that is, the person in the street reaction to the ads sounds like a person in the street ad, the neutral reporter ads sound like a neutral reporter.

3. The goal should be to clearly differentiate the news report from the ad content within it.

4. Suggested moves:

    a. Degrade the ad to push it into a background relationship with the foregrounded reporter:

        1) Take midrange and bass out,

        2) simulate dubbed quality,

        3) compress the ad's dynamic range,

        4) dampen the ad's resonance,

        5) but do not change volume level because change in volume angers listeners and attracts attention when we are trying to dampen attention.

    b. Create an audio stimulus that makes listeners conscious that an ad is about to play and has just ended.

        1) Wind up and wind down.

        2) Click before and after as if a tape recorder is being turned off and on.

        3) Create audio that suggests channel scanning (music—blur—talk—blur).

        4) Create a musical motif used only to signal ad.

    c. Create an audio stimulus that makes listener conscious that an ad is playing while it is playing by talking over the ad.

    d. Create clear contrasts between the ad and news voices. Use a female reporter when the ad voice is male, a male voice when ad voice is female.

After the conference, Chuck Sherman (Senior Vice President for Television of the National Association for Broadcasters [NAB], the broadcast stations' trade association headquartered in Washington, DC) agreed to review the guidelines, screen the accompanying tape, and, if both were of high quality, to distribute them at the annual meeting of the NAB in Las Vegas.

A rough cut of the tape was assembled at The Annenberg School. Permissions for use of copyrighted footage were secured from the stations and networks. A local video editing facility donated an editor and use of its broadcast quality equipment to produce the final cut of the tape.

Sherman and the NAB lawyers approved distribution of the tape and guidelines to those attending the NAB convention. Three of the graduate students who had worked on the experiments that led to creation of the guidelines attended the convention. After the breakfast meeting of station executives, the students answered questions which focused in the main on how the guidelines could be adapted to smaller stations with minimal computer-driven technical capacity.

A list of those attending was cross checked against the list of NAB members to determine which stations failed to receive a copy. Copies were mailed to those stations.

To determine viewer response to the guidelines, to refine them, and to employ empirical methods to assess their impact over time, a final test was performed. With supplemental support from The Annenberg Foundation, 165 subjects in 12 media markets were exposed to 6, 4, or 3 days of 1 hour of network television per day. Each day's prime time programming contained both political and regular commercial advertising. A half-hour CNN newscast was included in all conditions as well. In all conditions but the control, the newscast included an adwatch on one of the political ads seen in the prime time programming. Two forms of adwatch were tested. The study, whose procedures and results are detailed elsewhere, showed that the adwatches "affected attitudes toward the source of the ad and toward the perceived fairness and importance of the ad" (Cappella & Jamieson, 1994).

For the first time in 1992, the advertising of a presidential campaign was "policed" for fairness and accuracy by both print and broadcast reporters. As noted, CBS, NBC, ABC, and CNN followed the Annenberg guidelines. The most systematic and highest quality analysis was done by Brooks Jackson of CNN. On NPR Andy Bowers led analyses of radio, an important move because the most serious distortions of the campaign were found in the final weeks on local radio. Eric Engberg of CBS and Jackson of CNN performed yeoman service in locating and critiquing the radio ads on television.

It was in the adwatches that one learned that Democratic radio ads were falsely accusing Bush of wanting to "virtually eliminate all compensation for over one million disabled veterans." The watches also pointed out sins of omission. As a Clinton ad claims, George Bush did "sign the second biggest tax increase in American history." Unacknowledged, said the adwatchers, was the complicity of the Democratic Congress. And yes, as a Clinton ad avers, 17,000 Arkansans have moved "from welfare to work" since July 1989. But during that time, noted the reporters, the welfare rolls actually increased as new recipients of Aid to Families with Dependent Children and food stamps replaced the beneficiaries of the Clinton jobs program.

The real utility of the adwatches was not in their warnings to the readers and viewers of news—numbers that are necessarily small. The value comes instead in the ability of the other side to use the news corrections in counter advertising.

"George Bush is running attack ads," notes the unseen announcer in a current Clinton ad. "He says all these people [the ad shows those pictured in the Bush ad] would have their taxes raised by Bill Clinton." Not so, says the rebuttal. "Misleading," says *The Washington Post*. And *The Wall Street Journal* says, "Clinton has proposed to cut taxes for the sort of people featured in Bush's ad."

Reporters and consultants thought the adwatches made a difference in the conduct of the campaign. Reporters approved of press coverage of ads: 77% of the reporters surveyed approved of these policing efforts (*Times Mirror*, 1992, p. 7). One television newsperson told the *Times Mirror* that the debunking of the ads "is the primary reason why no Willie Horton ads or their cousins have appeared in this campaign. Our coverage is keeping the bastards honest" (p. 7). "We'll need a Teddy White to come along later to see if those who planned commercials really sat around worrying about whether we'd criticize them or not," another editor told the surveyors (p. 7).

The election debriefings provided an answer. "It was a terrible feeling when I used to open the [*New York*] *Times* and they used to take my commercial apart, or watch CNN and watch them take it apart. . . . I think these reality checks made our commercials less effective," observed Bush–Quayle adman Harold Kaplan at a debriefing held at the Annenberg School (December 12, 1992). "I spent more time talking about economics and the latest statistics from the Bureau of Labor statistics and the Bureau of Census than I thought a creative person every would in her lifetime," recalled Clinton–Gore ad director Mandy Grunwald at the same debriefing. She continued: "Gene Sperling (who was the economic director of the Clinton campaign) and I talked far more than almost any two people in the campaign [determining whether it was] appropriate to use this statistic or not."

CONCLUSION

A focus on individual genres of political discourse rather than on campaign discourse taken as a whole has made it more difficult for scholars to recognize that generic boundaries have blurred. Increasingly, political ads, debates, speeches, and news all share a common form. That form is the form once defined as *advertising*. Unbeknown to the reporters authoring the stories, beginning in the 1988 presidential campaign, broadcast and print news were infiltrated by the news ad. The Annenberg adwatch guidelines were an attempt to demarcate news ad content from news content, a move intended to restore integrity to the genre of news. In my view, scholarship should be guided by a methodological perspective that is pluralistic and opportunistic. The choice of method should be dictated by the question asked; scholarship should not only explicate the way things are but shape the way things should be. In this study, rather than exhort, I have described the development of guidelines that were used by newspapers, television, and radio reporters in the analysis of political advertising during the 1992 campaign.

REFERENCES

Beagles-Roos, J., & Gat, I. (1983). Specific impact of radio and television on children's story comprehension. *Journal of Educational Psychology, 75,* 128–135.

Buchholz, L. M., & Smith, R. E. (1991). The role of consumer involvement in determining cognitive response to broadcast advertising. *Journal of Advertising, 20,* 4–17.

Cappella, J. N., & Jamieson, K. (1994). Broadcast adwatch effects: A field experiment. *Communication Research, 21,* 342–365.

Edell, J., & Keller, K. L. (1989). The information processing of coordinated media campaigns. *Journal of Marketing Research, 26,* 149–163.

Hayes, D. S., & Birnbaum, D. W. (1980). Preschoolers' retention of televised events: Is a picture worth a thousand words? *Developmental Psychology, 16,* 410–416.

Hayes, D. S., Chemelaki, B. E., & Birnbaum, D. W. (1981). Young children's incidental retention of televised events. *Developmental Psychology, 17,* 20–232.

Hayes, D. S., & Pingree, S. (1982). Television's influence on social reality. In D. Pearl & J. Lazar (Eds.), *Television and behavior* (pp. 224–247). Washington, DC: U. S. Government Printing Office.

Hoffner, C., Cantor, J., & Thorson, E. (1989). Children's responses to conflicting auditory and visual features of a televised narrative. *Human Communication Research, 16,* 256–278.

Iyengar, S., & Kinder, D. (1987). *News that matters.* Chicago: University of Chicago Press.

Pezdek, K., & Hartman, E. F. (1983). Children's television viewing: Attention and comprehension of auditory versus visual information. *Child Development, 54,* 1015–1023.

Rolandelli, D. R. (1989). Children and television: The visual superiority effect reconsidered. *Journal of Broadcasting and Electronic Media, 33,* 69–81.

Times Mirror Center for the People and the Press (1992, Dec. 20). *The press and campaign '92: A self-assessment.* New York: Author.

Response to Jamieson:
The Scholarship of Application

Phillip K. Tompkins
University of Colorado

The letter inviting me to be one of the respondents at the 1991 SCA/USF conference, "Applied Communication in the 21st Century," seemed to assume a disciplinary consensus on the value and meaning of application. All that remained for the conferees was to decide what problems to tackle, what methodological strategies should be adopted, and how our collective efforts could best bring about significant social changes. Being unaware of any such consensus, my acceptance of the invitation was qualified by some small amount of skepticism. At times I find myself wishing that the field was more oriented to basic research and less eager to become "applied." I toyed with the idea of composing a strong counterstatement in response to the conference theme.

The process of thinking through the prospects of application changed my mind to some degree. I came to see that application can be desirable to some degree if we contemplate it in the context of our other responsibilities. This chapter, therefore, first attempts to develop a perspective on applied communication by considering it in relationship to the other major responsibilities we face. Second, it provides a tentative evaluation of Jamieson's specific project in applied rhetoric and communication. Third, it registers some objections to potential misapplications.

APPLICATION AS SCHOLARSHIP

Several years ago I was asked to participate in a research project undertaken by the Carnegie Foundation for the Advancement of Teaching. I agreed to do so, but after the long and searching interview about tenure and promotion practices in communication I promptly forgot about the study.

Recently the results of the forgotten project appeared in the form of a remarkable little book: Boyer's (1990) *Scholarship Reconsidered: Priorities of the Professoriate.* The book reported the results of "extensive conversations about standards for tenure and promotion with distinguished scholars and leaders of learned societies in five disciplines: chemistry, English, communications [sic], economics, and business" (pp. 28–29). Happily, the book is not limited to the statistical representation of our responses.

Boyer went beyond the many tables of data to offer new ways of thinking that might be of interest to those in communication research. For example, he argued that the relative emphasis on research, teaching, service, and application should not hold to a single model; it should vary from campus to campus. The Carnegie Foundation classifies institutions of higher learning into two categories each of research universities (I and II), doctorate granting universities (I and II), comprehensive colleges and universities (I and II), liberal arts colleges (I and II), and the single category of 2-year community, junior, and technical colleges. There are, of course, different strategies of emphasis appropriate to different categories of institutions. Surely the range of institutions represented in the Speech Communication Association (SCA) ought to enter into our analysis of applications needed in the 21st century.

The interests of Boyer and the Carnegie Foundation are both transparent: They want to improve and advance teaching. In this book, however, Boyer set aside the tired arguments about the relative importance of teaching versus research. Instead, he reframed and enlarged our perspective by shifting to the scholarships, plural, that make up the professoriate's professional responsibilities. The four scholarships are the scholarship of *discovery,* the scholarship of *integration,* the scholarship of *application,* and the scholarship of *teaching.*

The Four Scholarships

This new perspective caused me to see how unwise it would be for the Tampa Conference to concentrate on one of the four scholarships without giving some attention to its relationship to the other three. In an academic world of finite energy, which of the other three scholarships should receive less emphasis if we recommend more attention to application? And what is the proper mix of emphasis for each of the eight or nine categories of institutions represented in SCA and International Communication Association (ICA)? The scholarship of discovery and integration describe investigation and synthesis, and the scholarship of teaching reminds us that our classroom activities are not just a routine, tacked on function, but instead constitute the process that "both educates and entices future scholars" (Boyer, 1990, p. 23). My original skepticism about our conference theme was reduced by Boyer's redefinition of application:

> The scholarship of application, as we define it here, is not a one-way street. Indeed, the term itself may be misleading if it suggests that knowledge is first "discovered" and then "applied." The process we have in mind is far more dynamic. New intellectual understandings can arise out of the very act of application—whether in medical diagnosis, serving clients in psychotherapy, shaping public policy, creating an architectural design, or working with the public schools. In activities such as these, theory and practice vitally interact, and one renews the other.
>
> Such a view of scholarly service—one that both applies and contributes to human knowledge—is particularly needed in a world in which huge, almost intractable problems call for the skills and insights only the academy can provide. (p. 23)

Boyer even considered the practical problem of how the third and neglected criterion of academic personnel decisions, "service," could be revitalized by being linked to the scholarship of application. Applied work should be more than good citizenship; good citizenship has its own rewards. Application ought to advance our knowledge. The scholarship of application could be documented not only by a faculty member's record of a project but also by the evaluations of those receiving the service. Tenure and promotion committees might ask this question: "In what ways has the work not only benefitted the recipients of such activity but *also added to the professor's own understanding of his or her academic field?*" (p. 37, italics added).

The scholarship of application also has implications for graduate education in communication. "In the current climate, graduate study is, all too often, a period of withdrawal—a time when many students are almost totally preoccupied with academic work and regulatory hurdles" (Boyer, 1990, p. 69). The core of graduate education in communication ought to remain the disciplined inquiry into, and criticism of, rhetorical and communicative processes, but surely graduate students should also be pressed to reflect on the social consequences and implications of their work. "Field-based" projects might well become a systematic part of the postgraduate education of our successors.

Summary

The perspective recommended is to see application as one of the four aspects of scholarship incumbent on the members of SCA in ratios differing according to the type of institutions represented, the missions and make-up of academic departments, and, of course, the abilities and interests of researchers as individuals. No single model should be prescribed. Nor should application be construed as the second of a two-step process moving from discovery and integration to application. Rather, the scholarship of application should be seen as a dynamic, two-way process in which theory and practice interact, and in which new knowledge and new practices both emerge.

RESPONSE TO JAMIESON

My assignment was to respond to the paper by Jamieson, "Whipsmart Professor of Communication at the University of Pennsylvania."[1] The 25-page, single-spaced paper[2] was not at all what I expected, in that it did not directly address the questions Kenneth N. Cissna, Conference Director, said would be put to the authors of the main position papers at the conference. At first glance the paper seemed to be another project in the mainstream of Jamieson's research program. I have never thought of that program as "applied."

While reading Jamieson's paper I kept saying to myself over and over, finally writing it as a note to myself: "If this is applied communication research, then I'm all for applied communication research."

Jamieson has given us a brilliant study. If it qualifies as "applied" research, it does so because it is research in support of social advocacy. For some time now Jamieson has called for the reform of political communication in the United States. This study gave Jamieson additional evidence that political campaigns need to be reformed, both the reporting of the rhetoric as well as the campaign rhetoric itself. Her approach is similar to that called "action research," as practiced in organizational studies by Jaques (1987). It comes close to blurring the genres of scholarship defined above, combining as it does the scholarships of investigation and application.

Causality

Jamieson did not make a causal claim in this connection, but the paper seems to invite the reader to draw some inferences about cause and effect. As a citizen who usually votes for Democratic candidates, one who is tired of seeing Republicans win so consistently, I found myself wanting to urge Jamieson to "apply" her knowledge on behalf of what I suspect (from cues outside the paper) to be her favored party as well.

---

[1]David Broder awarded Jamieson this title in his column, "Language in the Service of Power," *Boulder Daily Camera*, January 8, 1990, p. 8A.

[2]Editor's note: The version of Jamieson's paper included in this volume is much abbreviated from her conference paper and focused on the implications of her work to news organizations.

Jamieson eschewed a partisan stance. Instead, she took the perspective of the public good and an implicit but normative model of political campaigns in which candidates of both parties make extended speeches to real audiences (or "nonpseudo-events"). In this model, speakers are expected to use evidence and argument in support of their claims. In addition, candidates of the contending parties engage in debates characterized by extended responses to each other's arguments.

Ideal Type or Model

Let's give this model a name: Jamieson's Ideal Type of Political Discourse. (The acronym is not very snappy—JITPD—and this may prevent it from catching on.) But Jamieson did assume an ideal type, one that has been construed from past practice: There is a trace of Athenian democracy perhaps, plus the Golden Age of Parliamentary Oratory manifest in Goodrich's (1963) *Select British Eloquence,* the Lincoln–Douglas Debates, and even some nostalgia for the Kennedy–Nixon Debates, if I have interpreted Jamieson properly.

It would have made my job easier if Jamieson had specified the model, or the practices to which she would have us return or create anew. (In trying to infer it I realized that I will have to teach the students in my undergraduate class in rhetorical criticism that presidential candidates once did debate and give speeches to real audiences.)

Some empiricists will complain that Jamieson did not provide the causal evidence that the new and changing practices make a significant difference in election results or in anything else of importance. However, I am convinced that her implicit causal indictments of recent practices are credible and grave.

The Absence of Theory

The data seem susceptible to a McLuhanistic theoretical perspective. Recall that the late media guru showed that new forms of communication cannibalize the content of older ones. Film appropriated the novel; television did the same with film. Something of that sort seems to be happening with the speeches, ads, and news-ads Jamieson worked with in this study. Notice also that film has a role; well, at least Clint Eastwood movies are a source of inspiration to Republican ads and news-ads—the reference here, of course, is to those breathless lines "Make my day" and "Read my lips." Burke's theory of form and Aristotle's enthymeme are also relevant—or so they were 15 years ago when Campbell and Jamieson wrote "Form and Genre in Rhetorical Criticism: An Introduction" (1976, p. 19).

Inconsistency?

Having raised the issue of form and genre, a second anomaly of Jamieson's paper should be examined. On one hand, Jamieson presented the claim that "generic boundaries have blurred." This quotation—or sight bite, the visual counterpart to the electronic "sound bite" Jamieson has helped make a household concept—was taken from the summary on the first page of her conference paper. A contrasting sight bite was taken from the conclusion: "This essay chronicles the emergence of a new genre of campaign discourse—the news-ad, a byproduct of reporters' focus on strategy and outcome and reliance on polls."

It appears on the surface to be an inconsistency to claim alternately that (a) genres have blurred but (b) a new genre has emerged with sufficient clarity of form for Jamieson to have identified and defined it. I believe that Jamieson can correct this impression with two temporally distinct arguments, that old genres began to blur in 1960, and that a new, distinct genre appeared in 1988. In addressing this apparent contradiction Jamieson ought to give more attention to *organizational* and *interactive* dimensions of the new genre.

Organizational Dimension

By the organizational dimension I mean the recognition that it is no longer possible for a politician to function as an individual candidate for the Presidency, even when assisted by logographers. Jamieson's research demonstrated that a modern campaign requires a complex kind of interorganizational communication, including organizations that interact with each other to create and deliver the messages to the audience.

For example, Bush's 1988 campaign required the efforts of Peggy Noonan (author of the statement, "I am that man"), the Republican National Committee, Bush's own campaign organization, plus their interaction if not cooperation with (a relationship I suggest be identified by the portmanteau "rapportage," suggesting a combination of *reportage* and *rapport,* a term coined by the Czech artist, Jiri Kolar [Dimitrijevic, 1990, p. 23]) Dan Rather, Leslie Stahl, Sam Donaldson, and their respective news organizations in order to produce the new genre, the news-ad, that Jamieson has identified. The necessary "cooperation" among organizations is probably inadvertent, at least on one side, but here is a case where the subdivisions of the field, organizational communication and political communication, do not serve us well. A deeper understanding might well accrue from combining the perspective of organizational and political communication in studying the processes that produce it.

Need and Plan

Let us acknowledge one more related and inevitable weakness in Jamieson's paper. The recommendations for reform of the electoral process are incommensurate with the diagnosis of the problems. Or, to put it in the debater's jargon, "Strong Need, Weak Plan." This encourages me to make bold this recommendation: that we establish a national taskforce of communication researchers to promote Jamieson's proposals and to monitor practices during campaigns. The task force should be empowered to cry "foul play" against the candidates, or their agents, of any political party.

OBJECTIONS TO "APPLIED" ORIENTATION

Now I turn to some possibilities of "applied communication" that I think would be damaging to the field. I register my objections in case my attempt to redefine the concept as the scholarship of application fails. If in fact the conference defines the concept as a two-step process in which conventional knowledge is slapped on an intractable social problem, I wish to warn about the dangers of misapplication. The first objection is an uncertainty about what is to be applied. Textbook knowledge? My favorite lecture? My favorite study in *Communication Monographs* or *Human Communication Research?* Before we endorse this kind of application we ought to certify what body of knowledge is secure and durable enough to be applied. Karl Weick (1979) inveighs against applied psychology on the grounds that it is an oxymoron, that the theory of psychology is not rigorous enough to stand application. If this is true for that field, can the situation be that much better in the field of communication?

The second objection is that an insufficiently reflective emphasis on application could divert the field from pursuing more basic questions. Here I wish to stress a distinction between what my colleague Robert Craig (1989) calls the practical nature and interests of the field and its applications. A practical field in Craig's way of thinking, and mine as well, is also inherently theoretical. As a practical field in a democracy our knowledge is potentially available to all citizens regardless of ideology and interest. To channel our applications to a segment of society could possibly violate the field's public trust established in Aristotle's *Rhetoric*. Both sides, if not all sides, should receive the presumed benefits of our pedagogy, the better that the truth may emerge.

Organizational communication, for example, lags behind where it should be because it has "applied" its knowledge inordinately to the "owner's" or "controlling" interests via consulting-for-fees rather than distributing the lore without prejudice. Workers and social/political agitators can rarely raise the money for fees commanded by the consultants. Rarely does the applied activity of consulting advance the common knowledge of the field through the publication of findings.

The third objection, and this may at first sound inconsistent with my second objection, is that as a field we are doing pretty well without a national revival of applied communication. Let me support this claim with a piece of reluctant testimony.

The testimony comes from Alvin Kernan, Avalon Professor of Humanities Emeritus at Princeton University. The title of Kernan's (1990) book, *The Death of Literature*, reveals his worst fear. University departments of literature are at risk of disappearing, partly because of the suicidal impulses of deconstruction, Marxist and Feminist criticism, partly because of the felonious assault of television and other nonliterary media. In addition, there is a threat from another branch of the tree of knowledge.

Kernan predicted who will likely benefit from the demise of the department of literature: "In its place, apparently, people are beginning to see 'communications,' a subject with both *practical* and theoretical dimensions, and considerable usefulness" (1990, p. 202, italics added).

Kernan understands the communication field surprisingly well: I have long considered it a serious structural problem that the field has no departments at Harvard, Yale, Princeton, and . . . my readers can complete the list. We have no one at such universities to produce PhD's, and serve as external evaluators in tenure cases and departmental reviews. Kernan (1990) transformed that weakness into a strength:

> The continuing shift in almost all colleges and universities away from the teaching of literature to the teaching of writing of various kinds signals a de facto change that manifests its direction clearly only in the very large number of universities where there are departments of communication but no departments of English or French literature. It is significant that communications [sic] departments appear in the newer and less prestigious educational institutions, for they are the only ones to be free enough of tradition to be able to do what makes sense, and they are the ones who have to satisfy the real and immediate market demands of their students. To those students and in their institutions, literature is disappearing into another category of reality where it is becoming only one technique for written communication, one among many ways, oral, pictorial, schematic, and many modes. (p. 201).

I think Kernan would prefer not to see literature departments disappear from universities. I know that is my preference and hope his prophesy is false in that regard. Nonetheless, he is correct in saying that departments cannot retain a place within the university unless they have a unique epistemological authority; I doubt we can certify the authority of our knowledge of communication on the basis of narrowly conceived applied activities. I am grateful to Kernan for his lexical choices in praise of our field: "practical," "theoretical," and even "useful." To be those things is different from being applied in the usual two-step definition of the term. And for the Greeks—as should be the case for us—*Praxis* operates within the realm of *phronesis* or practical wisdom. Too often our practices, our applications, neglect or forget the overarching role of wisdom. Those in the communication field ought to privilege wisdom, the practical and the theoretical, over the outmoded sense of application.

CONCLUSION

In conclusion, I express again my admiration for Jamieson's paper and recommend it highly. It helped persuade me to change my firm opposition against applied communication to a position of limited approval—limited, as indicated above, to theoretically informed action research in support of the common weal. Boyer's redefinition of application also changed my thinking. Application cannot be considered in isolation from the types of institutions represented in SCA and the scholarships of discovery, integration, and teaching. I recommend to the reader the view that application be defined as a form of scholarship that will be profitable as a field only if it can be shown to benefit society and add to the communication field's understanding of human communication.

ACKNOWLEDGMENTS

The author thanks John Waite Bowers, George Cheney, Robert Craig, Michael Pacanowsky, and Elaine Tompkins for comments about the first draft of this response.

REFERENCES

Boyer, E. L. (1990). *Scholarship reconsidered: Priorities of the professoriate.* Princeton, NJ: The Carnegie Foundation for the Advancement of Teaching.

Campbell, K., & Jamieson, K. (1976). Form and genre in rhetorical criticism: An introduction. In K. Campbell & K. Jamieson (Eds.), *Form and genre: Shaping rhetorical action* (pp. 9–32). Falls Church, VA: Speech Communication Association.

Craig, R. T. (1989). Communication as a practical discipline. In B. Dervin, L. Grossberg, B. O'Keefe, & E. Wartella (Eds.), *Rethinking communication: Vol. 1. Paradigm issues* (pp. 97–122). Newbury Park, CA: Sage.

Dimitrijevic, N. (1990). In the mirror of rhetoric. In D. Summerbell (Ed.), *Rhetorical image* [Exhibition catalogue]. New York: The New Museum of Contemporary Art.

Goodrich, C. (1963). *Select British eloquence.* Indianapolis: Bobbs-Merrill.

Jaques, E. (1987). *The changing culture of a factory.* London: Garland.

Kernan, A. (1990). *The death of literature.* New Haven: Yale University Press.

Weick, K. (1979). *The social psychology of organizing* (2nd ed.). Reading, MA: Addison-Wesley.

Response to Jamieson:
Radio's Oscillating Policies Jolt
New Zealand and Ireland—
An Applied Research Example

Thomas A. McCain
The Ohio State University

The purposes of the applied communication conference were articulated in a straightforward manner: What should be the topics, methods, and fora for applied communication research? Jamieson's answer was equally straightforward; they should be important, appropriate, and responsible. Her response to the charge of the conference was a manuscript of original work which provides leadership by example rather than precept. In the essay "The Blurring of Political Genres," Jamieson examined the political rhetoric of the television advertisements of the 1990 U.S. presidential campaign with insight, rigor and understanding. She argued that there is a blurring genre emerging as spot advertisements successfully make their way out of the clutter into the network newscasts. Political spots were not only important for placement in commercial clusters with side ads for cars and coffee, but were in search of replay in a more credible and useful forum—as "news" in the national network nightly newscast. And she described her recommendations to news organizations for reporting on political ads.[1] Jamieson's work is stunning. It challenges the communication field to be known by the quality of its insights and the rigor of its methods, rather than the seriousness of its intentions. Applied communication research should not legitimize its importance in a cluster of footnotes in other scholar's papers, but should be directed towards participation in a larger, more credible and useful social dialogue. Applied communication research should blur scholarly genres.

---

[1] Editor's note: The version of Jamieson's paper included in this volume is much abbreviated from her conference paper and focused on the implications of her work to news organizations.

We all know that appropriate methods will not rescue a vacant idea, nor will a pregnant thought have much impact if procedure is precarious. Do we really need this advice again? It is the stuff of every introduction to research course and text. What we need are scholars serious about their work and willing to engage the potential criticism which comes from acting like a scholar rather than advising others how to be one. This is the challenge Jamieson offers us.

So what was a respondent like me to do? Two options were considered. One, I could unpack the Jamieson piece to show how this provocative work identifies a social problem, uses appropriate methodological strategies and epistemological concepts, and how it can and should have an impact on public policy. Or, two, I could acknowledge that with the acceptance of Jamieson's implied premise, that applied communication researchers should be known by their works rather than their advice, I should share applied work of my own. This option I did not bargain for. I am much better at giving advice, though "door number two" beckoned.

RADIO'S OSCILLATING POLICIES JOLT
NEW ZEALAND AND IRELAND:
AN APPLIED COMMUNICATION EXAMPLE

The applied communication research reported here is about the evolving structures of telecommunications organizations and industries. It is about the relationships between communication technologies and dynamic social organizations. It is about radio. It seeks to describe why and how the same communication technology (in this case wireless radio) performs different social, economic and political functions in different societies and how changes in society and in communication technology influence existing radio broadcasting policies often in disruptive jolting ways. What follows are snapshots of radio/society relationships in New Zealand and Ireland. Its applied audiences are international and domestic policy makers and present and potential radio organizations. My goal in this work is to facilitate the emergence of new forms of radio broadcasting, while acknowledging and encouraging the legitimate existing uses of radio broadcasting.

Note on Methods

The example begins with an introduction to a theoretical framework for understanding radio broadcasting as a transforming telecommunications technology. This is followed by portions of two case studies focusing on different aspects of radio in two island countries, New Zealand and Ireland. The data were gathered during visits to these locations where interviews with key persons were conducted, visits to radio stations were numerous, and attempts at "cultural immersion" were undertaken. The key policy documents and histories of broadcasting in both countries have been examined extensively. Two different methods of presentation are used in reporting this field work. A case study description of the current state of affairs is used to describe New Zealand radio in the early 1990s. A different form is used to introduce Irish local radio. The beginnings of a "realist tale" and a "confessionalist tale," which are suggested by Van Maanen (1988), are used to suggest the relationships between radio and the Irish Society. These two different reporting methods are rather inelegantly shoved together; both are incomplete. The New Zealand case study is fully referenced in the traditional manner, the Irish tales are presented in narrative form without references. In a concluding theoretical section, I suggest that the contradictions of radio policy can help applied communication theorists understand the future of radio and other communication technologies.

A THEORETICAL PERSPECTIVE: CHANGING COMMUNICATION TECHNOLOGY AND SOCIETY RELATIONSHIPS

The communication media of a country are reflective of the institutions and values of that society. One of the reasons broadcasting and telecommunications infrastructures are the focus of examination is because the policies which guide these communication industries' form, function, and purpose are indicative of the values and ideology of the social organizations which created them. In an era of unprecedented change, understanding the value-laden imperatives of communication policy helps to identify and understand the conflicts inherent in the making of new policies which reflect social and technological developments. The history of modern communication forms is a history of changing political, social, and economic forces, swinging to and fro, left and right, within sovereign governing entities across the globe. Communication technology—transmitters, turntables, twisted pairs or transducers—becomes communicating media when standards are set and human rules relative to their use, purpose, and purview are enacted by a group. It takes human interaction and the larger needs of a collectivity of individuals to make communication technology a medium for communicating. Just as communication technology changes, so too do the social organizations which determine the parameters of use, purpose, purview, and philosophy. Nation-state and society were once interchangeable descriptors of the social organization whose province it was to write communication policy. This is less the case in the 1990s than it was at any previous time in the history of communication technology policy.

The 1990s found the political economy of the world experiencing contradictory movements towards both internationalization and localism (McCain, 1990). This is in sharp contrast to the ethos of colonialism which dominated the public conscience when broadcasting was introduced and was being initially regulated. The forces of nationalism, in colonial clothing, prevailed in most of the world, triumphing over more local agendas during the policy debates which made radio technology a communicating medium in its formative years in Europe.

In the countries of the globe which have experienced years of government regulation and practice in the Public Service Broadcasting (PSB) tradition, the relationship between new technology and society has become particularly perplexing for existing media forms (Avery, 1993; Rowland & Tracey, 1990). Where once radio broadcasting was seen as an agent for public service and extension of national agendas, the political economy and culture of smaller communities and "free-market" forces requires new conceptualizations of this technology. Radio of the 1990s is in many respects a new communicating medium. It is being prodded and pulled to the exigencies of cultural demands, political and economic opportunities and changing community realities on the one hand, and at the same time demanding attention, creating new shared understandings, pursuing agendas which are both complimentary and in conflict with radio broadcasting's original purposes (Lowe, 1992).

In an earlier paper, a typology for examining local radio broadcasting stations in the countries of Western Europe was developed in order to describe the varying ways governments were dealing with radio as a new communicating medium (McCain & Lowe, 1990). These radio types are national local radio, independent local radio, and community local radio. These same types are seen in most developed countries of the world and in a broad sense reflect the three ideological stances to the political economy and culture of broadcasting policy. Like most histories, the accounts of radio broadcasting in the world are by and large stories of majority structures, rather than minority ones. The policies and practices of broadcasting have by and large reflected the majority sentiment on issues of access, content, ownership, purview, philosophy, funding, purpose, and the like. Initial radio broadcasting policy was written at a time when the technology had a variety of potential applications important for a country's commerce, culture, education, governance, and defense. Each sovereignty has had its own unique application.

THE NEW ZEALAND RADIO ENVIRONMENT: A CASE STUDY

The purpose of this section is to provide a background and overview of New Zealand radio. It is a first step in the analysis of the changing nature of local radio in that island nation's attempt to refine the value issues which appear to be compelling the New Zealanders to shape communication technology to their situation.

New Zealand Radio History

Local radio began in New Zealand in November 1921 with an experimental broadcast from Robert Jack, a physics professor at the University of Otago. As Hall (1980) recounted, by 1925 a new corporation called the Radio Broadcasting Company (RBC) was established under a 5-year government contract. The RBC purchased and operated the four private stations then in existence in the four main population centers of the country. Seven years later the number of stations had grown to 39 and the New Zealand government, like its counterparts elsewhere in the world, decided that radio broadcasting was appropriate for federal government control. They established the New Zealand Broadcasting board in 1932 and in 1936 the National Broadcasting Service (NBS) was established with broadcasting becoming a Department of State reporting to a Minister of the Crown.

What is most unique about New Zealand radio's history is that in 1937, State owned and operated radio stations became commercial enterprises, reporting to a Minister of Broadcasting. This made the New Zealand government the first in the world to be in business as a broadcaster using paid advertising to partially fund the operation. By 1938, 12 noncommercial and 4 commercial stations, all government operated, were on the air (Radio New Zealand). Following World War II the commercial and noncommercial stations were amalgamated into a single company under the name of the New Zealand Broadcasting Service (NZBS) (Gregory, 1985; Hall, 1980). As radio developed and television was finding its way into the society, expansion occurred so that by the time of the next major restructuring in 1962, the number of stations had grown to 35 with their signals reaching the tips of both Islands and nearly all locations in between (see Gregory for a detailed account).

The next switch in the alphabet soup that has characterized the parent companies of radio was the establishment in 1962 of New Zealand Broadcasting Corporation (NZBC). At this time the operation of the broadcasting services shifted from direct government control by the Minister of Broadcasting to a public corporation which was seen as being at least an arm's length from direct government interference in daily affairs. Radio Hauraki, New Zealand's legendary pirate station, broadcast from international waters for 3 years, seeking a private warrant to broadcast legally. They came ashore in 1970 to become the first radio pirate to be awarded a legal tender (Blackburn, 1989; A. Blackburn, personal communication, May 9, 1990).

In 1973, a Broadcasting Act was passed, which again shifted the organizational structure of New Zealand radio and eliminated the position of Minister of Broadcasting altogether. This time NZBC was replaced with four new entities: a Broadcasting Council of New Zealand (BCNZ), Radio New Zealand (RNZ), and two television corporations, NZTV-1 and NZTV-2, beginning in 1975. The Broadcasting Council was responsible for infrastructure maintenance and shared functions such as research, whereas RNZ was charged with the operation of the public radio services for the whole country and to gather news for the two television stations which were at that time in their embryonic stages.

A change of government brought with it another restructuring of reporting lines for the government's radio in 1975 (Adam, 1973). The two television stations and RNZ retained their separate departmental status, the position of the post of Minister of Broadcasting was resurrected and the Broadcasting Council's tenure was ended quickly, being replaced by a new Broadcasting Corporation of New Zealand (BCNZ) which functioned as a single oversight board for public broadcasting in the country. BCNZ had a Director General as its principal administrative officer and a newly created Broadcasting Tribunal which was established to handle issues of broadcast Warrants (licenses) and other judicial and regulatory matters (Gregory, 1985). This organizational scheme worked for a decade, but changes both in the government and the communication industries brought to New Zealand yet another restructuring and organization which began in late 1988 (J. Hunt, personal communication, April 3, 1990; B. Wakem, personal communication, April 2 & 6, 1990).

The latest reorientation to broadcasting is among the most provocative approaches to deregulation of broadcasting in the developed world. The changes grew out of a series of government studies that were commissioned to dismantle the Government's ownership of the service and industrial sector of the country (Prebble, 1988). Privatization, New Zealand style, took the government owned and operated businesses in one of two directions. Previously public owned, operated, and funded services, from electric power to meat processing, became either State Owned Enterprises (SOEs) or were sold to private stockholders (Chapman, 1986; Rennie, 1988). The SOEs, like radio stations, were envisioned as for-profit corporations whose revenue should make money in the market place and help reduce taxes for the citizens (J. Hunt, personal communication, April 3, 1990).

What the new organizational schemes set about to do was to separate the social objectives and the economic objectives of broadcasting. The new structure for New Zealand dealt separately with issues of government needs, ownership, funding, programming, and distribution. The most controversial aspects of the changes were the auctioning of the electromagnetic spectrum to the highest bidders, the orientation of marketplace economics for all broadcasters, including the SOEs and the establishment of a separate authority to fund and insure that the full range of broadcast services needed by a society, including services to minority interests, was met through a system of grants and contracts (B. Impy, personal communication, May 8, 1990; National Economic Research Association [NERA], 1989; Independent Broadcasters Association of New Zealand [IBA], 1989).

New Zealand's Radio Structure

There are generally two groups of station constituencies in contemporary New Zealand, those owned by the State and those within the private sector. There is also a demarcation between stations based on sources of funding. Some of the stations are commercially funded, some are noncommercial with revenue coming either from the Government license fee, or from the ownership organization.

In the early 1990s there were approximately 98 radio stations which operated regular schedules. Of the commercial operations, 39 are operated and owned by Radio New Zealand (RNZ), the State Owned Enterprise. RNZ also owns a group of noncommercial stations which are linked in two networks— YA stations and YC stations. There are 24 Independent local radio stations which are operated by private commercial companies. There are 8 stations which are operated by nonprofit organizations, mostly church groups. There are also a variety of intermittent stations which are operated by groups such as student associations and by various Maori groups (Rennie, 1988).

Commercial Radio. For a relatively small country, New Zealand has a high number of commercial radio stations, especially when compared to Europe. For example, New Zealand has 53 commercial stations (not including repeaters) and a population of just over 3 million people, a ratio of 16 stations per million. Although this is decidedly less than the United States's 36 stations per million inhabitants, Germany has 4, Portugal 5, the UK less than 1, and France 18 stations per million (Saatchi & Saatchi European Market and MediaFact, in Rennie, 1988). Radio revenues were 13% of all media advertising expenditures, a share which had remained steady for the past 10 years. The level of radio advertising in New Zealand as a percentage of GDP is 19%, higher even than the United States's percentage of 17% according to Rennie. RNZ stations account for just over 60% of the total radio advertising revenues operating in 24 geographic markets. Most of the RNZ commercial stations (called community stations by RNZ) are mass appeal stations on the AM band. In Wellington, Christchurch, and Manawatu, the ZM stations broadcast on FM. Community stations, while assisted in developing their formats by RNZ in very sophisticated ways, do most of their programming locally (B. Wakem, personal communication, May 2, 1990; G. Duignan, personal communication, May 4, 1990). They broadcast 24 hours a day and are normally linked from 7 p.m. onwards to take the Network's *Tonight Show*. Some of the smaller mini stations combine local originated programming with a greater share of national networked programming (Rennie).

Most people are quite optimistic about the future of radio in New Zealand, as long as the future is seen in fairly expansive terms. The short range for the industry as a whole is flat due to several factors: the high level of radio advertising already, increasing competition from television, continued fragmentation and downward pressure on rates, economic factors related to the agri-economics of the country in the 1990s (Rennie).

The distribution of these stations follows the population densities of the country; 17 stations are located in the four largest metro areas of Auckland, Wellington, Christchurch, and Hamilton. All of the private stations are in the largest 14 New Zealand cities. RNZ earns on average $53 per listener compared with $39 per listener for the private stations. There is less difference in the value of the station and its earning capacity by market size than one would have suspected, with the smaller stations (35,000 listeners) earning about $4 per listener less than the medium and larger stations (Schmitt, 1988). RNZ in the past has cross subsidized its smaller community stations, but its organization and austerity moves, dramatically changed the fiscal nature of these stations, making them entirely self sufficient (B. Wakem, personal communication, May 2, 1990).

Changing Philosophies in New Zealand Local Radio.   This snapshot of the local public service radio operations of RNZ are quite different than a similar account might be of BBC local radio in Great Britain or RTE local radio in Ireland. The RNZ stations have been a mix of Government Local radio and Independent Local radio for over 30 years. In addition RNZ, or one of its similarly titled predecessors, have developed, funded, and operated what we have previously called Community Local radio stations (McCain & Lowe, 1990). These access stations and Maori language stations have been unique and successful compared to governmental attempts in other countries to accomplish these kinds of objectives. This does not mean to suggest that the Maoris are satisfied with their treatment (Fox, 1988; P. Walker, personal communication, May 1, 1990; Te Tino Rangatirattanga, 1988). But RNZ has seen as part of its mission providing relatively unrestrained use of radio to a variety of groups. The student radio stations are also quite successful for they are seen as an opportunity to both service a student audience and provide students with experience (M. McDonald, personal communication, May 2, 1990).

These and other cultural, economic and political exigencies greatly shape the face of New Zealand's radio services. There are structures and uses of radio in New Zealand found nowhere else in the world.

THE ENVIRONMENT FOR IRISH LOCAL RADIO: A REALIST TALE [2]

Radio Telefis Eireann (RTE) is the national public service broadcasting company of Ireland. It has a prestigious past and like most of its European counterparts, an uncertain future. Whether there will be an RTE in the future seems not in doubt. This company, started as Radio Telefis in the early 1930s, has a most resilient history. There is an expectation for government participation in broadcasting, given that such has been the pattern over the 70 years of RTE's existence. Some Irish governments have participated more than others. It appears to be part of the ethos of RTE and its associated enterprises to be both cooperative and in conflict with the government of the day, while at the same time preparing for better times in the future when a new government will meddle either less or at least differently.

Historical Context of Irish Broadcasting

The original broadcasting act that formed RTE had a view of public service broadcasting (PSB) which fostered an eclectic Irish approach. The news, public affairs, music, Irish language, drama, and educational programs of its beginnings were reflective of the De Valerian governments' view of how Ireland should cope with its new found independence as a sovereign state.

Certainly Irish broadcasting was influenced by its powerful, culturally and

---

[2]The fieldwork for this section on Irish Radio was begun in 1984 when I was on a research leave from Ohio State, living with my family in Howth, County Dublin and teaching at the National Institute of Higher Education (now Dublin City University). At that time the Irish Ministry of Communication asked me to prepare a report about the nature of local radio in Europe and the United States as background for the framing of legislation for introducing new broadcasting legislation. I have been following the developments of local Irish radio since that time through reading, observing, and conversing with a host of Irish broadcasters, scholars, audience members, friends, and acquaintances. The data for the Irish section were primarily gathered during trips to Ireland in 1984–1985, 1989, 1990, and 1992. The Irish Times, which was indexed and referenced at RTE, provided much of the background material for the sections on the present developments. I am particularly indebted to the librarians and researchers at RTE for their assistance. I also became a student of Irish custom and history under the tutelage of Peter Ash, Esq., of Dublin. He took this "Yank" under his wing in order that I might understand the beauty and pride of the Irish people. He also taught me, among other elegances, about Irish coffee, Georgian doors, and the pleasures of pork roll and gooseberry fool. A host of key informants from RTE, community radio supporters, and independent Irish broadcasters provided the background for the broadcasting system. Other helpful contributors included Harry Long, Peg and Pat Hodgson, Julian Walton, Ferrell Corcoran, Colm Kenny, Tony Fahey, Sean Connely, and countless publicans, greengrocers, butchers, musicians, and newsstand clerks who chatted with me at length about Ireland and broadcasting.

economically dominating neighbor to the East. Public service broadcasting as a philosophy was elaborately developed by the British Broadcasting Company, and transported to most corners of the globe as part of British colonialism. About one half of the Irish Republic's inhabitants can receive British television programs, and all can receive British radio. The Irish broadcasters at RTE have always paid attention to this force, be it as a competitor or as a cultural invader.

What seems clear from reading the histories of early Irish radio and by examining the elements of Irish policy for broadcasting, is that this country is not an exception for reflecting the politics of the country in its broadcasting service. In other words, radio can be viewed as a mirror of the country, its politics, and its government. To understand Irish broadcasting is to understand Irish politics, economics, culture, and power; Irish broadcasting is an Irish solution to an Irish problem.

Eamon De Valera, the Taoiseach (prime minister) of the Free State for most of its early years as a Republic (1932–1948) sought to make Ireland self sufficient. An island which experienced occupation and widespread cultural domination for most of the 1,000 years of its "modern" history yearned for self sufficiency. The Irish seem to ache for control of their own destiny, however modest. They needed to celebrate their ability to do things themselves during the early years of independence from England. The rally cry of the De Valera government was "Sinn Fein," in English, "ourselves alone." The political implications of Irish neutrality during World War II should be understood in this light. The need for and celebration of the family, the favoring of a subsistence agricultural economy, and the wide political correlates of such a policy in the 20th century are deeply ingrained in Irish affairs of state and in Irish broadcasting policy. "Ourselves alone" meant that there must also be a way to make the hundreds of rural and isolated communities come together in a national spirit. There was a great need to bring together the wide variety of local cultures, and to encourage and foster Irish patriotism, Irish traditional culture, Irish Catholicism, and Irish pride.

The one nation, ours alone, concept and the government and cultural policy which fostered it was the vision of De Valera and the Fianna Fail party. The political alliances which made the new nation were deeply entrenched in Irish history. The modern version of the alliances became the Republic of Ireland, whose constitution was adopted only in 1937. The balance of power at the time was a delicate and precarious one. A bitter civil war, fought in 1922–1923 over the issue of a peaceful settlement with Great Britain, which allowed the northern counties to remain part of Great Britain or to fight on for a totally "free" state, free of British rule, pitted neighbor against neighbor and families against each other.

The faction which favored the treaty for "peace now," not De Valera's Fianna Fail party, won the civil war, and won the national referendum which adopted the settled peace. But it was a high price and a deeply scarring settlement which intrudes on the politics and structures of Irish life into the 1990s. Although the parliamentary party ruled the day on the settlement, it was unable to rule the country following the civil war. It was Eamon De Valera, the son of a Mexican father and Irish mother who returned from exile to form a new government and lead the country through its early period as a sovereign state. As a general in the Irish Republican Army (IRA), De Valera fought hard but lost the big battle regarding one nation status for Ireland. He broke with the militant faction of the IRA in order to pursue Irish independence without the gun. His rise to power following the formation of the free state centered on a deeply held religious commitment to Catholicism and a strong alliance with the church, a dream of a pastoral and self-sufficient Ireland and the rhetorical vision to make the island one nation eventually.

The complicated set of circumstances, historical pressures, and scars that shaped trade policy and family policy (no contraception, no divorce, etc.) also shaped Irish radio broadcasting. The Irish version of the history of broadcasting credits the world's first broadcast to be in 1916 from the Dublin Post Office. This famous use of radio was from the Irish rebels who had occupied this grand public building on O'Connel Street, declaring the end of British domination and the beginning of Irish independence. The message was premature.

Value Issues in Irish Broadcasting

RTE's public service tradition has favored national, as opposed to a local or regional service. This is not to say that there has been no local service, but localism is less central than the mission of quality pluralism, offering the best of Irish entertainment, information and culture to all citizens. As one drives the remote regions of Donegal, 200 miles and 20 years from Dublin, the radio spots for film developing in downtown Dublin seem inappropriate somehow. The folk in the West learn to tune out that which is not appropriate to their lives, but not without some resentment and certainly not without notice. The radio choices for most Irish listeners prior to 1989 were either one of two RTE networks, or a radio pirate, broadcasting illegally.

The Dubs and the Culchies.   Ireland, as most countries, has rivalry between city and rural folk. This schism is traditionally between the capital city and other areas. The seat of government and the hub of commerce and trade is Dublin, the center of Ireland for nearly 1,000 years. There is a wonderful local chauvinism for both the urban and rural counties of the Republic of 3.5 million people. It is perpetuated in many respects by Irish sport, the Catholic church, and the pub rather than Irish radio.

One of the forces in Irish life, the Gaelic Athletic Association (GAA) has ancient beginnings that were fed by De Valerian cultural policy. Irish games of hurling, Irish football, and cammogie were the sports allowed in Irish National schools after independence. Rugby and cricket were viewed as English upper-class sports, soccer associated with European working classes; neither were deemed appropriate for Sinn Fein. The GAA thought that the Irish should play Irish games—other sports were discouraged. As the GAA became more and more powerful, their rulings prevented athletes who participated in rugby, cricket, or soccer from playing in Irish sports competitions. This assured that good athletes who also wanted to be good Irishmen would not participate in the international competitions which dominate most of European sport. If an athlete played rugby, cricket, or soccer, he or she was banned from GAA-sponsored activities. Because Irish heroes played Irish games, the Irish international sporting sides were structurally mediocre by European standards. The poor play of the Irish soccer teams before Jack Charlton became the coach perpetuated the Irish bumpkin image elsewhere in Europe, while the folks at home celebrated their sporting heroes—themselves alone.

This meander into sporting life is not unrelated to broadcasting and community purview. It helps to understand the importance of local regions in Ireland. The GAA-sponsored games are organized by villages, towns, counties, and provinces. Town and village sides play each other to find the best county team. The counties compete for championships of the province. When chatting in a pub it is quite common to have the conversation turn to discussion of some final match, or some great game between counties like Tipperary and Cork. The championships are matches in which the winners of the provincial competitions meet in the world series and super bowl of Ireland—the All Ireland finals.

Local and regional communities are as important to the Irish as they are to most populations. But public service radio has seldom been about this level of community for at least two important reasons. First, the funding of local stations to serve geographic areas the size of a county were problematic in the beginning. There were especially difficult economic imperatives working against local community stations during De Valerian economics. The small farmers and local retailers generated comparatively little capital to be spent on local news and entertainment vehicles like radio. Besides, they had pubs for this purpose. Whether local stations would be operated commercially or as municipal service of a region was not a considered alternative. But then, few countries opted for locally owned and funded community radio or television when original policy was written and radio became a mass media. It made little sense during the formative experimental years of radio. By the time it might have been economically viable in Ireland, the national public service broadcaster, RTE, had stakes in developing and maintaining a national service rather than a local service as its priority.

Radio Telefis Eireann

Radio Telefis Eireann (RTE), like any organization, has tremendous energy for self-preservation. It has marshaled its forces for doing things its way, for maintaining the public service concept of Irish broadcasting which it created and perpetuates. How could it be otherwise? The people of "The House," as RTE managers refer to themselves and their headquarters building in Donnybrook, have carefully considered alternative structures and broadcasting formats and sought the best solution for Irish broadcasting. RTE's vision of Irish radio's future includes itself as the biggest, most central player; at the heart of power and control. Once RTE became synonymous with broadcasting, other approaches, other programs, other owners, other funding schemes were in conflict with their own visions for the future. RTE quite naturally came in conflict with other pretenders to the broadcasting throne. To behave otherwise would be to not protect the employees of The House. To endorse competition would be to encourage losing revenue. To encourage local ownership and control would be to step away from quality and the ideals of public service broadcasting. It would be a step towards dismantling the power and influence which they grew to enjoy, having been the only game in the country for half a century. The policies and stances of the original RTE, like the early GAA, have been in the interest of keeping the Irish, themselves alone. RTE has been a natural and persistent force against Independent local radio and Community local radio, because their ethos and their own self preservation favored a national as opposed to a local purview.

Independent Local Radio

Sean Connely was the first secretary of the Independent Radio Television Commission (IRTC), which is Ireland's version of New Zealand's Independent Broadcasting Association (IBA). The IRTC was formed by the Broadcasting Act of 1988, which was companion legislation to a bill that silenced 30 years of Irish pirate broadcasting.

The commission has a chair and eight other members. The Honorable Charles Healy stepped down from the Irish supreme court to become the first Chair of the IRTC. The other members of the Commission represent various business, geographic, cultural, and media interests of the country. The Broadcasting Act created them as a body and spelled out their procedures for operation. Their mission and structure is in a document only a few pages long. The bill generated hundreds of pages of debate in daily proceedings in the Dail (parliament) over the course of 15 or more years, though its final form is slight and in some important ways meaningfully ambiguous—another Irish solution for an Irish problem.

Because Ireland was entering the local and private broadcasting arena at a different time from other countries, it faced different exigencies and mixes of technology than had been faced by other countries when making similar decisions. The procedures and means for silencing some 70 pirate radio stations and bringing on board replacements suitable for the audience was to be no small feat. The Irish audience had, of course, grown to depend on the illegal broadcasters during their raid on the island. The previous governments had all vainly tried to silence the pirate radio stations. How and why the IRTC was able to accomplish this is in many respects due to the pragmatic way in which the commission and its staff proceeded to bring private broadcasting to the listeners who were used to having it, but whose government had not licensed or regulated it in any way.

At the center of things was Sean Connely, a slightly built, energetic man probably in his late 30s. He spoke candidly, practically, and eagerly about the local broadcasting emergence. His guidance and shaping of the decision making resulted in a four stage process which brought private broadcasting to the country. The first phase was the awarding of a license to a national radio competitor to RTE's national service. Next the Commission took up the awarding of a television franchise to compete with RTE's Channels 1 and 2. Those decisions were made by the end of 1988. (Neither of these decisions provided competition to RTE of any importance. Century Radio was unable to attract an audience and left the air; audiences were still waiting for the third television channel to begin programming in 1995.)

The Commission then turned its attention to the business of licensing 24 local stations, one each for geographic regions of the country that were by and large identifiable as counties. The exceptions were the counties where cultural identity within the county made awarding a single franchise politically impractical in a short time span. The newly formed Commission assumed the position that it was first and foremost there to put local radio stations on air where previously there had been illegal operators. Speed was also a consideration. Those stations which were not to be economically viable over the long haul would, it was thought, sort themselves out eventually. Two licenses were awarded in Dublin City, to the first of the stations to go on the air. They began broadcasting in less than 1 year after the pirates were silenced. The Commission moved confidently and with breath-taking speed for a regulatory group. By July 1990, there were licenses awarded to 24 local operators, representing 24 different ownership groups.

The Commission accomplished this feat through a variety of tactics. First, they encouraged input from citizens in the nation and in the local regions which were to have their own stations. The response was astounding. In the first 4 months of existence responses averaged 2,000 letters of comment a week. Eight large file cabinets full of letters and comments were accumulated, 75% of which could be and were answered with a stock reply. All Irish lobby groups were represented among the respondents. A staff of eight people answered every letter within the same week of its receipt. The self-selected players in this new regulatory game felt that they were having a say in the proceedings.

The Commission and Sean Connely were very accessible to the press both at RTE and the national and provincial papers. Connely noted that it was not unusual for him to do three to four interviews a week. He established a high profile with the press and was viewed positively by media professionals at RTE, in the ad industry, at the Communications Minister's office, and with the trade press. Typical comments about Connely included: an "excellent source," a "straight-ahead guy," "a person of enormous energy," "open and honest," "helpful." The organizational ability, the refreshing candor, and the strategic decisions regarding the pragmatics of getting radio stations on the air appeared remarkably uncontroversial for such sweeping changes in Irish broadcasting.

In addition, the IRTC held public hearings. This was rather without precedent in Irish regulatory politics, but was a strategically gifted move on the part of the Commission. It helped to mute the conspiracy theories, of which typically there would be dozens. It provided a venue where journalists and government lobbyists could witness the quality of the applications. Colm Kenny, an excellent journalist and university lecturer who has written widely on the politics of local radio in Ireland, noted that "there is little doubt in my mind that the best applicants were awarded the franchises" (C. Kenny, personal communication, July 23, 1990). His coverage in the *Irish Independent,* along with Ronan Foster's writing in the *Irish Times,* kept the public at large, politicians, and media personnel well informed on this process. The hearings were held in public, although no transcript or critical documentation was kept, nor were the documents of all applicants reproduced. (Financial and privacy considerations notwithstanding, it just didn't seem necessary to the IRTC or others involved.)

The IRTC's fourth contribution to making the Broadcasting Bill work was to deliberate in private and provide no reasons for why particular applicants were chosen over others. No records of the deliberations were kept, the winners were announced after careful, but immediate deliberation. The commission saw no advantage in allowing the public or the failed applicants to second guess the decisions. Sean Connely's view was that "the commission was appointed by the government to perform a deliberative function, it was not something they could shirk, nor would publishing a reason or two, facilitate the pragmatics of their implicit goal of getting stations on the air quickly" (S. Connely, personal communication, July 26, 1990). The final phase for the commission was to make a matter of public record the final negotiated contracts for each franchise.

These procedures, a mixture of public and private deliberations of wide access for input but limited oral public hearings, of access to the media at all stages is quite remarkable to this observer, especially given the history of hostage holding which previous governments had experienced.

Perhaps most remarkable is that there was but one denied applicant who pursued a legal redress. Only the owner of the popular Dublin pirate *Sunshine Radio* fought to have the Commission decision overturned and the whole of the IRTC halted, as he pursued his case through the supreme court. However, Robinson failed in his appeal.

The people who thought less well of Connely and the IRTC were the broadcast interests of the small voices, the community local radio advocates. Awarding licenses for community radio groups was taken up as the last bit of new business. The IRTC chose to segregate the community local radio interests to the backwaters of Irish radio policy and to deal with the problems of finding a community radio presence only after the economics of the marketplace had some shape to it.

IRISH COMMUNITY LOCAL RADIO: A CONFESSIONALIST TALE

Beginning in 1878 and continuing for a century, young boys without social anchors or support were sent to the Industrial School in Letterfrack, County Galway, where they went to learn a trade and some discipline. This, in order to be meaningful members of the community. The building which housed this orphanage/reform school sits at the crossroads in Letterfrack in the heart of Connemara, dominated by the starkly beautiful mountains which rise majestically from the barren landscape. Most of the three-story stone structure was refurbished and modernized in the 1980s by Connemara West Development Corporation. It houses a successful woodworking school, agricultural development office, and an industrial development office. This one-time home for boys who had to develop a sense of community in difficult, near prison-like surroundings, is also the home of Connemara Community Radio. This small local station was seeking to develop and nurture a sense of community utilizing radio technology. In a rather ominous and ironic way Connemara Community Radio, like other community broadcasters, are prisoners of the establishment media who set the rules for what is acceptable broadcasting. People who work in The House at RTE seldom acknowledge the legitimacy of local community radio operators like John and Erin and the others who work at Connemara Community Radio.

"If you don't behave, we'll send you to Letterfrack," was a common phrase in Irish households when boys were bad or did not do what their parents said they should. What is stifling to the current inhabitants of the Letterfrack Industrial School are the rules and conceptions of radio in which the community local radio volunteers must find a way to operate. In a very real sense community radio advocates are prisoners to conceptions of radio from another era, for another purpose, for another kind of community.

The folk at Connemara Community Radio seemed happy to be there. They were highly motivated and talented people. The local community radio enthusiasts did not feel that they were isolated from the geographical community, in fact, quite the opposite. The love for the region, its people and problems, was infectiously obvious with their every story and action. The dedication of these volunteers and the one employee of the station was nearly overwhelming to me.

This was home. This was community. Connemara, a place of anchor and refuge. In Connemara there are stories to tell and retell. Important social histories are waiting to be told and understood. Social issues brought on by the information age and industrial development need a forum and some perspective taking. This is a magnificent and awesome geography which has supported small communities of people for perhaps 9,000 years. A place whose destiny must include its past and its present inhabitants. This community local radio station is like a newsletter of the air. Announcements of upcoming church supers, musical groups playing their tunes, community development people, and county agents with the latest word on fish farming are among the stories of this station, on the air during the weekends. Folk of the region use microphones and tape recorders in local and innovative ways, finding Connemara solutions for Connemara problems.

THEORY AND POLICY IMPLICATIONS FOR RADIO

These brief accounts of some of the changes in radio in New Zealand and Ireland are meant to reveal the communication policy process as a human activity. People struggle to find ways for communication technology to facilitate and strengthen existing relationships, whether political, economic, social, or cultural. As the times when policy decisions concerning communication technology are somewhat serendipitous, the structures of communication media like radio have a variety of shapes and uses by a society. It is inevitable that societies constantly examine the changing relationships in communication technology as it changes, and as society also changes. In this process fundamental conflicts regarding communication policy are revealed and the media–society relationship is transformed.

Radio broadcasting and other media that individuals and societies use are inherently value laden and power differentiating. Not only does policy need to be developed for the new technologies and their opportunities and threats, but existing policy and definition for established communication media must also be examined. In the case of radio, such remarkable changes occurred in the 1980s that this old technology needs perhaps to be seen as a new communication medium. New relationships with new forms of a society are resulting in radio technology being used differently. Public service broadcasting models, designed for this technology in the 1920s and 1930s, are hardly relevant for the multifaceted and differentiated communities of the 1990s. Market defined models of broadcasting, driven by audience size designed for current radio technology in the 1960s, are equally irrelevant for the current milieu.

Irish and New Zealand society and the functions to be performed by radio as a communication technology in these states has been and continues to be altered. There have been alterations in sending and receiving technology, changes in social problems, changes in geographical boundaries, changes in ideology, changes in audience uses, changes in economies, and changes in the problems of private and public life. As these countries change, their media and communication systems must likewise transform. It is difficult to imagine that there would be a society whose communication infrastructure, rules, regulations, laws, and policy were not reflective of the rest of the power structure of that society. This is so because communication technology is a mediator of these structures.

The relationships individuals have and develop with radio and other media organizations are one crucial way which societies define themselves. Societies and communities are more than arbitrary groups of individuals. They share common and discrete histories, locations, sense of boundary, cultural practices, religious experiences, educational patterns, folklore and heroes, games and entertainments. The relationship individuals have with their communities is in one sense a feeling of belonging or not belonging with this collective of individuals which share so many common practices and exigencies. Common practices and perspectives result in particular shared views of what is good and bad for not only personal needs but also for shared or community needs. These commonly held orientations are known as social values. They are the result of constant interaction between an individual's personal life experiences within self, between self and significant others, and the shared feelings people know exist among those with whom they share a community. Because communities are at once both homogeneous and heterogeneous, differences in social values result in varying perspectives on ways to organize communication policy. Communication policy must, at an arbitrary point in time, resolve the tensions people feel for needing both individual freedom and collective recognition. This paradox or dialectic is the most fundamental contradiction of human experience and can be seen to be at the root of communication policy debates since the telegraph was introduced.

The critical value debates of each of the past waves of communication policy were at the heart of the radio debates in Ireland, New Zealand, and elsewhere in the world. The key policy conundrums include technological standards and compatibility, ownership and access, funding and subsidy, purview and coverage, speaker versus audience conceptions, and content debates between information and entertainment orientations. The social value conflicts tend to turn on whether the greatest good comes for both individuals and the collective by favoring the individual or favoring the collective. It can be understood as the traditional and inevitable clash between left and right, liberal and conservative, and perhaps, between socialism and capitalism.

The mediascape of Europe, Asia, Africa, and the Americas is in the process of a significant transformation by a complex of new communication technologies in a milieu of changing political and economic realities. We need structures that will preserve the best of the past while creating a pluralism of structures which are appropriate for the 21st century. We can expect to see continued growth of small community radio stations across the globe as well as new international radio services. National radio stations will assume a remarkably altered role in most corners of the world, wielding less influence than they have in the past.

APPLIED RESEARCH

This example of applied research suggests that communication scholars should be focusing on the problems of communication for which people and societies are grappling for answers. Policy research in telecommunications and mass media is of critical importance and of some urgency. The convergence of technologies, markets, and policies which form the communication infrastructure of societies is being negotiated in this latter part of the 20th century. Applied communication research is needed which is theoretically grounded and culturally situated. Mostly it requires that communication scholars address the communication problems which people have. If communication research, labeled as applied or pure, does not help society solve the problems which it identifies as communication related, then the relevance of communication as a field or discipline is of modest consequence. If people are not coming to communication scholars to help them with their communication problems, then perhaps it is time for us to go away.

REFERENCES

Adam, K. (1973, July). *The broadcasting future for New Zealand.* Paper presented to the House of Representatives, New Zealand.

Avery, R. K. (Ed.). (1993). *Public service broadcasting in a multichannel environment: The history and survival of an ideal.* New York: Longman.

Blackburn, A. (1989). *The shoestring pirates* (2nd ed.). Auckland: Hauraki Enterprises.

Chapman, R. M. (1986). *Report of the Royal Commission of inquiry.* Auckland: Royal Commission on Broadcasting and Related Telecommunications in New Zealand.

Fox, D. T. (1988). The mass media: A Maori perspective. In *Report of The Royal Commission on Social Policy (Te Komihana A Te Karauna Mo Nga Ahuatanga-A-Iwi)* (pp. 483–499).

Gregory, R. J. (1985). *Politics and broadcasting: Before and beyond the NZBC.* Palmerston North, New Zealand: The Dunmore Press.

Hall, J. H. (1980). *The history of broadcasting in New Zealand, 1920–1954.* Wellington: Broadcasting Corporation of New Zealand.

Independent Broadcasters Association of New Zealand (IBA). (1989). *Don't pull our plug! Independent Broadcasters Association radio spectrum deregulation proposals.* Position summary and IBA case for Members of Parliament, Auckland.

Lowe, G. F. (1992). *Value and meaning transformation in public service broadcasting: Competition and legitimacy in the Finnish radio renaissance.* Unpublished doctoral dissertation, University of Texas, Austin.

McCain, T. A. (1990). *Telecommunications and community: The global village and other myths* (Center for Advanced Study in Telecommunications [CAST] working file 1990–003). The Ohio State University, Columbus.

McCain, T. A., & Lowe, G. F. (1990). Localism in Western European radio broadcasting: Untangling the wireless. *Journal of Communication, 40*(1), 86–101.

National Economic Research Association (NERA). (1989). *Summary of proposals on alternative methods of spectrum management.* Report to New Zealand Government, Department of Trade and Industry.

Prebble, R. (1988, December). Broadcasting in New Zealand: A complete restructure. *Combroad, 36*–39.

Rennie, H. B. (1988, July). *Report of the steering committee on the restructuring of the Broadcasting Corporation of New Zealand on state owned enterprise principles.* Report to The Minister of Broadcasting, The Minister of Finance, New Zealand.

Rowland, W. D., & Tracey, M. (1990). Worldwide challenges to public service broadcasting. *Journal of Communication, 40*(2), 8–27.

Te Tino Rangatirattanga o o ratou whenua [The choice between networked and regional radio for Maoridom]. (1988, June). Huirangi, Waikerepuru. (unpublished)

Van Maanen, J. (1988). *Tales of the field: On writing ethnography.* Chicago: The University of Chicago Press.

II

REFLECTIONS

6

Applied Communication Research in a Practical Discipline

Robert T. Craig
University of Colorado at Boulder

The 1991 Tampa conference on "Applied Communication in the 21st Century" generated considerable light and even a certain amount of heat but was not, as I recall it, an event highly charged with collective excitement. Notably, one cannot say of this gathering what Simons (1985) wrote concerning an Iowa symposium on the rhetoric of inquiry, that "[a] movement-like tone pervaded the conference from the very first" (p. 52). No "movement-like tone" emanated from Tampa.

There was, to be sure, a collective recognition that we had been assembled to stamp the disciplinary imprimatur on applied communication research, which we did. Our recommendations, especially in the reduced and clarified form in which they emerged from the postconference Delphi process, should neither offend nor inspire anyone but will surely prove useful for their intended purpose. Predictably, they urge "increased recognition" and "greater influence" for applied communication research while insisting that such studies "use the best available research methods," "be based on a solid disciplinary grounding," "be sensitive to . . . ethical and value issues," and be disseminated "in a style and manner that is accessible" to relevant audiences.

The voice of the conference as expressed in these recommendations is resolute but thin and unpenetrating; resolute because it announces a consensus perhaps too easily achieved; thin and unpenetrating because it emerged from a process that necessarily filtered out as noise most of the conference's various, dissonant energies. Thus our recommendations bear only faint traces of the tensions that recurrently troubled us, tensions expressed less often in overt conflict than in a certain mutual wariness among the diverse applied behavioral scientists, postmodernist and/or critical interpretivists, disciplinary stalwarts, and interdisciplinary visitors assembled. There was little point in trying to persuade such a group to adopt one's own perspective on applied communication research. Civility, punctuated by moments of exasperation and tempered by wariness lest the official vocabulary be co-opted by some opposing tendency, was the attitude generally sensed from where I sat. The recommendations we crafted, however predictable, were well balanced and certainly appropriate to the occasion.

More interesting, if less harmonious, than the consensual voice of the recommendations, is the cacophony of the chapters in the present volume. The tensions that troubled us—and should continue to trouble us, for they are inherent in the practice of applied research within our discipline—are at least partly reflected in differences among the conference papers.

The following pages offer a perspective on applied communication research that does not deny or attempt to eliminate those differences. In a practical discipline that derives its theoretical substance from the study of communicative practices applied research can play an important mediating role between theory and practice, but only if the tensions inherent in such a role are understood and their generative possibilities realized.

A PERSPECTIVE ON
APPLIED COMMUNICATION RESEARCH

What distinguishes applied communication research for me is that its immediate top priority is to address problems that emerge in the practical world rather than those that emerge within the internal conversation of the communication discipline itself. *Disciplinary research*—a term I use in preference to more familiar terms such as basic or pure research—reverses those priorities; its immediate top priority is to address theoretical problems and controversies, fill gaps in knowledge, and in general, to advance the discipline. This is not, of course, the end of the story but only the beginning. Complications ensue; the relationship between applied and disciplinary communication research is, and ought to be, more complex than any such simple reversal of priorities can suggest. As we further explore that relationship, we encounter fundamental questions about the character of our discipline and the role of applied research within it.

From a pragmatic standpoint, applied communication research can be thought of as a professionalized extension of an impulse toward "reflection-in-action" (Schön, 1983, 1987) that arises naturally within the communication process as within any practical activity (Dewey, 1933/1989).

As Schön (1983) observed, a person involved in doing something may engage in reflective thinking whenever faced with "some puzzling, or troubling, or interesting phenomenon. . . . As [the person] tries to make sense of it, [he or she] also reflects on the understandings which have been implicit in [the] action, understandings which [the person] surfaces, criticizes, restructures, and embodies in further action" (p. 50). Reflection-in-action is not necessarily a rapid or continuous process. "It is bounded," wrote Schön, "by the 'action-present,' the zone of time in which action can still make a difference to the situation. The action-present may stretch over minutes, hours, days, or even weeks or months, depending on the pace of activity and the situational boundaries that are characteristic of the practice" (p. 62).

Although these descriptions of reflection-in-action make reference to individuals engaged in practical activities, reflective processes also occur at a broad societal level and within formal organizations, and professional consultants or researchers may become involved. Communicative practice naturally requires ongoing surveillance and interpretation of situations, occasional reflection on purposes and values, practical reasoning about possible courses of action, and so on. Applied communication research potentially brings to this natural reflective process the methodological principles and techniques of formal research along with the conceptual resources of an academic tradition of communication studies. In this sense, applied communication research can be thought of as a process requiring collaboration between academically trained researchers and persons engaged in reflection-in-action in the course of some practical communicative activity.

Communication research that is not applied in this sense might be called pure research. This distinction strikes me as highly problematic in the context of our discipline, however. The notion of pure research evokes a scientific-technological model of theory and practice, a model derived from the physical sciences and their relationship to applied technological fields. Pure research in physics has but one essential purpose: to seek the best possible theoretical explanations of physical phenomena. Since Francis Bacon, we have understood that knowledge is power, that knowing the laws of nature makes it possible to control natural processes, hence that pure science can yield hard, economic payoffs in the long run, as Watson and Crick's discovery of the double helix structure of DNA in the 1950s eventually made possible the flourishing biotechnology industry of today.

This is an interesting case because it illustrates the difficulty of keeping pure research pure in the face of pressing practical needs or the prospect of big, short-term profits. Cries are currently raised against the progressive commercialization of research in molecular biology. Why? Because the research most needed to advance our theoretical understanding of nature is unlikely to yield the biggest economic profits in the short run. Commercialization thus distracts pure science from its central purpose—quite possibly to the detriment of its long-term economic payoff to society. Pure science must be kept pure, on this view. Applied research enters the picture as a distinct, socially important though scientifically lower order enterprise of developing useful, science-based technologies.

The question in a field like human communication studies is not whether it is possible to pursue pure research in this sense—for it is certainly possible—but whether it is worthwhile to do so on a large scale. This is finally a matter of prudential judgment. We cannot know in advance what knowledge might emerge from a pure science of communication. The search for "laws of communication" like those of theoretical physics is now generally dismissed as an absurdly improbable, pseudoscientific fantasy. But still, communication research is supposed to "build theory," and "theory" still means, for most social scientists in the field, scientific explanations that, if only more successful than they currently are, would be functionally similar to those of the "more advanced" sciences. How much we have to show for these efforts to date is open to dispute. Meanwhile, human communication in our present era of social fragmentation and inequity, global interdependence, and exploding information technologies more than ever confronts us as a practical problem of great moral, political, and economic urgency. Where should we direct our efforts? Should we devote much of our resources to pure, scientific research in the faith that the best possible technological applications will emerge in the long run? Or should we focus more centrally and immediately on communication as a practical, human problem?

But is there ultimately any real difference between these two approaches? Didn't Kurt Lewin (1951) tell us that "there is nothing so practical as a good theory?" (p. 169). What could be more practical than research that increases our ability to predict and control communication outcomes? In fact there are other and arguably better ways of being practical, but in order to grasp this possibility it is necessary to adopt a different way of thinking about theory and practice. It is necessary to see beyond the scientific-technological model of theory and practice in which practice is thought of only in terms of the application of science-based technologies to predict and control events.

Instead, we might better think of practice as *praxis:* reflectively informed, prudential human conduct. This model of theory and practice draws upon the ancient, Aristotelian distinction between a scientific discipline (*theoria*) that pursues apodictic theoretical knowledge (*episteme*) for its own sake and a practical discipline (*praxis*) that pursues a more limited kind of theory that, although not worth knowing for its own sake (because of its limited character), is worth pursuing insofar as it can be of some assistance in one's efforts to achieve greater practical wisdom (*phronesis*). Practical knowledge, in what Bernstein (1971) has called "the 'high' sense of practical" (p. x), involves more than just knowledge of techniques for achieving specific results (*techne*). It involves reflection on ends (purpose, value, *telos*) as well as means (technological know-how). It is limited by the irreducibly particular, contingent nature of practical situations. It can, however, be theoretical insofar it incorporates concepts and principles relevant to a broad range of situations.[1] In this alternative model, then, a practical discipline does build theory but of a kind essentially different from scientific theory. Practical theory is adapted to the requirements of practical reflection whereas scientific theory is adapted to the requirements of scientific explanation.[2] Those requirements are not the same.[3]

The distinction between pure and applied research is not very relevant to a practical discipline conceived on this alternative model. All research in a practical discipline is ultimately pursued not for its own sake but for the sake of practice. Strictly speaking, pure research is not typically done. Nevertheless, some research is relatively more applied (oriented to solving immediate practical problems) while other research is relatively more disciplinary (oriented to advancing the discipline itself, though ultimately for the sake of advancing the practice of communication).

It may be helpful to imagine a continuum in terms of Schön's (1983) notion of "action-present," the scope of the "situation" in which action can make a difference. Research in a practical discipline can be characterized generally as an effort to inform processes of reflection-in-action. Disciplinary research is oriented to an action-present that encompasses a broader sociohistorical situation. As compared to applied research, it strives for longer term, more nearly universal, applicability. It addresses problems at a higher level of abstraction, reflecting on purposes, processes, and methods of communication in general. At the other end of the continuum, applied research assists the reflection-in-action of particular persons, groups, and agencies in a shorter term, more closely circumscribed action-present, but in doing so it makes use of (applies) whatever disciplinary resources may be relevant and helpful within the situation.

To further illustrate the continuum, research on the intellectual history of rhetorical theory typically falls near the disciplinary end. It addresses no immediate practical problem although it enriches disciplinary thought on broader questions about the practice of rhetoric in society. Jamieson's study

---

[1]Seibold (chapter 2, this volume) uses the language of *praxis*. It is important to understand that this shift in language involves more than just the substitution of certain fashionable Greek words for "theory" and "practice." It entails a fundamentally different way of thinking about theory and practice.

[2]The distinction necessarily has a different meaning now than it did for Aristotle. Modern science is not Aristotelian science, and key terms such as *episteme* and *telos* must be reinterpreted in light of a long history of subsequent thought. Much work remains to be done in order to elaborate a satisfactory concept of "practical discipline" for present day use.

[3]As Goodall (chapter 3, this volume) notes, people seldom actually use theory for predicting and controlling outcomes in everyday life. Instead, they use theoretical concepts to articulate their own experiences and make them meaningful in broader contexts. For an alternative perspective on "theory," see Craig (1993).

of political campaign discourse (chapter 5, this volume) occupies a middling position in that it addresses an immediate practical problem but on a broad social level, from an independent, academic disciplinary perspective, and in such a way that disciplinary thought is not only applied but markedly advanced. At the applied extreme of the continuum we might find an academically trained rhetorician doing issues research and speech writing for a particular political campaign with an eye to the relevance of disciplinary knowledge. All of these forms of research deserve to be called practical, but some are clearly more applied whereas others are more disciplinary in orientation.

TENSIONS INHERENT IN APPLIED RESEARCH

Applied and disciplinary research differ, then, not dichotomously, but by degrees along a continuum. For applied research to have a role within the communication discipline requires traffic along that continuum. Potentially, it would seem, if we think of ours as a practical discipline, traffic should be heavy in both directions and the role of applied research therefore quite significant. Unlike the scientific-technological model in which information flows one way only, from pure research into applied fields, in a practical discipline theory must be informed by, and relevant to, the requirements of practical reflection. Applied research should thus serve as a vital source of insight into the contingencies of practice. Disciplinary and applied research should be in constant dialogue. Such dialogue, however, is not easily achieved, and is inherently problematic. To understand the role of applied communication research within a practical discipline, we must understand the tensions that make it difficult as well as the potentials that make it possible and worthwhile. Finally, we must understand that those tensions and potentials are really the same; that the tensions that make the role of applied research problematic are in fact the very potentials that make it possible and useful. It is a mistake, therefore, to think that those tensions should somehow be eliminated; instead they should be understood and even cultivated.

What I have in mind are tensions like those described by Conquergood (chapter 4, this volume) in his model of the engaged intellectual whose *praxis* attempts to reconcile opposing tendencies towards rigor and relevance, discipline and solidarity.[4] For Conquergood, "relevance" means sociopolitical struggle as distinct from politically disengaged conceptual analysis and professional practice ("rigor"); and "discipline" means introspective critical reflection as distinct from public action in "solidarity" with a professional or

---

[4]Conquergood and I define the term *praxis* somewhat differently. His use of the term alludes to a Marxist critical tradition, whereas my own alludes to an Aristotelian tradition of practical philosophy.

political group.[5] Even if many applied communication researchers do not wish to see themselves as "engaged intellectuals" in precisely Conquergood's sense, still they must sometimes experience an impulse towards advocacy that they must balance against conflicting commitments towards professionalism and dispassionate inquiry. The desire to do research that addresses specific practical problems or meets the requirements of specific clients must also sometimes conflict with an academic discipline's strong impulse toward intellectual rigor. In an academic discipline, theory spins off into metatheory and intellectual history, scholarship into arcane critiques of texts and interpretations, lines of investigation into tangled arguments about the interpretation of experimental results. Indeed, we know more and more about less and less as disciplinary research becomes progressively involuted, specialized, and remote from everyday practical concerns. The concerns that drive disciplinary research are not irrational or trivial; they typify the reflective questions that would arise in any serious attempt to assess the merits of discursive claims. They do, however, conflict with the defining impulse of applied research, which is to grapple with immediate practical problems and which may necessitate putting aside conceptual and methodological questions that, however important in principle or in the long run, are not immediately pressing.

The tensions of applied and disciplinary research in a practical discipline arise from the awareness that in pursuing one set of priorities a researcher necessarily neglects, to some degree, other, equally important, priorities. Disciplinary research, in pursuing self-reflective problems, diverges from the practical relevance that is the raison d'être of such a discipline; applied research, in pursuing immediate practical problems, diverges from the rigorous self-reflection that warrants the study of communication as a discipline.

Although such tensions were much in evidence at the Tampa conference, they were more frequently denied than deeply explored. A view often expressed was that applied research should be theoretically grounded and should adhere to the highest standards of research methodology. Miller (chapter 3, this volume) goes so far as to deny any real distinction between applied and pure communication research on the grounds that all good communication research addresses socially significant problems and should be

---

[5]Conquergood's distinction between "critical reflection" and "analytical rigor" can be questioned. Critical reflection has its private, introspective moments to be sure, but it arises from and erupts into discourse not only outside but within academic disciplines insofar as their norms legitimize, and their professional practices facilitate, the discussion of normative questions. Although it is true that academic disciplines must stand somewhat apart from political struggle in order to retain their institutional legitimacy, I see no reason why critical reflection in Conquergood's sense cannot be incorporated into the professional practices of an academic discipline as an integral component of the discipline's norms of "rigor." There seems no place for a practical discipline in Conquergood's scheme.

theory-based as well as ecologically valid (see also Miller & Sunnafrank, 1984). It is, of course, possible to do research that addresses disciplinary and applied concerns simultaneously. Jamieson's work on political campaign rhetoric (chapter 5, this volume) is, again, a noteworthy example, as is Miller's own research on the effects of videotaped trial testimony (Miller & Fontes, 1979). Not all studies do or should occupy this middle range of the applied-disciplinary continuum, however. Broader disciplinary as well as more narrowly applied questions remain worthy of investigation. What is necessary—and inherently difficult—is to conduct disciplinary as well as applied research in such a way that the other end of the continuum is not entirely forgotten, so that the vital link between theory and practice that warrants the pursuit of both types of work within a practical discipline is not broken.

The tensions between applied and disciplinary concerns are also denied, in rather different ways, by Argyris (chapter 1, this volume) and Goodall (chapter 3, this volume). In Goodall's postmodernist perspective, all forms of research can peacefully coexist in a pluralistic discipline, so there is no need of tensions. Argyris, on the other hand, mounts a direct assault against disciplinary rigor. Like his colleague Schön (1983, 1987), Argyris (e.g., Argyris, Putnam, & Smith, 1985) has been highly critical of discipline-based, "rigorous research." Academic disciplines can be faulted for their insularity and fragmentation of knowledge and for following self-generated research agendas that diverge from practical concerns. When standard academic research practices are applied in practical situations, according to Argyris, an ethically questionable ("Model I") relationship between researchers and practitioners tends to result. On this view, applied research is more useful as well as ethically better when it takes the form of a collaboration characterized by fully open communication between researcher-consultants and their clients.

The norms of such academic-practitioner collaboration require more careful consideration than is possible within the bounds of this brief chapter. Although the top priority of applied communication research is to address practitioners' problems, such research would seem to be useful in large part because academically trained researchers can offer resources and perspectives that differ in certain ways from those of practitioners. It is because the applied researcher is steeped in a tradition of disciplinary thought that she or he can bring to a practical situation a critical difference in perspective that can render collaboration with practitioners potentially informative to both sides. This principle applies to human communication in general: The differences among people that make communication difficult are precisely those that make the process necessary and potentially fruitful. I believe we should acknowledge essential tensions between disciplinary rigor and practical relevance that Schön and Argyris as well as Miller and others fail to appreciate adequately. Rather than deny or attempt to suppress those tensions, we should acknowledge them and learn to exploit the creative potentials that they generate.

Creative potentials are generated by a sort of disciplinary "superego" that reminds us of neglected priorities. Disciplinary research, in its pursuit of intellectual rigor, must worry lest it drift too far from practice, must justify itself by establishing its relevance, however indirect, to the problems and requirements of application. Applied research, in its pursuit of usefulness, must worry lest it become entirely routine and thus lose its critical edge, must justify itself by establishing its accessibility to disciplinary thought as a source of depth, rigor, and novelty of insight. Hence, disciplinary and applied researchers in a practical discipline need each other in order to justify their work, a need that if openly acknowledged impels them toward intradisciplinary dialogue. If the Tampa conference did not spawn a new movement in the field, we may yet come to see it as a turning point in that dialogue.

REFERENCES

Argyris, C., Putnam, R., & Smith, D. M. (1985). *Action science: Concepts, methods and skills for research and intervention.* San Francisco: Jossey-Bass.

Bernstein, R. J. (1971). *Praxis and action: Contemporary philosophies of human activity.* Philadelphia: University of Pennsylvania Press.

Craig, R. T. (1993, Summer). Why are there so many communication theories? *Journal of Communication, 43*(3), 34–41.

Dewey, J. (1989). *How we think* (rev. ed.). In J. A. Boydston (Ed.), *John Dewey; The later works, 1925–1953: Vol. 8. 1933* (pp. 105–352). Carbondale: Southern Illinois University Press. (Original work published 1933)

Lewin, K. (1951). *Field theory in social science: Selected theoretical papers* (D. Cartwright, Ed.). New York: Harper & Row.

Miller, G. R., & Fontes, N. E. (1979). *Videotape on trial: A view from the jury box.* Newbury Park, CA: Sage.

Miller, G. R., & Sunnafrank, M. J. (1984). Theoretical dimensions of applied communication research. *Quarterly Journal of Speech, 70,* 255–263.

Schön, D. A. (1983). *The reflective practitioner: How professionals think in action.* New York: Basic Books.

Schön, D. A. (1987). *Educating the reflective practitioner.* San Francisco: Jossey-Bass.

Simons, H. W. (1985). Chronicle and critique of a conference. *Quarterly Journal of Speech, 71,* 52–64.

7

Theorizing Practice, Practicing Theory

Julia T. Wood
The University of North Carolina at Chapel Hill

Pursuing a goal more modest than Goodall's deconstruction of Kansas or Jamieson's reformation of political communication, I engage issues raised by other conferees as entry points to my argument that applied communication research is practicing theory and theorizing practice. I am not contending merely that a dynamic dialectic of theory and practice should characterize applied scholarship, but that it necessarily does. Theorizing depends on practice to provide its subject matter and verify its claims. In addition, theorizing is in itself a practice consisting of activities that sustain academic ideologies, for example, theory is privileged by the very act of discursively distinguishing it from practice even, ironically, as practice informs theorizing. At the same time, concrete experience enacts and speaks back to implicit theoretical stances, which infuse material life and scholars' efforts to interpret its rhythms.

Germane to my discussion of intersections between theory and practice are questions regarding the interests served when research and its outcomes directly affect people's lives: What impacts, intended or not, does applied communication research have? Without proposing specific criteria to evaluate impact, I identify heuristics that might direct reflection about commitment to particular audiences, goals, and interests. Along the way, I insert a few caveats about applied researchers' increasing interest in altering savage oppressions that infect social life.

THEORY AND PRACTICE

Whereas most conferees contend theory and practice are mutually enhancing and both enrich applied scholarship, some stake out less moderate stances perched on contestable conceptions of theory and/or practice. At one extreme, Miller reprises the traditional refrain that theory is the primary goal of scholarship. Aided and abetted by Tompkins and others, Miller seems to sanction practical research so long as it is theoretically grounded and pays homage to conventional shibboleths such as generalizability and objectivity.

Anchoring the other side of this debate are renegade scholars who counsel against continued allegiance to the goals, methods, and evaluative criteria of science-as-usual. Goodall, for instance, makes a cartographic excursion that transforms the U.S. map along with principles of scholarship. Meanwhile, Conquergood names engagement and passion as benchmarks of exemplary applied research, and Argyris enjoins us to accent usability in evaluating the results of inquiry. Within this debate, theorizing and practice are depicted as distinct. Resisting this discursive framework, I aim to recast the conversation by refusing to grant the separation or separability of practice and theory.

Historically, of course, communication is an applied field in which theories arise out of discursive activities. Aristotle, Plato, and Socrates all taught rhetoric as a practical art—a way to influence the *polis*. The theoretical principles they developed grew directly out of close inspection of actual communication practices. Roughly 2,000 years later when the modern discipline of Speech Communication was born, members chose to designate themselves the National Association of Academic Teachers of Public Speaking, thereby affirming pragmatic skills as the heart of the field. Commitment to practice subsided during the middle part of this century as faculty sought to prove they could do "real research" guided by the positivist model rooted in philosophies of Bacon, among others, and epitomized by the natural sciences, which enjoyed a premiere position in mid-century universities. Research was the search for capital-T Truth in the form of universal laws discovered via value-free inquiry in which knower and known are presumed independent, objectivity is paramount, and explanation, prediction, and control are guiding goals. This view of scholarship assumes the separation of theory and practice and elevates the former while disparaging the latter and its offspring, applied research.

Of late, however, the sanctity of capital-T Truth has fallen on hard times. In a postmodern era, we find ourselves enmeshed in myriad contexts, engaged with diverse people, and surrounded by multiple, sometimes contradictory horizons. As our increasing and increasingly disparate involvements divulge multiple knowledges that make sense in specific contexts, we are led, however unwillingly, to surrender faith in a single Truth. Addressing this earlier, Browning and Hawes (1991) noted that the grand narrative is dead and, with it, laws, master theories, and the like. As belief in universal, transhistorical Truth erodes, the academy confronts a fundamental crisis (Gergen, 1991). If we are not discoverers of Truth, who are we? If we do not profess discovered Truth to students, what is the purpose of teaching? If what we know is not broadly generalizable, is it knowledge?

In other quarters of academe, celebration greets the demise of Truth and its disciple, generalizability. Scholars who find postmodernity refreshing often regard the debilitation of universals as an invitation to notice and affirm multiplicity. All is a matter of perspective: What is true from one standpoint is blatantly false from an alternative one, and no position enjoys unequivocal privilege. If all experience is materially and epistemologically situated, then concrete activities in particular settings emerge as a legitimate focus of research.[1] Many scholars embracing this tradition nurse a thorough distrust of theory. As Pollock and Cox (1991) wryly remarked, " 'theory' has become a dirty word . . . arcane, elitist, even corrupt" (p. 170). Because theory is often inaccessible to all but the chosen few, and because it may be accused of distorting actual experience, some practitioners believe it has little place, function, or value in efforts to understand human activities and may even contaminate the intrinsic integrity of subjective experience.

At this crossroads in intellectual life modernity and postmodernity eye each other in uneasy, frequently strained encounters. Proponents of the two world views scramble to establish which is better and, thus, which has authentic claim to real scholarship. It would no doubt cause Burke to chuckle smugly to see that we seem goaded by the hierarchy in scholarship, and even more so by the quest to establish our positions toward the top of whatever hierarchy is certified. This hegemonous impulse is embodied in debates between researchers who proclaim situated engagement the raison d'être of scholarship and modernists who grumble such work is "an intellectual whorehouse" (Ellis, 1982). Because divisive discourse incites efforts to defend the primacy of either theory or practice, it stifles appreciation of how the two activities impregnate, invigorate, and re-form one another.

Like most polarities, the schism between application and theory withers upon close inspection. Kurt Lewin (1951), a premiere theorist of his day, insisted "there is nothing so practical as good theory" (p. 169). The converse is also true: There is nothing so theoretical as good practice. Literary critic Robert Scholes (1989) eloquently described the dialectic between theory and practice. "It is true," he wrote, "that there is no place outside of prac-

---

[1]I do not imply all postmodern academics would define themselves or be defined by others as applied researchers. Postmodernism and its relative, poststructuralism, in fact, have thus far prospered primarily at theoretical levels while pragmatic applications and implications of postmodernity have been less articulated. (For an exception, see Gergen, 1991, which probes personal and social implications of postmodern life.)

tice where theory might stand. . . . But there is no place outside of theory
for practice to stand, either. Theory is not the superego of practice but its
self-consciousness" (p. 88). As the self-consciousness of practice, theory is
immanent in material activities and acts to expose less than conscious, less
than obvious patterns in experience by offering conceptual accounts of how
overall social systems shape social life and individual consciousness. As Bannerji (1992) noted, "the social and historical always exist *as* and *in* 'concrete'
forms of social being and knowing" (p. 94). Studying situated, pragmatic
communication, then, is a primary portal to insightful theorizing.

Theorizing Practice

Practices are theoretical, inescapably, inevitably, necessarily. The most basic
kind of practice—everyday activity—resonates at every juncture with explanatory and conceptual overtones. Practices of applied communication research are theoretical in two senses: First, the activities applied researchers
study as well as the process of inquiry itself are informed by theory; second,
practical activities reverberate back into theory, informing and reforming it
continuously.

Theoretical positions inhabit the process of all practices, because who we
believe ourselves to be and what we imagine we are doing are framed by interpretive patterns authorized by larger contexts in which we and our activities are embedded. Engraved in practice are tacit theories that direct us and
those we study to see some phenomena but not others, to regard some perspectives, relationships, positions, and codes of conduct, thought, and feeling as normal and others as aberrant, and to take for granted certain arbitrary but normalized values, assumptions, and beliefs on which collective life
depends (Wood, 1994b).

Theories inflect not only social actors' everyday conduct, but also the performances of researchers. As scholars go about their business, they decide
what to study, what counts as significant data, and how and for whom to interpret findings. Each of these decisions is theoretical in the sense that it is
guided by understanding how things work, including especially the grounds,
assumptions, and conditions that authorize knowledge. No less than a Nepal-
ese woman who automatically balances a 50-pound basket off center on her
head to distribute weight evenly, applied communication researchers make
choices based on usually less than conscious beliefs about what leads to understanding or knowledge. I am not arguing that theory could or should
guide applied work, but that it inevitably, unvaryingly does. Echoing this is
Hennessy's (1993) observation that "theory is inescapable in the sense that
every discourse assumes a frame of intelligibility which contributes to the
construction of what counts as 'the way things are.' It is in this productive

sense that theories matter" (p. 36). Applied researchers value particular perspectives, methods, interpretive frameworks, subjects, and forms of presentation, all of which reflect unvoiced and typically unquestioned theories of how knowledge is generated and shared.

A second way in which theory is implicated in practical research is that material life both informs and is informed by explanatory schema. In elucidating conditions that structure experience, theories enrich both understanding and effective intervention. Applied researchers' growing interest in addressing oppression illustrates how research focused on concrete, embodied experience depends on and nourishes theory. Efforts to understand and alter the lived realities of oppressions require more than respecting difference or giving voice to those heretofore silenced. Theory is necessary quite simply because sources of oppression often are not transparent, relationships between marginality and cultural ideology not obvious, and reasons for silence neither self-evident nor likely to disappear solely because someone is now willing to listen.

Addressing aching inequities requires discovering how sense-making systems authorized by discourses at local and cultural levels create and sustain hierarchical social arrangements and constitute subject(ivitie)s (Geertz, 1973; March, 1991; Smith, 1987). Discussing theory as cultural narrative, Hennessy (1993) suggested "theories themselves can be considered to be the effects of struggles over what meanings are allowable and endorsed at any given time" (p. 7). Informed efforts to uncover and contest tyrannical ideologies, structures, and practices rely on sophisticated, careful theoretical work, such as that begun by a handful of scholars (Althusser, 1970; Gramsci, 1971; Hennessy, 1993).

To study oppressive practices and liberatory alternatives is to theorize them. Research focused on particularistic interactions in specific settings often begets insight into relationships between activities in local sites and broader ideologies that reflect and uphold systems of uneven social relations. Consider, for instance, the genesis of much feminist theorizing: Attention to what at first seemed personal discontent of individual women unveiled dominant social ideologies that produce and reproduce "woman's place in man's world" and, with it, dissatisfactions that proved to be political, which is to say, generalizable. Intense focus on individuals' lived experiences forged new theories of cultural life and the gender ideologies inscribed within it. To recognize the reliance of practice on theory and the debt of theory to practice is not to dilute respect for experience. Rather, it reminds us that theories have palpable power to illuminate and change concrete life, and experience may re-form theoretical understandings of how things work.[2]

---

[2]What I have said here only hints at relationships between concrete experience and larger systems in which it is embedded. A fuller discussion of this nexus and how tension between experience and theory may inform research is in Wood and Cox (1993).

Practicing Theory

Theory is practice or, if you prefer, *theoria* is *praxis*. Whatever else it may be, theory is an activity with rules that define what one does, why and how one does it, what it means, and how it is to be interpreted and evaluated. Highlighting theory's potential to reflexively comment on its own operation, Hennessy (1993) defined theory as "a critical practice" (p. 8) borne of discourses in circulation at a given moment in a culture's life. Within academe, discourses authorize forms of thinking, writing, and inquiry to count as producing knowledge. Yet McKenna (1992), among others, argued that the practice of academic theorizing more often regulates than produces knowledge by excluding anything that does not follow conventional academic doctrines. For instance, prevailing ideology values publication and incestuous conversations among academics more than using knowledge to improve concrete communication (listed as "community service" on vita) or writing in styles and forums accessible to laypersons (McKenna, 1992; Wood & Cox, 1993).

Understanding theory as itself a practice suggests it is essential to understand how we and our work are situated within particular discursive fields that promote certain practices and devalue others. The identity of applied scholarship is constrained by institutional structures and practices that legitimize and reproduce particular understandings of the academic enterprise (Browning & Hawes, 1991; Ehrenhaus, 1991). This directs us to identify and critique practices that produce and reproduce understandings of academic life (Ehrenhaus, 1991). If the next generation of theory is not unquestioningly to reinscribe currently privileged paradigms, we must theorize critically our own practices to consider whether they merit continued adherence. If not, then the task is to rewrite the practice of theorizing by inserting alternatives into discourses that construct and justify academic ideologies (Hennessy, 1993).

THE INTERESTS OF
APPLIED COMMUNICATION RESEARCH

Related to affiliations between practice and theory is an issue ascendant in an era when diverse interests competing in a stratified social order assume unprecedented salience: What and whose interests are to be served by applied communication scholarship? Diverse answers have been offered by conferees. Professor Miller holds that building theory is the titular objective of research, Conquergood prioritizes fomenting positive social change, Argyris favors empowerment, Jamieson rehabilitation of political communication, and so on. Evaluative standards accompanying these goals, while more implicit, similarly traverse a range. Whereas Miller champions generalizability,

Argyris prescribes usability, Conquergood argues for impassioned engage-ment with lived experience, and Goodall prefers to turn his rollicking ad-ventures into stories people enjoy reading.

More urgent than consensus on interests and evaluative criteria for ap-plied communication research is attention to the issues themselves. Although I resist any mandate for applied researchers as an intellectual community, as individual scholars we might reflect on who is served and who might be af-fected (exploited, mystified, empowered, changed) by particular research projects. Of the number of questions suggested by conferees to launch in-trospection, I note only four, one of which I elaborate:

1. Do we define our work as opportunistic and reactive, which would in-cline us to respond to events of the times as, for instance, Seibold implies and McCain and Jamieson exemplify in their research on current topics?

2. Do we rely on a Kantian criterion, invoking the greatest good for the greatest number or a variation, the greater the generalizability the better the research, as Miller urges?

3. Is usability an important criterion for assessing applied communication research? Argyris's insightful distinction between applicable (relevant to practice) and usable (potential to implement applicable knowledge) findings has been largely inanimate to date. To illustrate, Jamieson's study of politi-cal news ads is clearly applicable since it addresses goings-on in the real world and argues that news-ads affect voters. Yet, the usability of her work hinges on whether those who could implement her advisories have (a) access to her work, (b) requisite skills to enact advice, and (c) motivational disposition (what Argyris calls "theories in use") to do so. My hunch is that her work is more applicable than usable. Is that a problem? Should this affect judgments of the merit of her research?

4. The fourth issue, which I will discuss in greater detail, concerns using research to empower others. If this is an appropriate goal, is it somehow more legitimate if those others are members of some designated oppressed group?[3] If so, do we assume the prerogative to speak for others, defining what they need, how they are oppressed, and even what counts as oppression and empowerment? How might we justify presuming a right to speak for others? Is doing so ever inconsistent with the professed valuing of historically si-lenced voices (Alcoff, 1991; Borland, 1991)?

I confess to being somewhat troubled by an inclination to assume that in-volvement with social problems and marginalized people presumptively in-vests work and those who do it with integrity. Clearly, the commitment of

---

[3]No less than other ideas, "oppression" and "oppressed groups" are social-symbolic con-structions. It is curious that women, lesbians and gays, people of color, and those of low so-cioeconomic status have been declared oppressed, whereas routinely abused people have not be systematically labeled as such (e.g., retarded and elderly citizens).

many contemporary scholars to multicultural study and social justice can be liberatory and socially reformative, and I count myself among those engaged in this pursuit.[4] It is naive, however, to suppose empowerment arises naturally out of well-intentioned celebrations of difference/differance. Lest we presume that commitment to social reform and good intentions exonerate us from harming and misrepresenting, we should be mindful of what paves the proverbial road to hell.

Profound and enduring change in hegemony requires critical perspectives on the means and motives that reproduce differences (Hennessy, 1993). Addressing the need to go beyond honoring diversity, Bannerji (1992) insisted that "beginning and ending with difference . . . merely hinders us from facing/uttering the fact that a whole social organization is needed to create each unique experience" (p. 85). More than learning to recognize and appreciate diversity, critical postures toward difference take on moral and political force, impelling those who hold them to confront their own complicity in structures and practices that create and sustain difference and its derivative, inequality. I now circle back to a point upon which I touched earlier.

CRITICALLY THEORIZING OUR OWN PRACTICES

As part of the effort to direct applied communication research in the coming years it may be valuable to ferret out and inspect taken for granted values and beliefs that define "how we do things" in academe, what Gramsci (1971) called cultural common sense. For starters, we might ask questions such as these: Why is it that we study certain people and topics? Why is publication, particularly by university presses and peer-refereed national journals, the ultimate certification of scholarly merit? Why are rules concerning manuscript length and style as they are? Why do .05 and .01 define significance? Why are findings of difference regarded as more important than ones of no difference? Why is credibility with academic peers too often inversely related to accessibility? Naming and questioning received truths of academic traditions enable us to appraise and, if appropriate, re-form who we are and what we do.

Those who study historically marginalized groups and issues might extend their scrutiny to the means by which prevailing ideologies have consistently

---

[4]I am not indicting the desire to empower historically oppressed individuals or groups, nor am I suggesting that existing scholarship is disrespectful of the subjective experience of those who have been and are marginalized. My own work (Wood, 1992, 1993, 1994a, 1994b; Wood & Cox, 1993; Wood & Inman, 1993) has consistently focused on practices and situations in which oppression operates. I am, however, suggesting that I and others committed to social change ought be aware of how our motives and experience as well as our situatedness within academe shape our work.

marginalized certain topics, goals, and methods within the ivory tower. At a minimum, this requires identifying practices that define and reproduce scholarship as usual. For instance, perusal of published works reveals that research traditions of the social sciences enjoy a dominant position. Marginalized intellectual practices associated with hermeneutics, folklore and oral tradition, interpretive scholarship, and critical perspectives have much to learn from and offer to the theory and practice of applied communication.

Consider an example: West (1993) thoughtfully pointed out implicit barriers to ethnomethodolgical work when he notes that not only must ethnomethodologists devote space in every manuscript to explaining and defending their theory and methods, but also that journals' standard page limitation accommodates quantitative studies and mitigates against interpretive work which requires more space to present analyses and findings. A second example: Many consider performance different than and apart from knowledge and research. Yet I recently visited a colleague's class and witnessed performance leading students to new understandings of their subjects of study. Something happened in the doing. It is a kind of learning not routinely realized by privileged teaching methods such as lecture and discussion and not fully understandable within explanatory systems of social science. Applied communication would benefit from the contributions of performance scholars who can theorize the practice of performance to help us understand its epistemological capacities. In sum, we need to probe how taken-for-granted academic practices define and reproduce intellectual hegemony.

Whether contesting sociopolitical oppression in the streets or taken-for-granted hierarchies that govern academic routines, applied communication scholars might bear in mind that passion alone is no guarantee of positive results, nor does the intent to empower oppressed peoples necessarily cohabit with genuine understanding of and respect for others and their interpretations of their lives. Such passion and intents are most effective when they are infused by theoretical understandings. Thus, theorizing everyday life, including our own academic practices, is integral to efforts to understand and improve communication both within and beyond the ivory tower.

CONCLUDING COMMENT

In this chapter I argue that in applied communication research, as in other forms of scholarship, practices are theoretical and theory is practical. Whenever applied communication scholars study concrete experiences, they do so from implicit theoretical frameworks; in turn, their findings reverberate consequentially back into those frameworks. At the same time, theory is itself a practice in which normalized understandings regulate conduct to maintain particular views of what theory and applied research are, what they accomplish, and where each ranks in the academic hierarchy. The essence of my argument is twofold: Theories arise from and are informed by study of practical activities; and practices are guided, understood, and altered by theoretical understandings.

At this juncture in our history, applied communication scholars might profit from directed self-reflexivity. Understanding our own situatedness and how it shapes our work begins with questioning the sedimented separation between theory and practice and, relatedly, what we have defined as scholarship and what and whom we have left out. We can only enrich our work by rethinking the views of center and margins we have normalized and how our own practices ratify, reproduce, and, if we choose, may refashion these placements.

ACKNOWLEDGMENTS

I gratefully acknowledge Bill Eadie and Ted Zorn for their insightful readings and comments on an earlier draft of this chapter.

REFERENCES

Alcoff, L. (1991). The problem of speaking for others. *Cultural Critique*, Winter, 5–32.

Althusser, L. (1970). *Reading capital*. (B. Brewster, Trans.). London: NLB.

Bannerji, H. (1992). But who speaks for us? Experience and agency in conventional feminist paradigms. In H. Bannerji, L. Carty, K. Dehlik, S. Heald, & K. McKenna (Eds.), *Unsettling relations* (pp. 67–108). Boston: South End Press.

Borland, K. (1991). "That's not what I said": Interpretive conflict in oral narrative research. In S. B. Gluck & D. Patai (Eds.), *Women's words* (pp. 63–75). New York: Routledge.

Browning, L. D., & Hawes, L. C. (1991). Style, process, surface, context: Consulting as postmodern art. *Journal of Applied Communication Research, 19*, 32–54.

Ellis, D. G. (1982, March). The shame of speech communication. *Spectra, 18*, 1–2.

Ehrenhaus, P. (1991). Co-opting the academy: On the urgency of reframing "applied". *Journal of Applied Communication Research, 19*, 123–128.

Geertz, C. (1973). *The interpretation of cultures*. New York: Basic.

Gergen, K. (1991). *The saturated self: Dilemmas of identity in contemporary life*. New York: Basic.

Gramsci, A. (1971). *Selections from the prison notebooks*. (Q. Hoare & G. N. Smith, Trans.). Newark, NJ: International.

Hennessy, R. (1993). *Materialist feminism and the politics of discourse*. New York: Routledge.

Lewin, K. (1951). *Field theory in social science: Selected theoretical papers* (D. Cartwright, Ed.). New York: Harper & Row.

March, J. G. (1991). Organizational consultants and organizational research. *Journal of Applied Communication Research, 19*, 20–32.

McKenna, K. (1992). Subjects of discourse: Learning the language that counts. In H. Bannerji, L. Carty, K. Dehlik, S. Heald, & K. McKenna (Eds), *Unsettling relations* (pp. 109–128). Boston: South End Press.

Pollock, D., & Cox, J. R. (1991). Historicizing 'reason': Critical theory, practice, and postmodernity. *Communication Monographs, 58,* 170–178.

Scholes, R. E. (1989). *Protocols of reading.* New Haven: Yale University Press.

Smith, D. (1987). *The everyday world as problematic: A feminist sociology.* Boston: Northeastern University Press.

West, J. (1993). Ethnography and ideology: The politics of cultural representation. *Western Journal of Communication, 57,* 209–220.

Wood, J. T. (1992). Telling our stories: Narratives as a basis for theorizing sexual harassment. *Journal of Applied Communication Research, 20,* 349–363.

Wood, J. T. (1993). *Who cares: Women, care and culture.* Carbondale: Southern Illinois University Press.

Wood, J. T. (1994a). *Gendered lives: Communication, gender and culture.* Belmont, CA: Wadsworth.

Wood, J. T. (1994b). Saying it makes it so: The discursive construction of sexual harassment. In S. Bingham (Ed.), *Discursive conceptions of sexual harassment.* New York: Praeger.

Wood, J. T., & Cox, R. (1993). Rethinking critical voice: Materiality and situated knowledges. *Western Journal of Communication, 57,* 278–287.

Wood, J. T., & Inman, C. C. (1993). In a different mode: Masculine styles of communicating closeness. *Journal of Applied Communication Research, 21,* 279–295.

8

Making a Difference:
The Status and Challenges of Applied
Communication Research

William F. Eadie
Speech Communication Association

I enjoyed being at the Tampa Conference; the papers reflected the diversity of opinion about the nature of the term *applied* and the proposed agenda for applied communication research, both within the field and in "making a difference in the real world." It was perhaps most fun to participate in a small group where Chris Argyris, Kathleen Hall Jamieson, and Robert Norton went at it, while the rest of us (and "the rest of us" were no slouches as scholars) could do little more than sit and listen. As the vitality of this volume testifies, applied communication research is a "hot" topic. Perhaps because it is a focus of intense interest and heated opinion, it arouses strong arguments and equally strong disagreements, many of which are apparent in the chapters comprising this volume. My chapter takes a somewhat different perspective, that of one who is differently involved from the other authors.

I attended the conference as the first editor of the *Journal of Applied Communication Research* (*JACR*) since the Speech Communication Association (SCA) had purchased it and brought it from semiannual to quarterly publication. As I saw it, I was there both to gain ideas about the direction in which the journal should travel and to report to the conferees on the journal's progress (the first issue under my editorship appeared 3 months after the conference concluded). As I write these words, I have just put my final issue of *JACR* into press, so I am in a position to take a retrospective look at what has gone on since the conference. I intend to do so here first by analyzing the trends I see as having emerged from the first three volumes of *JACR* as a journal published by our largest professional association and then by offering some commentary about how we as a field can work to engage in scholarship that more clearly delineates a distinctive purview for applied communication research, one that privileges making a real difference in the real world.

WHERE DO WE STAND? AN ANALYSIS OF *JACR*

One measure of the status of applied communication research is gained by examining the last several volumes of *JACR*, the outlet devoted to publishing this sort of work. Although there may be problems relying on the validity of such a measure (e.g., the journal just became a quarterly 3 years ago, its status as a publication of the SCA is also that recent, and I have served as editor for that period of time), it is still an indicator of the kinds of research that a group of the field's professionals considered worthy of publication.

Looking at this 3-year corpus, I see three major themes emerge. First, as a field we have difficulty addressing social concerns. Second, a debate is emerging over the degree to which communication skills training is helpful. Finally, a good deal of our work is focused on internal communicative processes within individuals and organizations, and it is the exception to read in our journals explicit consideration of the social implications of the work we do. I will elaborate on each of these themes.

Difficulty Addressing Social Concerns

When I was first appointed editor, Robert Avery, the chair of the SCA Publications Board and the founding editor of *Critical Studies in Mass Communication,* approached me much like the man who approached Dustin Hoffman at the party in *The Graduate.* He didn't, however, have "just one word" for me, he had two—"social issues." Bob fervently believed that *JACR* would make its greatest difference if it could publish research that would address social concerns by investigating their origins and the processes that sustain them and by attempting to resolve the issues through communicative means.

Even a cursory look at the topics covered by research reports published in *JACR* between 1991 and 1993, however, indicates that most of the social problems being addressed would not be rated as major ones. The largest number of articles dealt with factors affecting the development of individual communication skills and/or increased communication effectiveness (Ayres et al., 1993; Ayres & Hopf, 1991; Bruschke & Gartner, 1991; Hopf & Ayres, 1992; Kalbfleisch, 1992; Palmerton, 1992; Petronio & Bradford, 1993; Plax, Beatty, & Feingold, 1991; Powell, 1992; Richmond & Roach, 1992; Seibold, Kudsi, & Rude, 1993). There was also some tendency to address various problems resulting from cultural differences (Banks & Banks, 1991; Bantz, 1993; Brown, 1992; Hammer & Martin, 1992), or gender differences (Bingham, 1991; Gayle, 1991; Wood & Inman, 1993). Although these problems clearly interest communication researchers, they would not rank high on the average person's list of contemporary social problems.

The studies that addressed specific societal problems were fewer and farther between. Four studies reported on attempts to prevent drug use, alcohol consumption, or HIV infection among adolescents. Two of these reports (Alberts, Miller-Rassulo, & Hecht, 1991; Krizek, Hecht, & Miller, 1993) came from the same large-scale study funded by the National Institute on Drug Abuse and focused on how adolescents talked about drug use. The 1991 study inferred adolescents' strategies for resisting drug offers from interview data, whereas the 1993 study correlated language use in those same interviews with degree of risk the subjects had for drug use. The alcohol study (Snyder & Blood, 1992) found results parallel to those of Feingold and Knapp (1977): The use of warnings in alcohol commercials had a boomerang effect of actually making consumption *more* attractive to adolescent viewers. The HIV education study (Brown, 1992) showed how different strategies were needed to reach Asian-American college students effectively than to reach students of other ethnicities.

Three studies dealt with some aspect of the environment (Cantrill, 1993; Krendl, Olson, & Burke, 1992; Renz, 1992). Of these, however, only Krendl et al. (1992) reported results of a specific intervention that had consequences for the environment. Cantrill (1993) reviewed the literature on environmental advocacy and found that most of that substantial body of work originated outside the field of communication. Renz (1992) studied a city council's decision-making process regarding an environmental issue, and the study's focus was more on decision-making than on the environmental issue involved.

Individual studies reported on attempts to change physicians' attitudes toward working with HIV patients (Vanderford, Smith, & Harris, 1992), how employees deal with invasions of their privacy in the workplace (Le Poire, Burgoon, & Parrott, 1992), the relative compliance of children's advertisers with voluntary guidelines regarding advertising content (Kunkel & Gantz, 1993), how family interaction affects adjustment of cancer patients (Gotcher, 1993), how chronically ill individuals believe that they are perceived by the world at large (Hayden, 1993), and communication predictors of nurse burnout (Ellis & Miller, 1993). Of these five studies, three could be considered health related and social issues to the extent that many in society are concerned about health care.

Perhaps the most studied single social issue, however, was sexual harassment. Such was the case primarily because, under the guest editorship of Julia Wood, most of one issue was devoted to the topic. But sexual harassment is also a natural for our field's researchers, because it is itself, among other things, a communication phenomenon. One of the early pieces accepted by the board was Bingham's (1991) analysis of strategies for dealing with sexual harassment, and Le Poire, Burgoon, and Parrott's (1992) study on privacy had sexual harassment as a subtext. But, *JACR*'s special section on sexual harassment, with a set of stories recounting the sexual harassment experiences of communication professionals, Wood's (1992) essay setting them into a communication context, and Strine's (1992) and Taylor and Conrad's (1992) pieces providing insightful analysis, was the high point of the 1991–1993 term.

Analysis of even the best of these studies on social issues reveals a certain amount of uncertainty regarding methodology and desired outcomes. The two adolescent drug use studies, for example (Alberts et al., 1991; Krizek et al., 1993), came from interviews with a modest sample of adolescents from one area of the United States. Although the grounded theory approach seemed appropriate, because of lack of theoretical development, and especially because communication patterns seemed to vary as the subjects moved from describing one relationship to describing another, these findings need to be replicated with larger, more diverse samples in order to assure their accuracy.

On the other hand, Snyder and Blood's (1992) study used an experimental methodology and tested hypotheses carefully derived from previous research results. Their finding of a boomerang effect when alcohol advertising contained a government mandated warning label, has limited potential for use by policy makers, however, because in the tightly controlled atmosphere of the laboratory subjects may have paid more careful attention to the advertising than under more routine conditions.

The classic methodological solution to problems of too little theory on one hand and too much control on the other has been the field experiment. Krendl et al. (1992) was *JACR*'s only example of this genre during the 1991–1993 period. Studying ways to increase recycling behavior in a small city in the midwestern United States, the authors relied on the message and channel effects literature, which predicted differences in behavior change based on type of argument contained in the message and the channel that was used to carry it. Results indicated that all of the argument/channel combinations tested raised recycling participation levels above the 33% target level (and significantly better than participation of controls) but that none of the argument/channel combinations were superior to the others. The authors attributed their failure to support the theoretical predictions to the fact that recycling was a high-interest topic to the city's residents and therefore all messages on that topic were influential.

This study raises an important distinction between applied research and theory-testing research. When one is doing applied research for a specific client, achieving the client's goals are an important part of the project. When one is doing theory-testing research, the major goal is to find the best set of conditions for testing the theory. These competing motivations are many times incompatible. Communication researchers have been trained to value the latter approach, so doing applied research often does not come naturally to them. For that matter, reviewing applied research reports does not come naturally to journal reviewers; perhaps we need more substantive agreement on what constitutes "good" applied communication research.

The most important insight to be gained from this analysis comes from what is not present in the 1991–1993 volumes of *JACR*. There are no articles on ways of increasing public safety (though, more than one article on hostage negotiating was submitted), no articles on helping individuals cope with pressures brought upon by recessionary times (such as job searches or coping with creditors or families when money is tight), no articles on alleviating homelessness or helping people deal with the homeless individuals they encounter in their daily lives (though one article on homelessness was submitted), and only one piece, a commentary, on domestic violence (Whitchurch & Pace, 1993). All of these would surely be social issues of some long-term standing with the public in this country, but if communication researchers are addressing these issues they are not submitting their research reports to *JACR*.

In summary, we seem to have difficulty with researching social issues because we have not seen the communication aspects to some of our most pressing social problems, with the exception of sexual harassment, which can be cast easily as a communication problem. It seems that we often find ourselves with either a lack of relevant theory to guide our research or with theory that, to be tested fairly, might keep us from producing results that could be immediately useful. Moreover, perhaps our traditional taxonomy of subfields (interpersonal, group, public, organizational, mass) pulls us away from social issues and allows us to concentrate on internal processes more than we should.

Debate Over Skills Training

Although *JACR* has not been the sole forum for the debate on the effectiveness of training in communication skills (cf. Ford & Wolvin, 1993; Hart, 1993; Sprague, 1993), the issues surrounding the controversy over the effectiveness of communication skills training has been raised in three *JACR* commentaries. Palmerton (1992) argued that the traditional focus on developing skill in public speaking courses actually might do disservice to developing students' thinking processes. In a companion piece, Powell (1992) argued similarly that critical thinking, as contemporary researchers have come to understand it, may not be taught with the kind of effectiveness necessary for today's students merely by placing them in traditional argument and debate courses. On another front, Whitchurch and Pace (1993) challenged the assumption of several communication researchers that between-spouse violence could be alleviated via communication skills training.

And yet, *JACR* has published ample evidence that specific training for specific purposes can be effective. In an extremely careful study, Seibold, Kudsi, and Rude (1993) found that a public speaking training program was effective in both the short and long terms in making observable changes in specifically targeted behaviors. Vanderford, Smith, and Harris (1992) showed how a carefully constructed series of ethical interventions could change both the attitudes expressed by physicians toward HIV patients in their care and the ways in which those patients perceived the quality of care being provided them. And Plax, Beatty, and Feingold (1991) determined that both business students (who, in general, had only been the object of appraisals in their organizational affiliations) and senior executives (who were very experienced in conducting such appraisals) used the same thought processes in making decisions about how to communicate their appraisals, a finding that has implications for training strategies for handling one of the most difficult communication situations faced in the work environment.

Although the challenges to our traditional mantra that "better communication will fix it" may be warranted, we should remember that even the most ardent critic did not propose that skills training be done away with, just that the assumptions about what is going on in such training and what its goals are should be thought through better. The studies supporting positive impacts of skills training were careful not to overgeneralize their findings nor overstate the applicability of their training methods. What this debate probably illustrates best is that we have to get around the "communication is good; good communication is even better" mentality and define our terms and expectations precisely in order to achieve results that can be applied effectively.

Focus on Internal Communicative Processes

The third group of studies published in *JACR* during 1991–1993 focused on factors influencing message construction and message perception and how those factors influenced and were influenced by the environments in which they occurred. These studies often came in the form of case studies or multiple case studies and were often qualitative, rather than quantitative, in methodology.

Examples of these types of studies are scattered throughout the three volumes examined. Short analyses of several of these studies follow.

Banks and Banks (1991) recorded a hotel manager speaking in English to a group of employees about a new frequent guest awards program. Because most of the employees spoke Spanish as their first language, another manager provided simultaneous translation. As it was learned later that the employees were quite confused about the program being described, the authors decided to compare the two versions of the speech. They had the Spanish version "backtranslated" into English and in comparing language use and structure of the two versions they were able to draw some inferences about where the problems might have occurred.

Barge and Musambira (1992) interviewed faculty members about their relationships with their department chairs. They inquired about "turning points" in the relationship, and followed up the interview with a questionnaire assessing quantitatively the degree to which the turning point episodes positively or negatively affected the relationship. Results indicated that chair–faculty relations were most positively affected when the chair was either able to orient the faculty member to some hidden aspect of the university or when the chair provided some special recognition to the faculty member. Chair–faculty relations were most negatively affected when the chair appeared to be helping the faculty member but it was later discovered that the chair had ulterior motives for appearing to provide the help.

Nicotera and Cushman (1992) did a double case study considering the ethical issues involved in IBM's and General Electric's handling of similar plant closings. Although the two large corporations dealt with the closing situation in nearly opposite manners, Nicotera and Cushman (1992) argued that both behaved in an ethical fashion. In both cases, corporate ethics were shown to be well known to employees and consonant with commonly accepted American values. In closing the plants, both corporations behaved consistently with their ethical standards. The fact that the resulting patterns of corporate behavior were so different, the authors argued, results from inconsistencies in American values themselves, inconsistencies which are tolerated until such specific cases come along.

Bantz (1993) applied Hofstede's (1984) work-related values and four group communication variables (language, cultural norms, status, and politics) to the analysis of communication difficulties (and strategies for overcoming those difficulties) of a multinational research team. Bantz found that Hofstede's dimensions were helpful in understanding and predicting how differences would occur among the individuals of varying cultures on the team, and he described the varying techniques that this group of communication specialists used to overcome those differences.

Barker, Melville, and Pacanowsky (1993) studied a key communication incident in the conversion of the XEL corporate culture from using traditional manufacturing assumptions to using those of "Just In Time" manufacturing. The authors found a variety of riches in examining a short incident where the manufacturing vice president was confronted by one of the work teams over a misunderstanding about whether he had ordered them to resolve a problem in a certain way (the old culture) or whether he was coaching them toward a solution (the new culture).

Finally, Nelson and Polansky (1993) conducted a rhetorical analysis of the decision-making dynamics that were employed in the selection of music to be included on the Voyager Interstellar Record probe that NASA launched in 1977 in hopes of encountering other life forms and providing those it encountered with information about our nature. The authors fleshed out the principal issue underlying the question, "How is it that music reflects our own humanity?" and pointed to cultural and personal considerations as means of probing this question.

These are the sorts of studies that Hickson (1973) hoped *JACR* would specialize in when he began the journal. And, in many ways, these sorts of studies are an editor's dream. They are clearly communication based, they tackle interesting issues occurring in real situations, and, most importantly, they make for both compelling and fun reading. They are also suggestive rather than directly instructive, their insights may not generalize beyond the cases examined, and their social relevance is often limited. But, they will be read, discussed, and eventually they will influence work that may lead to more broadly applicable results. I must admit that when it came time to nominate articles for association-wide awards I tended to pick these studies over others that *JACR* published.

Given the limitations of this sort of work (and those limitations have been pointed out by others contributing to this volume), it is fair to ask whether the field ought to encourage such work by publishing it in *JACR* as examples of applied research. My response is an affirmative one. Even though these studies often do not have clear and immediate relevance to social problems, nor do they have immediately applicable results their unique depictions of actual events allow us to connect *theoria* with *praxis* in unique and potentially useful ways. Too, studies such as these may help us find our way to undertaking socially relevant research more directly. Clearly, we are better off from a social standpoint by doing exploratory work in the field than by administering to one more group of students one more relatively hypothetical questionnaire.

Summary

In my admittedly biased "insider's" analysis, I have attempted to describe the current state of applied communication research by examining trends in what was published during the first 3 years of *JACR* as a Speech Communication Association journal. My analysis indicated some confusion, both in what to study and how to study it, when it came to work on social issues. I also saw a budding conflict on the horizon, as research continued to support the viability of a skills training approach to the improvement of communication ability while at the same time critics were calling for rethinking the assumptions underlying the skills training approach. Finally, I looked at a category of studies, many times case studies, often done qualitatively or ethnographically, which examined specific communication situations from a critical/analytic perspective. I attempted to point out both the problems and the prospects for this sort of "intermediately applied" work.

CONCLUSION: HOW CAN OUR WORK BE NOTICED?

One of the positive effects of this conference, to my mind, has been the bringing of added momentum for the creation of a position at the Speech Communication Association whose duties include promotion of the field's scholarship. As the initial occupant of this position, I have needed to give some thought to this matter, and some of what I will say stems from an essay Avery and I (1993) had included in the *Journal of Communication's* special issue on "The Future of the Field."

First, our work need not be applied or on social issues to be noticed. New insights into history are oftentimes of interest to both the press and the public at large. For example, Medhurst's (1993) collection of essays on the Eisenhower presidency might be material for news or feature stories if some of those essays provide insights considered to be significant. Because the media do tend to focus on current issues, however, more and better research into matters potentially affecting public policy will be the most likely to be covered.

Second, we need to learn to write and speak for audiences other than ourselves. This is not an easy task. I remember Kathleen Hall Jamieson, one of our more eloquent and publicly visible spokespeople, when she started doing next day analysis of presidential speaking for National Public Radio's *Morning Edition* some 20 years ago. To be kind, let's just say that her oral commentaries have improved dramatically over the years, despite Jamieson being a capable and insightful scholar even then. To be effective, we need to learn to make our points quickly and in language that listeners or readers will understand, and doing so takes practice. I do not mean by this suggestion that we aim for slick sound bites instead of substance, but rather that we learn how to make substance more engaging.

Finally, we need to make ourselves available. I imagine that most of us would be happy to talk with the reporter for *Time* who was doing a story on a topic we have researched, but what about the reporter for the hometown paper, radio or television station? We can make ourselves available by writing for popular publication. A year before Kunkel and Gantz' (1993) findings on children's advertisers' compliance with voluntary standards was published in *JACR*, an op-ed piece on the matter was published by Kunkel in the *Los Angeles Times*. We may not be called to testify in front of Congress immediately, but what about matters that come before city councils, county governments, or state legislatures? If we have some expertise to share, it need not matter whether we have a national forum for that expertise. Information reaching national levels often trickles up from state and local levels. By being available, we begin to be involved.

As Hart (1993) indicated, we have one element in our favor: Students are already on our side. As the study of communication continues to be popular on university campuses and as students are able to take what they learn in our classrooms and talk about it to others, our reputation with the general public will become more favorable. When we are able to compliment our fine teaching with what the public will consider as breakthrough research we will be well down the path toward our goal of being recognized and respected for the work we do.

ACKNOWLEDGMENTS

Thanks to Julia T. Wood for her insightful comments on and arguments with an earlier version of this chapter.

REFERENCES

Alberts, J. K., Miller-Rassulo M. A., & Hecht, M. L. (1991). A typology of drug resistance strategies. *Journal of Applied Communication Research, 19,* 129–151.

Avery R. K., & Eadie, W. F. (1993). Communication research: Making a difference in the real world. *Journal of Communication, 43*(3), 174–179.

Ayres, J., Ayres, F. E., Baker, A. L., Colby, N., De Blasi, C., Dimke, D., Docken, L., Grubb, J., Hopf, T., Mueller, R. D., Sharp, D., & Wilcox, K. (1993). Two empirical tests of a videotape designed to reduce public speaking anxiety. *Journal of Applied Communication Research, 21,* 132–147.

Ayres, J., & Hopf, T. (1991). Coping with writing apprehension. *Journal of Applied Communication Research, 19,* 186–195.

Banks, S. P., & Banks, A. (1991). Translation as problematic discourse in organizations. *Journal of Applied Communication Research, 19,* 223–241.

Bantz, C. R. (1993). Cultural diversity and group cross-cultural team research. *Journal of Applied Communication Research, 21,* 1–20.

Barge, J. K., & Musambira G. W. (1992). Turning points in chair–faculty relationships. *Journal of Applied Communication Research, 20,* 54–77.

Barker, J. R., Melville, C. W., & Pacanowsky, M. E. (1993). Self-directed teams at XEL: Changes in communication practices during a program of cultural transformation. *Journal of Applied Communication Research, 21,* 297–312.

Bingham, S. G. (1991). Communication strategies for managing sexual harassment in organizations: Understanding message options and their effects. *Journal of Applied Communication Research, 19,* 88–115.

Brown, W. J. (1992). Culture and AIDS education: Reaching high-risk heterosexuals in Asian-American communities. *Journal of Applied Communication Research, 20,* 275–291.

Bruschke, J. C., & Gartner, C. N. (1991). Teaching as communication: Advice for the higher education classroom. *Journal of Applied Communication Research, 19,* 197–216.

Cantrill, J. G. (1993). Communication and our environment: Categorizing research in environmental advocacy. *Journal of Applied Communication Research, 21,* 65–95.

Ellis, B. H., & Miller, K. I. (1993). The role of assertiveness, personal control, and participation in the prediction of nurse burnout. *Journal of Applied Communication Research, 21,* 327–342.

Feingold, P. C., & Knapp, M. L. (1977). Anti-drug abuse commercials. *Journal of Communication, 27,* 20–28.

Ford, W. S. Z., & Wolvin, A. D. (1993). The differential impact of a basic communication course on perceived communication competencies in class, work, and social contexts. *Communication Education, 42,* 215–223.

Gayle, B. M. (1991). Sex equity in workplace conflict management. *Journal of Applied Communication Research, 19,* 152–169.

Gotcher, J. M. (1993). The effects of family communication on psychosocial adjustment of cancer patients. *Journal of Applied Communication Research, 21,* 176–188.

Hammer, M. R., & Martin, J. N. (1992). The effects of cross-cultural training on American managers in a Japanese-American joint venture. *Journal of Applied Communication Research, 20,* 162–183.

Hart, R. P. (1993). Why communication? Why education? Toward a politics of teaching. *Communication Education, 42,* 97–105.

Hayden, S. (1993). Chronically ill and "feeling fine": A study of communication and chronic illness. *Journal of Applied Communication Research, 21,* 263–278.

Hickson, M., III. (1973). Applied communications research: A beginning point for social relevance. *Journal of Applied Communications Research, 1,* 1–5.

Hofstede, G. (1984). *Culture's consequences: International differences in work-related values* (abridged ed.). Beverly Hills, CA: Sage.

Hopf, T., & Ayres, J. (1992). Coping with public speaking anxiety: An examination of various combinations of systematic desensitization, skills training, and visualization. *Journal of Applied Communication Research, 20,* 184–198.

Kalbfleisch, P. J. (1992). Distrust and the social milieu: Application of deception research in a troubled world. *Journal of Applied Communication Research, 20,* 308–334.

Krendl, K. A., Olson, B., & Burke, R. (1992). Preparing for the environmental decade: A field experiment on recycling behavior. *Journal of Applied Communication Research, 20,* 19–36.

Krizek, R. L., Hecht, M. L., & Miller, M. (1993). Language as an indicator of risk in the prevention of drug use. *Journal of Applied Communication Research, 21,* 245–262.

Kunkel, D., & Gantz, W. (1993). Assessing compliance with industry self-regulation of television advertising to children. *Journal of Applied Communication Research, 21,* 148–162.

Le Poire, B. A., Burgoon, J. K., & Parrott, R. (1992). Status and privacy restoring communication in the workplace. *Journal of Applied Communication Research, 20,* 419–436.

Medhurst, M. J. (Ed.). (1993). *Eisenhower's war of words: Rhetoric and leadership.* East Lansing: Michigan State University Press.

Nelson, S., & Polansky, L. (1993). The music of the Voyager Interstellar Record. *Journal of Applied Communication Research, 21,* 358–376.

Nicotera, A. M., & Cushman, D. P. (1992). Organizational ethics: A within-organization view. *Journal of Applied Communication Research, 20,* 437–462.

Palmerton, P. R. (1992). Teaching skills or teaching thinking? *Journal of Applied Communication Research, 20,* 335–341.

Petronio S., & Bradford, L. (1993). Issues interfering with the use of written communication as a means of relational bonding between absentee, divorced fathers and their children. *Journal of Applied Communication Research, 21,* 163–175.

Plax, T. G., Beatty, M. J., & Feingold, P. C. (1991). Predicting verbal plan complexity from decision rule orientation among business students and corporate executives. *Journal of Applied Communication Research, 19,* 242–262.

Powell, R. G. (1992). Critical thinking and speech communication: Our teaching strategies are warranted—not! *Journal of Applied Communication Research, 20,* 342–347.

Renz, M. A. (1992). Communication about environmental risk: An examination of a Minnesota county's communication on incineration. *Journal of Applied Communication Research, 20,* 1–18.

Richmond, V. P., & Roach, K. D. (1992). Willingness to communicate and employee success in U.S. organizations. *Journal of Applied Communication Research, 20,* 95–115.

Seibold, D. R., Kudsi, S., & Rude, M. (1993). Does communication training make a difference?: Evidence for the effectiveness of a presentational skills program. *Journal of Applied Communication Research, 21,* 111–131.

Snyder, L. B., & Blood, D. J. (1992). Caution: Alcohol advertising and the surgeon general's alcohol warnings may have adverse effects on young adults. *Journal of Applied Communication Research, 20,* 37–53.

Sprague, J. (1993). Retrieving the research agenda for communication education: Asking the pedagogical questions that are "embarrassments to theory." *Communication Education, 42,* 106–122.

Strine, M. S. (1992). Understanding "how things work": Sexual harassment and academic culture. *Journal of Applied Communication Research, 20,* 391–400.

Taylor, B., & Conrad, C. (1992). Narratives of sexual harassment: Organizational dimensions. *Journal of Applied Communication Research, 20,* 401–418.

Vanderford, M. L., Smith, D. H., & Harris, W. S. (1992). Identification in narrative discourse: Evaluation of an HIV education demonstration project. *Journal of Applied Communication Research, 20,* 123–161.

Whitchurch, G. G., & Pace, J. L. (1993). Communication skills training and interspousal violence. *Journal of Applied Communication Research, 21,* 96–102.

Wood, J. T. (1992). Telling our stories: Narratives as a basis for theorizing sexual harassment. *Journal of Applied Communication Research, 21,* 349–362.

Wood, J. T., & Inman, C. C. (1993). In a different mode: Masculine styles of communicating closeness. *Journal of Applied Communication Research, 21,* 279–295.

9

A Bridge to Be Crossed:
Levels of Social Control in Future Applied
Communication Theory and Research

Louis P. Cusella
Teresa L. Thompson
University of Dayton

As we began to write this chapter, we were struck by the number of communication scholars, and others, who have recently addressed issues related to the future of applied communication research (ACR). For example, Krayer (1988) observed that applied communication scholars can be categorized into one of two groups, "those who are interested in *contexts* and those who are interested in *practical results*" (p. 339, italics original). ACR stemming from an interest in contexts involves the testing or translation of existing research knowledge into specific field sites (e.g., medical, business, educational, etc.). Practical results oriented ACR involves employing research knowledge for the instruction of others or personal development. However, as a PhD corporate training and development manager, Krayer observed that many of the managers he trained are "disenchanted with what academic research provides them today" (p. 340). In reaction to the recent challenges faced by the field of sociology, James Coleman, 1992 President of the American Sociological Association (ASA), and himself a formidable social theorist and scholar, has stated that it is "extremely important for sociology to demonstrate its utility to society if it's going to be viable in the long run" (Kantrowitz, 1992). Most recently, Planalp (1993) has argued that "research is, above all, seeking solutions to problems. . . . Although an individual researcher may lean toward one type of research, the research enterprise as a whole thrives on the 'how to' informing the 'how' and the 'how' informing the 'how to'" (p. 3). For Planalp basic research explores the "how" while applied research addresses the "how to," and both are essential and interdependent as the interplay between problems and solutions is explored.

These authors and other astute observers intimate the general parameters for ACR in the 21st century. The need to produce practical results, to demonstrate their utility, and to generate solutions lead to our central contention: Practical applications must be a crucial outcome of future ACR. Although it may appear obvious to some and old news to others, recent critiques of ACR suggest a goal not yet achieved (e.g., Krayer, 1988; Pettegrew, 1988).

The goal of practical results is also not a new challenge to anyone interested in the building and testing of communication theory. Thus, the future goals of applied communication research and communication theory (CT) are, de facto, isomorphic: to explain, predict, and control communication process and related phenomena in field contexts. In reality, the generation of solutions to problems and concerns for disciplinary utility have always shadowed those devoted to theory construction and basic research. As such, the chasm between CT and ACR should not be appreciable or significant. For example, in the area of organizational communication theory, Cusella (1984) has argued that theory must have an impact on actual organizations:

> No area of scholarship should advance a concept that does not have an impact on the real world. Impact essentially means that a change in a variable makes a *difference* in an organization. If the concept, as operationalized, does not have much of an impact on an organization it may not warrant the time and effort required for investigation. Identifying communication concepts that cause change and not solely those which are caused by or correlate with other variables should be a major concern of organizational communication scholars. (p. 297)

Thus, while the pathways taken in pursuit of ACR are manifold, they all must eventuate in the ability to directly influence and control phenomena, which necessitates the development of sound theory. Thus, ACR is herein synonymous with the control of phenomena directly related to sense making, meaning creation processes in symbolic contexts. Consequently, this paper suggests that future ACR must be conducted in the field, where the interplay between context and process is an ever present empirical concern. The contextual imperative of ACR is of such importance that it must be addressed immediately, before other issues are considered.

CONTEXT

As Bateson (1935) has established, the context in which behaviors occur determines the meaning of these behaviors. This paper assumes that ACR generally focuses on participants of communication systems who must share information transmitted symbolically. According to Haslett (1987), context is "the knowledge humans have about how to interact in a specific setting" (p. 85) and can precede communication action or evolve from it. As such, context can be viewed as both a medium and outcome of communication. But, although Pettegrew (1988) agrees that communication varies as a function of context, situation, and time, his indictment of current ACR is stinging in this regard: "Even the most legitimate applied communication research usually fails to consider the context in which the interaction is taking place" (p. 334). A review of ACR since 1988 indicates that not much has changed since Pettegrew's observation. Consequently, the contextual imperative in future ACR occupies a central role in the current argument.

RELEVANT MEANINGS:
APPLIED AND APPLIED RESEARCH

Before we develop our argument further, the implication surrounding the operative term *applied* in ACR and a discussion of the meaning for the expression *applied research* must be considered. Tracing back through the Middle English *applie* to the Latin *applicare* brings us to the original root *plicare*, which meant to fold, bend, or mold something to a desired purpose (Stein, 1973). Just what is being applied or bent to a desired purpose is made clear by examining definitions of applied research in various fields of study. In essence, theory and knowledge are applied to the solution of a variety of practical problems. An even more precise definition of an applied area is provided by Fairchild (1966), who notes that "applied sociology" is:

> the deductive phase of scientific sociology. The accurate and precise use of sociological generalizations to assist in the solution of social problems. The application of social laws and principles to particular cases. May be an instrument of either social reform or social engineering. (p. 302)

Fairchild's focus on social reform or social engineering returns us to the primary focus of the present essay, the notion of control.

Although the goals of science are many, it is generally agreed that scientific knowledge should provide: (a) typologies; (b) predictions of future events; (c) explanations of past events; (d) a sense of understanding about what causes events; and (e) the potential for control of events (Reynolds, 1971). There are, of course, some variables that cannot be controlled, so control is not a necessary criterion for accepting knowledge as scientific. "However, it will be assumed that, if a theory related to a particular phenomenon is scientifically useful, then scientists and 'men of action' can examine their ability to influence the variables that will affect the events they wish to control" (Reynolds, 1971, p. 10). Other philosophers of science concur. For example, Kaplan (1964) advocates an instrumentalist view of theories, such that "their significance lies in the action they guide" (p. 310), while Meehan (1968) distinguishes between strong and weak explanations, where "a strong explanation provides accurate and reliable control over substantial parts of the environment" (p. 23). Finally, while focusing particularly on systems theory explanations, Miller and Nicholson (1976) argue that the paramount function by which such an explanation is judged is its ability to provide control.

Although some may focus on explanation of past events or the prediction of future events as a goal of theory, it was Argyris (1979) who cogently observed that this

> leaves us with the puzzle that explanatory models cannot be used to alter the variables whose relationships they describe. Is this not like maintaining that a model that explains cancer cannot be used to design its cure? Theoretical models for informing practice must be designed, I believe, to make implementation the ultimate, and explanation the penultimate, objectives. (p. 689)

Here, Argyris states the case cogently: without the ability to control phenomena, and implement theory, ACR will fail to fulfill its promise. In essence, the future of ACR necessitates theoretically rich frameworks that facilitate the rational control of communication phenomena and the consequent implementation of utilitarian models.

Thus, both theory development and ACR should have "control" as the ultimate purpose. In this chapter, control is essentially the ability to provide purposeful direction to phenomena, and will be discussed at length later.

CONTROL IN ACR

In simplest terms, we argue that any future agenda for ACR must eventuate in the control of communication phenomena for desirable ends. In this sense, control will be defined as the intentional enactment of a known set of causal relations. In defining control in this fashion, the current authors are employing portions of an already established intellectual framework that treats a power relation as a type of causation. Based on the conceptual work of Simon (1957), Nagel defines an actual or potential power relation as a causal relation between an actor's preferences regarding an outcome and the outcome itself. For Nagel (1975), "In social power relations, the *outcome* must be a variable indicating the state of another social entity—the behavior, beliefs, attitudes, or policies of a second actor" (p. 29). In the present analysis, the contention is that, de facto, control is enacted power and that ACR should enable actors to control communication phenomena. Simon (1957) and Nagel (1975) refuse to define control per se because it conceptually muddles their definition of power, whereas we define control as an enacted causal (i.e., power) relation, intentionally set into motion by a researcher, or one who bases actions on ACR findings, for the purpose of attaining outcomes deemed desirable in field contexts. By intentional we mean deliberate, purposeful, consciously directed action. By enactment we mean behavior that serves to bracket (isolate) and construct (create) "portions of the flow of experience" (Weick, 1979, p. 147) in field contexts.

One important implication of this notion of control in ACR is the necessity of specifying the scope and domain of a causal relationship. This is a requirement for any meaningful statement, at any level of abstraction in ACR (Baldwin, 1989). Following Nagel (1975), it must be emphasized that, if control is enactment, ACR must state the outcome caused. Thus, future ACR must stipulate domain and scope answers to the question "control over what?". Finally, although space limitations preclude further discussion, it is also important to note that, as a future goal of ACR, control of communication phenomena must be specified in terms of four principles implicit in the logic of causal inference: temporal sequence, possibility of intervention, prepotence, and known mechanism (Simon & Rescher, 1966).

TYPES OF CONTROL IN ACR

One can seek to control phenomena based on a variety of goals. Various extant frameworks address the issue of types of control in social contexts. These frameworks may help sensitize ACR scholars to the type of control most relevant to their theory and research goals. One framework has had a substantial influence on organizational communication research.

Burrell and Morgan (1979) have attempted to characterize organizational research. Briefly, they try to make sense out of the different ways and forms of theory building. Their framework classifies theories according to their inherent assumptions about the nature of social science and the nature of society. Paradigms of social theory are based on two interacting dimensions: (a) the objective/subjective nature of reality, and (b) the radical change/regulation aspect of social order. An objectivist approach views reality as external to the individual, where social phenomena constitute objective facts that occur independent of the individual. A subjectivist view sees reality as a socially created phenomenon, that is interpreted by those who participate in the process. Here social reality does not exist independent of the interpretations of events, especially symbolic action. A regulation stance focuses on the role of social order in society. Here order is essential for the maintenance of social stability, where the fundamental building blocks of social systems are orderly patterns, integration, consensus, and stability. A social theory of radical change rests on premises of societal conflict, disintegration, and coercion (Louis, 1983).

When the two dimensions intersect, four theoretical paradigms result. Functionalists view society as objective and orderly, wherein behavior is concrete and oriented toward stability of the status quo. Interpretivists assume that subjective reality is socially constructed, with interests in regulation or a lack of interest in changing the status quo. The radical humanist paradigm takes a subjectivist view of reality and is focused on the radical change of socially constructed realities. Finally, the radical structuralist occupies an objectivist stance, with an ideological concern for the radical change of the social order.

Examples of the four theoretical paradigms can be found in all areas of ACR. However, we draw for a moment upon the research in health communication. Much of the research on the impact of communication on compliance with medical regimens, especially that published in medical journals, can be characterized as functionalist. It takes an objective perspective with a goal of improving compliance with health care providers—maintaining the societal status quo (e.g., Pruyn, Ruckman, van Brunschot, & van den Borne, 1985). Research on control patterns in provider–patient interaction is objective, but is focused on changing the status quo by changing control patterns (e.g., O'Hair, 1989), characterizing it as radical structuralist. Research such as that conducted by Cherry and Smith (1993) examining the loneliness of AIDS patients is subjective, in that it attempts to understand the reality of the patient, but works toward the goal of social change. Finally, work similar to that conducted by Wyatt (1991) appears to be interpretivist, in that it focuses on the perspective of physicians, but evidences little interest in societal change. All four types of research make contributions on their own level.

Although criticisms of this typology abound (Louis, 1983; Rosengren, 1983), especially regarding terminology and the taxonomic requirements for a consideration of any theory, the Burrell and Morgan (1979) framework is an inventive heuristic that provides a neat structure when considering future ACR questions and the theoretical perspectives upon which they will be based. Through this framework, ACR scholars may gain a heightened awareness of the paradigm to which they have, perhaps tacitly, subscribed. At a fundamental level, Burrell and Morgan (1979) have provided a structure for a consideration of one's explicit or implicit research focus: Does my ACR seek to change or regulate the status quo, and is the status quo an objective or subjective reality?

ELIMINATION, PREVENTION, AND MANAGEMENT AS CONTROL TYPES

In earlier writings (Thompson & Cusella, 1991a, 1991b) it has been argued that communication researchers concerned with social problems (e.g., drug abuse) may strive to control the problem in different ways. Control by elimination would concern itself with the resolution of a problem such that its causes are addressed after it has already become a problem for some actors in certain contexts. In the present context, as a result of specific ACR findings, a known set of causal relations would be intentionally enacted and the social problem would disappear. Control by prevention would attempt to eliminate the causes of a social problem before certain actors in specific contexts experience the problem. From this control perspective, based on adequate forecasting, a social problem would never emerge as a reality for actors in a specific field site. Control by problem management would seek to lessen the magnitude or intensity of a social reality by containing its causes after the problem has emerged in a social collectivity. Here control of the progression of the problem would be sought. These three levels of control vary such that the causes of the problem are either eliminated a posteriori (elimination), a priori (prevention), or the causes are contained a posteriori (management).

This framework has its roots in the work of Hawes and Smith (1973) in the area of communication and conflict. The authors observed that strategies for normative theories of conflict typically stress means by which the conflict may be brought to an end (resolved), because "the only good conflict is a resolved conflict" (p. 424). Alternatively, Hawes and Smith argue that, if a conflict is not destructive, it may be best to manage it and, in so doing, maintain a level of conflict and ambivalence that guarantees some productive outcomes (e.g., group creativity).

Thus, ACR may be used to control social phenomena at different levels. Not much worthwhile will emerge, however, if ACR and communication theory are not conducted in concert. This is because a lack of a deep understanding of the causal nature of problem phenomena may only produce shallow, short-lived "solutions." Argyris (1979) makes a related observation regarding the separation of theory from practice:

> This separation between theory and practice may be counterproductive to the progress of both. For example, there is danger that practitioners may focus their attention upon advice that, in the short run may solve some of the problems but, in the long run, drives the basic causes even further underground. This may result in legacies about organizational, political, and interpersonal activities that become more inbred and camouflaged. (p. 679)

VALUES IN ACR

This discussion of levels of social control in ACR leads to the necessary and unavoidable question of values and their impact on the research process. Although somewhat obvious, it is important to note that ACR, as with all research, is based on numerous decisions made in an effort to reach certain goals. For example, Winer (1971) holds that it is the researcher's task to reach the final decision about the conduct of his or her study. Metaphorically, the setting of specific research goals provides a window to the researcher's values. Simon (1964) contends that goals are value premises that serve as inputs to a decision. In this view, a goal can be operationalized as the criterion a researcher as a decision maker uses to order his or her preferences. Simon argues further than motives are the underlying causes that lead a decision maker to select some goals rather than others as value premises for decisions.

If research goals are tantamount to values, the argument can be forwarded that all ACR is, in a sense, ideological, since the values embedded in select goals serve to justify the research conducted. For ACR this begs the question, whose values are of central concern during the conduct of ACR? Given the likelihood that ACR will be conducted in the field, amidst "real" people, living "real" lives, facing "real" problems, and concomitantly, the findings from ACR will be used to frame solutions to the problems of real people (Planalp, 1993), the values of those real people must also be taken into account.

As an example, consider the work of Pondy (1967), who asserts that organizational conflict can be functional, dysfunctional, or simultaneously both, depending on the values that are employed as criteria for the assessment of conflict outcomes. The organizational values Pondy uncovers are: productivity, stability, and adaptability. These values also serve as implicit or explicit levels of control. For Pondy, other things being equal, an organization is "better" (p. 308) if it: produces more at a higher quality and is more innovative, increases its cohesiveness and solvency, and can adapt to internal and external organizational pressures. Importantly, these values are not always compatible (Pondy, 1967) and, as such, an organization may have to sacrifice one for another. The issue of ACR is which value will be sacrificed and which will be upheld?

Suppose one has the opportunity to conduct ACR in profit seeking organizations experiencing conflict. An applied researcher emphasizing the Deming Method of statistical quality control (Walton, 1986) will likely start by emphasizing productivity, where working smarter and better are the "cornerstones" of ACR. On the other hand, a critical theorist, who sees organizations as political and linguistic structures that are potentially repressive (Mumby, 1988), begins his or her ACR effort by assuming that capitalist work organizations are incapable of meeting worker needs, as long as workers are used the most effectively and efficiently. Consequently, the values of productivity, stability, and cohesiveness are rejected, out of hand, as long as the business of management is about safeguarding the interests of shareholders by controlling the productive capacity of workers (Alvesson & Willmott, 1992). For the critical communication theorist, the goal of ACR is not productivity but worker emancipation. Our point is that these divergent approaches to ACR are based on different values held by the two researchers, neither of whom have taken into account the values of organization members experiencing the organizational conflict. Now, if the essence of ACR is the creation of solutions to problems through the control of communication phenomena in field contexts, both researchers have missed the point, since both have failed to consider the motives of the actors in context. Future ACR must be a social construction (Smircich & Calas, 1987), where, in known field contexts, the researcher must be sensitive to the motives of self (researcher) and other (those being researched). Thus, control must be calibrated to the needs and motives of those for whom the ACR is intended.

Goodall and Phillips (1981) neatly address this concern by citing the work of Blumer (1969):

> Blumer (1969, p. 24) . . . claims that empirical research in social behavior must be based on an initial picture, or scheme, of the world under consideration, literally a point of view. Later on, Blumer (p. 33) points out that once viewing is constrained by a point of view, the nature of what can be observed is limited. (p. 286)

An awareness of the actors' needs and motives may serve as a corrective check on the applied researcher's "point of view" (p. 24), and on discourse directed at actors in the field while ACR is conducted.

PARTICIPATORY RESEARCH

As a critical communication theorist with an interest in research benefitting organization members, Mumby (1988) sketches a research method called participatory research that offers a mechanism for checking a researcher's motives and point of view vis-à-vis those being researched. Doing participatory research involves four aspects. First, the researcher conducts open-ended interviews with organization members to collect their stories of and meanings for organizational phenomena. Second, the researcher interprets the dominant organizational meaning structures that produce and reproduce social systems in the organization. Third, the researcher feeds back these interpretations to organization members for reactions. Lastly, organization members are encouraged to undertake their own "constraint free" analysis of relevant organizational communication phenomena. What is striking about this approach is Mumby's care to check his interpretations with those of actual organization members. However, if this method is to be truly participative, ACR scholars who employ it must take pains to free organization members of the constraints posed by the researcher's values and discourse, conveyed while the actual research is conducted.

Finally, as previously stated, future ACR should seek to understand the causal dynamics of communication processes in field contexts, because the overarching goal of control is necessary if solutions to problems are to be found. As future work in ACR proceeds, scholars in the area would do well to heed the advice of Weick (1979) to strive always to partially discredit what we know to be past knowledge and also treat as certain those things which we doubt: "The nuance we wish to preserve is that there are good reasons to question the accuracy and reliability of enacted environments, that one should be suspicious of any private version of the world, and that the credibility of that enacted environment is not guaranteed" (p. 221).

CONCLUSION

The central thesis of this chapter is that future ACR, not unlike CT, should strive to control communication process in the field. As we have discussed, social control may take the form of regulation, radical change, prevention, elimination, management, productivity, stability, cohesiveness, and emancipation. All of these levels of social control require an understanding of the causal relations that produce the problems on which future ACR will be focused.

In his 1992 ASA presidential address, Coleman (1993) argued that societal transformation is so basic as we approach the 21st century, that "it may require a change in the very stance of the discipline to its subject matter" (p. 1). This observation can also be made of ACR, because its ultimate justification will be its contribution to the optimal design of communication systems of the future. Communication theory must also be directed toward this charge, because we have argued that both need to focus on social control. The transformation of society will proceed whether or not ACR and communication theory are bridged. It is the task of ACR to aid in that construction.

REFERENCES

Alvesson, M., & Willmott, H. (1992). On the idea of emancipation in management and organization studies. *Academy of Management Review, 17,* 432–464.

Argyris, C. (1979). Richard Neustadt and Harvey V. Fineberg: The swine flu affair: Decision making on a slippery disease. *Administrative Science Quarterly, 24,* 672–679.

Baldwin, D. A. (1989). *Paradoxes of power.* New York: Basil Blackwell.

Bateson, G. (1935). Culture contact and schismogenesis. *Man, 35,* 178–183.

Blumer, H. (1969). *Symbolic interactionism.* Englewood Cliffs, NJ: Prentice-Hall.

Burrell, G., & Morgan, G. (1979). *Sociological paradigms and organisational analysis.* London: Heinemann.

Cherry, K., & Smith, D. H. (1993). Sometimes I cry: The experience of loneliness for men with AIDS. *Health Communication, 5,* 181–208.

Coleman, J. S. (1993). The rational reconstruction of society. *American Sociological Review, 58,* 1–15.

Cusella, L. P. (1984). Conceptual issues in organizational communication research: Elements of a model of conceptual authenticity. *Communication Quarterly, 32,* 293–300.

Fairchild, H. P. (1966). *Dictionary of sociology.* Totowa, NJ: Littlefield, Adams & Co.

Goodall, H. L., & Phillips, G. M. (1981). Assumption of the burden: Science or criticism? *Communication Quarterly, 29,* 283–296.

Haslett, B. J. (1987). *Communication: Strategic action in context.* Hillsdale, NJ: Lawrence Erlbaum Associates.

Hawes, L. C., & Smith, D. (1973). A critique of assumptions underlying the study of communication in conflict. *Quarterly Journal of Speech, 59,* 423–435.

Kantrowitz, B. (1992, February 3). Sociology's lonely crowd. *Newsweek,* p. 55.

Kaplan, A. (1964). *The conduct of inquiry: Methodology for behavioral science.* New York: Chandler.

Krayer, K. J. (1988). Whither applied interpersonal communication research: A practical perspective for practicing practitioners. *Southern Speech Communication Journal, 53,* 339–343.

Louis, M. R. (1983). Gibson Burrell and Gareth Morgan: Sociological paradigms and organisational analysis. *Administrative Science Quarterly, 28,* 153–156.

Meehan, E. J. (1968). *Explanation in social science: A systems paradigm.* Homewood, IL: Dorsey Press.

Miller, G. R., & Nicholson, H. E. (1976). *Communication inquiry: A perspective on a process.* Reading, MA: Addison-Wesley.

Mumby, D. K. (1988). *Communication and power in organizations: Discourse, ideology and domination.* Norwood, NJ: Ablex.

Nagel, J. H. (1975). *The descriptive analysis of power.* New Haven, CT: Yale University Press.

O'Hair, D. (1989). Dimensions of relational communication and control during physician–patient interactions. *Health Communication, 2,* 97–115.

Pettegrew, L. S. (1988). The importance of context in applied communication research. *Southern Speech Communication Journal, 53,* 331–338.

Planalp, S. (1993). Communication, cognition, and emotion. *Communication Monographs, 60,* 3–9.

Pondy, L. R. (1967). Organizational conflict: Concepts and models. *Administrative Science Quarterly, 12,* 296–320.

Pruyn, J. F. A., Ruckman, R. M, Van Brunschot, C. J. M., & van den Borne, H. W. (1985). Cancer patients' personality characteristics, physician–patient communication and adoption of the Moerman diet. *Social Science and Medicine, 20,* 841–847.

Reynolds, P. D. (1971). *A primer in theory construction.* Indianapolis, IN: Bobbs-Merrill.

Rosengren, K. E. (1983). Communication research: One paradigm or four? *Journal of Communication, 33*(3), 185–207.

Simon, H. A. (1957). *Models of man.* New York: Wiley.

Simon, H. A. (1964). On the concept of organizational goal. *Administrative Science Quarterly, 9,* 1–22.

Simon, H. A., & Rescher, N. (1966). Cause and counterfactual. *Philosophy of Science, 33,* 324–340.

Smircich, L., & Calas, M. B. (1987). Organizational culture: A critical assessment. In F. M. Jablin, L. L. Putnam, K. H. Roberts, & L. W. Porter (Eds.), *Handbook of organizational communication* (228–263). Newbury Park, CA: Sage.

Stein, J. (1973). *Random House dictionary of the English language.* New York: Random House.

Thompson, T. L., & Cusella, L. P. (1991a). Communication and drug abuse prevention: Information, incentives, and metaphors. *Health Communication, 3,* 251–262.

Thompson, T. L., & Cusella, L. P. (1991b). Muddling through toward small wins: On the need for requisite variety. In L. Donohew, H. E. Sypher, & W. J. Bukoski (Eds.), *Persuasive communication and drug abuse prevention* (pp. 317–333). Hillsdale, NJ: Lawrence Erlbaum Associates.

Walton, M. (1986). *The Deming management method.* New York: Perigee.

Weick, K. E. (1979). *The social psychology of organizing* (2nd ed.). Reading, MA: Addison-Wesley.

Winer, B. J. (1971). *Statistical principles in experimental design* (2nd ed.). New York: McGraw-Hill.

Wyatt, N. (1991). Physician–patient relationships: What do doctors say? *Health Communication, 3,* 157–174.

III

Appendixes

Appendix A:
Recommendations Formally Adopted
by the Tampa Conference
on Applied Communication

Kenneth N. Cissna
Conference Director

This appendix contains the recommendations that were adopted by the participants of the Tampa Conference on Applied Communication, co-sponsored by the Speech Communication Association (SCA) and the Department of Communication of the University of South Florida (USF). These recommendations are those approved by the majority of the conference participants, and are not necessarily the views of the members of SCA or of USF's Department of Communication.

These recommendations are the work, initially, of six Recommendation Drafting Groups, with two groups focusing on each of three areas, Issues and Responsibilities in the Field, Research Priorities, and Graduate Education. Each conference participant was assigned to one of these six groups, which met for most of one day. Following each set of recommendations are the names of the members of the original groups that drafted the recommendations.

The following day, time was allotted for the two groups generating recommendations within one area to meet in order to compare recommendations and to reconcile their products into a single report to the Conference. Those three reports were then distributed to conference participants. Each report and its accompanying recommendations were considered at a general session of the Conference. Recommendations of the drafting groups were often modified or amended, and each was voted on by conference participants.

Because deliberation time was relatively short (1 hour, 45 minutes for each area), each recommendation that received majority approval was then submitted to a postconference Delphi procedure, which was conducted among the conference participants. Three Delphi rounds were conducted. The present set of recommendations emerged from that process.

RECOMMENDATIONS CONCERNING ISSUES
AND RESPONSIBILITIES OF THE FIELD

1. The discipline should encourage its members to engage in research that (a) illuminates specific communication contexts or situations, (b) provides insight into the solution of social problems, or (c) leads to interventions that make a difference in people's lives.

2. Applied communication research should receive increased recognition within the academy. Achievement of this goal can be facilitated by:
   a. Having editors of scholarly journals and planners and readers for scholarly conventions and conferences include a contribution to application as a criterion for evaluating papers, manuscripts, and proposals;
   b. Creating professional awards that recognize outstanding applied communication research, and adding contribution to application to the criteria for existing awards;
   c. Having scholarly organizations and research institutions make acquisition of funding for applied research projects a high priority;
   d. Having departments note the value of applied communication research in their criteria for promotion and tenure.

3. Applied communication research should achieve greater influence in public policy discussions and decisions. Achievement of this goal can be facilitated by:
   a. Improving the communication of the results of applied communication research to policy makers, practitioners, and the general public;
   b. Sponsoring conferences and workshops to discuss how research can be applied;
   c. Encouraging publication of review essays that synthesize a body of theory and research and indicate how the findings can be applied;
   d. In conferences, journals, and other forums, discussing explicitly the ethical, economic, ideological, and political issues surrounding applied communication research.

4. The priorities of the discipline should include the cultivation of potential sources of funding for applied communication research to bring levels of support up to that needed for its growth and greater usefulness to society.

5. The Speech Communication Association should seek to collaborate with other professional and scholarly communication societies to develop appropriate organizational structures to implement the recomendations of this report.

Issues and Responsibilities of the Field
Recommendation Drafting Committees:

Group A	Group B
Arthur P. Bochner	James L. Gaudino
Mark L. Knapp	H. L. Goodall
James C. McCroskey	John (Sam) Keltner
Gerald R. Miller	Dale G. Leathers
	Kathleen Hall Jamieson
	Robert Norton
	David H. Smith

RECOMMENDATIONS CONCERNING RESEARCH PRIORITIES

6. Through conferences, workshops, convention programs, and published commentaries, the discipline should regularly identify the most critical issues, problems, and contexts for applied communication research.

7. Applied communication researchers should use the best available research methods to answer the particular research questions asked and should, whenever feasible, use multiple methods. To assist researchers:
   a. Professional organizations should sponsor methodological and research development workshops;
   b. Editors and reviewers of scholarly publications and convention program submissions should rigorously evaluate not only the applications being claimed but also the methods used to arrive at the knowledge claims.

8. Applied communication researchers, like all scholars, should strive to develop and refine theory so that insights gained are useful in situations beyond the specific ones studied.

9. Researchers should be sensitive to ethical and value issues in designing, conducting, and reporting applied communication research, as well as in introducing interventions. These issues include:
   a. Protecting the rights of subjects;
   b. Monitoring and evaluating the consequences of interventions;
   c. Protecting the interests of relevant publics;
   d. Recognizing the political and economic implications of applied communication research.

10. Researchers should assume responsibility for the dissemination of applied communication research to relevant and concerned publics in a style and manner that is accessible to those publics.

11. Researchers should consider the imperative for change in policy or practice inherent in their findings, reporting their best estimates of the economic and social costs of these changes, as well as the benefits.

Research Priorities Recommendation Drafting Committees:

Group C	*Group D*
Samuel L. Becker	Robert K. Avery
David Bender	Dwight Conquergood
William F. Eadie	Vicki Freimuth
Gary L. Kreps	Loyd S. Pettegrew
Jon F. Nussbaum	Barbara F. Sharf
Frederick Steier	
Janet Yerby	

RECOMMENDATIONS CONCERNING GRADUATE EDUCATION

At the Master's and Doctoral Levels

12. Graduate education in communication should be based on solid disciplinary grounding in communication theory and research that includes social relevance and applicability as inherent components of this disciplinary grounding.

13. Graduate education in communication should encourage students to become better acquainted with applied research contexts by, for example:

   a. Providing opportunities for students to experience internships, externships, and practica;

   b. Inviting non-academic applied researchers, action role models, and practitioners to campus as guest speakers.

14. Graduate education in communication should emphasize the social, political, economic, and ethical implications and responsibilities of doing applied research, including interventions that may be recommended or implied.

15. Graduate education in communication should institute appropriate curricular innovations such as:

   a. Offering research seminars that examine exemplars of applied communication research;

   b. Developing courses or course components that critically examine the concept applied;

   c. Utilizing case studies;

   d. Providing training in the design of research-based interventions and ways to determine the applicability of theory;

e. Considering the impact of cultural differences on applied research;

f. Allowing individualized, problem-centered programs of study.

16. Graduate education in communication should recruit students with interests in socially relevant research and include relevant nonacademic work and life experiences among the important indicators of preparation for graduate study in communication.

17. Graduate education in communication should expand our efforts to recruit a graduate student body that is diverse ethnically, culturally, and in age and experience, because these factors may influence the likelihood of attracting students motivated to do socially relevant research.

At the Doctoral Level

18. Doctoral education in communication should emphasize theory construction and methodological training, and acquaint students with a broad variety of methodological orientations and theoretical perspectives.

19. Doctoral education in communication should provide each student training in depth in at least one methodological approach.

20. Doctoral education in communication should expand opportunities to become acquainted with applied communication research contexts through such programs as doctoral seminars, funded research projects, and course work in cognate fields.

Post-Doctoral Education

21. Postdoctoral education in communication should be expanded by:

a. Having professional associations expand their continuing education programs for members of the discipline, including programs with applied communication foci;

b. Having research universities initiate and develop opportunities for postdoctoral research experiences that include applied communication.

Graduate Education Recommendation Drafting Committees:

Group E	Group F
Michael Burgoon	Chris Argyris
Donal A. Carbaugh	Joseph N. Cappella
Kenneth N. Cissna	Thomas A. McCain
Robert T. Craig	Michael Pacanowsky
Lewis Donohew	Sandra L. Ragan
Kathleen M. Galvin	Everett M. Rogers
David R. Seibold	

Appendix B:
List of Conference Participants

Chris Argyris Harvard University, Presented Keynote Address
Robert K. Avery University of Utah, Member of Conference Steering Committee and Issue Identification Group Reporter
Samuel L. Becker University of Iowa, Respondent
David Bender Bruskin Associates Marketing Research, Issue Identification Group Recorder
Arthur P. Bochner University of South Florida, Member of Conference Steering Committee and Moderator
Michael Burgoon University of Arizona, Recommendation Drafting Group Leader
Joseph N. Cappella University of Pennsylvania, Issue Identification Group Recorder
Donal A. Carbaugh University of Massachusetts, Issue Identification Group Leader
Kenneth N. Cissna University of South Florida, Conference Director, Member of Conference Steering Committee, and Moderator
Dwight Conquergood Northwestern University, Presented Position Paper
Robert T. Craig University of Colorado, Recommendation Drafting Joint Group Reporter
Lewis Donohew University of Kentucky, Issue Identification Group Leader
William F. Eadie California State University, Northridge, Issue Identification Group Recorder
Vicki Freimuth University of Maryland, Respondent

Kathleen M. Galvin Northwestern University, Issue Identification Group Leader

James L. Gaudino Speech Communication Association, Member of Conference Steering Committee and Recommendation Drafting Joint Group Reporter

H. L. Goodall Jr., University of Utah, Respondent

Kathleen Hall Jamieson University of Pennsylvania, Presented Position Paper

John (Sam) Keltner Consulting Associates, Recommendation Drafting Group Leader

Mark L. Knapp University of Texas, Member of Conference Steering Committee

Gary L. Kreps Northern Illinois University, Recommendation Drafting Joint Group Leader

Dale G. Leathers University of Georgia, Issue Identification Group Leader

Thomas A. McCain Ohio State University, Respondent

James C. McCroskey West Virginia University, Recommendation Drafting Group Leader

Gerald R. Miller Michigan State University, Presented Position Paper and Member of Conference Steering Committee

Robert Norton University of Oklahoma, Respondent

Jon F. Nussbaum University of Oklahoma, Recommendation Drafting Group Leader

Michael Pacanowsky University of Utah, Recommendation Drafting Group Leader

Loyd S. Pettegrew University of South Florida, Member of Conference Steering Committee and Moderator

Sandra L. Ragan University of Oklahoma, Recommendation Drafting Joint Group Leader

Everett M. Rogers University of Southern California, Issue Identification Group Leader

David R. Seibold University of Illinois, Presented Position Paper

Barbara F. Sharf University of Illinois at Chicago, Recommendation Drafting Joint Group Reporter

David H. Smith University of South Florida, Moderator

Frederick Steier Old Dominion University, Respondent

Janet Yerby Central Michigan University, Issue Identification Group Reporter

---

Note. In addition, James Fletcher (University of Georgia), Lynne Webb (University of Hawaii and University of Florida), Teresa L. Thompson (University of Dayton), Phillip K. Tompkins (University of Colorado), and Karl E. Weick (University of Michigan) were scheduled to participate but at the last minute were unable to attend. Affiliations listed are those at the time of the Conference.

Appendix C:
Instructions Sent to Conference Participants and Conference Format

DEPARTMENT OF COMMUNICATION
UNIVERSITY OF SOUTH FLORIDA

MEMORANDUM

March 22, 1991

TO: Participants
     Tampa Conference on Applied Communication

FROM: Kenneth N. Cissna
      Conference Director

SUBJ: The Conference

This memo is intended to collect in one place information, which you may or may not have acquired elsewhere, about the Tampa Conference on Applied Communication and about your roles and responsibilities in it.

General Information

We will be meeting at the Wyndham Harbour Island Hotel in Tampa. Please arrive in Tampa in time to be at the hotel by 5:00pm on Wednesday March 27th; the first event begins at 6:00pm. The conference will conclude at 5:00pm Saturday, March 30th. We will have an informal session over breakfast Sunday morning for those who wish to stay over Saturday night. The hotel has a complimentary limousine to the airport. One-half hour for the trip from airport to hotel will be plenty to allow.

There are 40 participants in the Conference. The roster and the complete conference schedule are included in the Conference Program. All participants will serve in a formal role in the conference.

Sponsored by the Research Board of SCA, the Conference is intended to parallel in scope and function the national SCA research conferences at New Orleans and Wingspread. Our purpose will be to set a research and practice agenda for applied studies in communication.

It is my hope and intention that a significant volume will result from the Conference. I anticipate that the volume will include at least the keynote address, the four position papers and responses, and a charge to the field of communication, including definitions, issues, and responsibilies; the development of research priorities; and the implications for graduate education. The recommendations may be disseminated through other publication outlets as well. Finally, I anticipate that one or more programs at the November, 1991, SCA Convention will be based on the Conference.

You have received a packet of materials containing the keynote address, the four position papers, and most of the responses. Please review the materials carefully, as the presentations will be brief summaries of the papers.

An IBM compatible computer and NEC printer will be available for the use of conference participants in the Conference Office (Room 315).

I will be able to cover many of your expenses while you are here. At minimum, every participant will receive two nights lodging (double occupancy), three breakfasts, three lunches, one dinner, a cocktail party, and sodas and snacks at break times.

Format of the Conference

The format is designed to produce a set of recommendations regarding applied studies in communication that can be widely disseminated within the field.

A rather structured format has been provided for the Conference. We are a relatively large group with relatively little time together. As such, the format requires the active participation of each and every participant if we are to accomplish our objectives.

Each participant serves in one of several formal roles, as speaker, moderator, group leader, or group reporter.

In addition to the keynote address, four position papers and two responses to each paper will be briefly summarized. These will begin on Thursday and be completed Friday. These are intended to stimulate discussion and suggest productive avenues for exploration. The presentation of each position paper and of the two associated responses will occur in one-hour blocks, including a brief opportunity to ask questions of the three presenters. The moderators assigned to these sessions are asked to help maintain the time schedule.

Each participant has been assigned as a member of two distinct groups. First, the Issue Identification Groups will meet on Thursday, and will report to the General Session of the Conference Thursday evening regarding the issues, concerns, or topics that need to be addressed by the Conference.

Second, the Recommendation Drafting Groups meet most of the day Friday and report their written recommendations as motions to be considered by the Conference on Saturday. We will consider recommendations concerning: (a) issues and responsibilities of the field, (b) research priorities, and (c) graduate education. Two groups will work independently to draft recommendations concerning each area. The two parallel groups will meet in joint session Saturday morning to reconcile their reports and to determine the recommendations to be presented to the Conference.

Most of Saturday will be devoted to deliberating on the reports of the Recommendation Drafting Groups. Each written recommendation will be considered and amended, adopted, or rejected as the conference participants see fit. Those recommendations that receive the support of the majority of the participants will be considered part of the official report of the Conference.

Responsibilities of Participants

Presenters of position papers and the respondents to them will make oral presentations of their papers that should not exceed twelve minutes.

The moderators for the General Sessions will introduce each session, manage the time appropriately, and help keep the session on the topic.

The chairpersons of the Issue Identification Groups and Recommendation Drafting Groups should do what is necessary to organize the work of their groups and assure the successful completion of their tasks.

The reporters for the Issue Identification Groups will keep a record of the work of their groups and report on their discussion to the General Session.

The chairpersons of the joint meetings of the Recommendation Drafting Groups will help integrate or reconcile the recommendations of the two separate groups. Hopefully, similar recommendations can be collapsed, and redundancy reduced as much as possible. If necessary, opposing recommendations can be forwarded to the General Session.

The reporters of the joint groups will keep a record of their group's deliberations and report the recommendations as agreed by the group to the General Session.

All participants are expected to be the best conference participants and group members that they can be. In the event that the structure of the Conference seems counter-productive, we can modify it. The commitment of each participant to making this Conference a success is essential.

Group Assignments

Issue Identification Groups

The Issue Identification Groups will meet Thurday, March 28th, 11:00am to 12:30pm and 4:15pm to 5:15pm, and will report to the General Session at 7:30pm to 9:30pm that evening.

> *Group 1* (Chapin Room)
>
> Lewis Donohew (Leader)
> David Bender (Reporter)
> Art Bochner
> Michael Burgoon
> Jon Nussbaum
> Barbara Sharf
> Fred Steier
> Karl Weick
>
> *Group 2* (Ybor Room)
>
> Kathy Galvin (Leader)
> Bill Eadie (Reporter)
> Chris Argyris
> Kathleen Jamieson
> Bob Norton
> Michael Pacanowsky
> Loyd Pettegrew
>
> *Group 3* (Plant Room)
>
> Ev Rogers (Leader)
> Joe Cappella (Reporter)
> Dwight Conquergood
> Jim Fletcher
> Mark Knapp
> Thom McCain
> Jim McCroskey
> Sandra Ragan
>
> *Group 4* (Fletcher Room)
>
> Dale Leathers (Leader)
> Janet Yerby (Reporter)
> Sam Becker

Ken Cissna
Buddy Goodall
Sam Keltner
Gary Kreps
Dave Seibold

Group 5 (Jackson Room)
Donal Carbaugh (Leader)
Bob Avery (Reporter)
Bob Craig
Vicki Freimuth
Jim Gaudino
Gerry Miller
Dave Smith
Lynne Webb

Recommendation Drafting Groups

The Recommendation Drafting Groups will meet Friday, March 29th, 10:30am to 11:30am and 1:00pm to 5:00pm. The joint meetings will be held Saturday the 30th 8:30am to 9:30am, which will report to the General Session as indicated below.

Issues and Responsibilities of the Field Recommendation Drafting Groups

Group A (Ballroom II)
Jim McCroskey (Leader)
Lynne Webb (Joint Group Leader)
Art Bochner
Mark Knapp
Gerry Miller
Karl Weick

Group B (Chapin Room)
Sam Keltner (Leader)
Jim Gaudino (Joint Group Reporter)
Buddy Goodall
Dale Leathers
Kathleen Jamieson
Bob Norton
Dave Smith

Joint meeting room is Ybor. General Session deliberations on the reports of Groups A and B are scheduled for Saturday the 30th from 10:00am to 11:45am.

Research Priorities Recommendation Drafting Groups

> *Group C* (Ybor Room)
> Jon Nussbaum (Leader)
> Gary Kreps (Joint Group Leader)
> Sam Becker
> David Bender
> Bill Eadie
> Fred Steier
> Janet Yerby

> *Group D* (Plant Room)
> Jim Fletcher (Leader)
> Barbara Sharf (Joint Group Reporter)
> Bob Avery
> Dwight Conquergood
> Vicki Freimuth
> Loyd Pettegrew

Joint meeting room is Fletcher. General Session deliberations on the reports of Groups C and D are scheduled for Saturday the 30th from 1:00pm to 2:45pm.

Graduate Education Recommendation Drafting Groups

> *Group E* (Fletcher Room)
> Michael Burgoon (Leader)
> Bob Craig (Joint Group Reporter)
> Donal Carbaugh
> Ken Cissna
> Lewis Donohew
> Kathy Galvin
> Dave Seibold

> *Group F* (Jackson Room)
> Michael Pacanowsky (Leader)
> Sandra Ragan (Joint Group Leader)
> Chris Argyris
> Joe Cappella
> Thom McCain
> Ev Rogers

Joint meeting room is Jackson. General Session deliberations on the reports of Groups E and F are scheduled for Saturday the 30th from 3:15pm to 5:00pm.

Please call me if you have any questions, concerns, or suggestions. I am looking forward to working with you in Tampa.

Author Index

Subject Index

Printed and bound by CPI Group (UK) Ltd, Croydon, CR0 4YY

17/10/2024

01775684-0006